REA

ACPL ITEM
DISCARDED

Opening Doors to Reading

Opening Doors to Reading
Building School-to-Work Skills

Dee L. Fabry

Sally A. Seier

Foreword by Gwen Sonnenburg

Illustrator Amilee J. Seier

2001
TEACHER IDEAS PRESS
A Division of
Libraries Unlimited, Inc.
Englewood, Colorado

To Jim and making dreams come true.

To my parents, Max and Marge Crist, for their encouragement, support, and unwavering **faith***.*

To my children, Dan, Ami, Tim, and Crissy for their clear-eyed belief in the future and their **hope** *in the goodness of the world. 1434!*

To my husband, Dave, for his shoulder, his meals, and his **love***.*
FAHOLO!

Teacher Ideas Press
A Division of
Libraries Unlimited, Inc.
P.O. Box 6633
Englewood, CO 80155-6633
1-800-237-6124
www.lu.com/tip

Library of Congress Cataloging-in-Publication Data

Fabry, Dee L.
    Opening doors to reading : building school-to-work skills / Dee L. Fabry, Sally A. Seier ; foreword by Gwen Sonnenburg ; illustrator Amilee J. Seier.
        p. cm.
    Includes bibliographical references and index.
    ISBN 1-56308-775-8 (softbound)
    1. School-to-work transition--United States. 2. Middle school education--United States--Curricula. 3. Reading--Remedial teaching. I. Seier, Sally A. II. Title.

LC1037.5 .F32 2000
373.19--dc21   00-055976

CONTENTS

3—Speaking, *Technology*, Analysis, and Reading Through Research 47

4—Speaking, Technology, *Analysis*, and Reading Through Research 79

5—Speaking, Technology, Analysis, and *Reading* Through Research 99

6—Speaking, Technology, Analysis, and Reading Through *Research* 143

8—STARR MULTIDISCIPLINARY UNITS 241

9—MANAGEMENT, ASSESSMENT, AND EVALUATION 269

FOREWORD

Feelings of frustration rarely lead to outstanding creations, but that is at the core of the innovative STARR program (Speaking, Technology, Analysis, and Reading through Research). In 1991, seventh grade teachers at Horizon Community Middle School in the Cherry Creek School District outside Denver, Colorado, were feeling less than successful. For many years, the small affluent district had been strictly Anglo. During the late 1980s those demographics changed drastically. Horizon found itself a pioneer in what the district was rapidly becoming. Cherry Creek transformed into a large, diverse, and mobile district, with residents in the lower socio-economic levels. Some of the present curriculum and instructional strategies were not meeting the needs of these new students. As building administrator, I shared that frustration with the staff. On the day of a seventh-grade-level meeting, I had just finished observing an outstanding lesson in a reading classroom. Dee Fabry, the reading teacher and seventh grade team leader, conveyed her insights about our new learner and how she was using information from the *Goals 2000* report as a guide. At the grade level teachers' meeting, I posed the question: "What do our seventh grade students need that we presently do not provide?" That led to brainstorming sessions on identifying what these students require to prepare them for the twenty-first century and how we can provide it. Dee Fabry facilitated those discussions and the proposal for STARR was created. That summer, curriculum-writing committees, master schedule revisions, and teacher hiring all occurred to prepare for STARR in September.

Principals rarely have the opportunity to implement outstanding teacher concepts. We had a talented teacher with the curriculum and instructional knowledge to bring her visionary insights to life. Since Dee Fabry would willingly devote the necessary time and energy, we had to do all within our power to remove any obstacles. Our students were the winners because of Dee Fabry, the dedication of the first new STARR hire, Sally Seier, and the support and hard work of the teacher team, both then and now.

Gwen Sonnenburg

ACKNOWLEDGMENTS

If you are a believer in synchronicity, as the authors and editor of this book are, you will fully understand the wonderful events that have happened to make this labor come to fruition. Thanks to Gwen Sonnenburg, the former principal of Horizon Community Middle School, for sharing the vision for STARR and providing the nurturing learning environment to make it happen. Thanks to all those teachers who worked on the STARR team then and now.

Sally Seier is one of the most dedicated professional teachers I have ever had the privilege of working with, and her constant support and long hours in the initial writing of STARR years ago was a gift. Her invaluable contributions during the co-authoring of this book are evident in the final product. She is an amazing colleague and friend.

Over the years of teaching this curriculum we were given feedback from some very special students and parents. In particular, Carla and Kyra Dougherty lent their voices in its ongoing development. Thanks to both of you.

As I learned when I was writing my dissertation, it takes a village to create substantial projects, this book being one of them. Betty J. Morris, Acquisitions Editor for Libraries Unlimited, is one of the very special synchronicities that happened along the way. Thank you for your friendship and resounding enthusiasm about this book. My husband Jim has endured my writing passion for years and it doesn't look like either the passion or the support will fade anytime soon. I appreciate the many cups of tea and neck rubs.

Dee L. Fabry, Ph.D.

Grateful thanks to Kathie Jenkins for her contributions of the Research Roundup unit on research. Her untiring assistance is appreciated by many, but spoken by few.

Also, our heartfelt appreciation to Ami Seier for her joyous approach to adding graphics to our project. (Darn those circles!)

Sally A. Seier, M.A. Ed.

CHAPTER 1

STARR Design and Development

> *The principal goal of education is to create (people) who are capable of do-ing new things, not simply of repeating what other generations have done—(people) who are creative, inventive, and discoverers. The second goal of education is to form minds which can be critical, can verify, and not accept everything they are offered. . . . So we need pupils who are active, who learn early to find out for themselves, partly by their own selves, partly by their own spontaneous activity and partly through material we set up for them; who learn early to tell what is verifiable and what is simply the first idea to come to them.*
>
> —Jean Piaget, *The Origins of Intelligence in Children*, 1952.

THE DESIGN AND DEVELOPMENT OF THE STARR CURRICULUM

STARR—Speaking, Technology, Analysis, and Reading through Research—is an inquiry-based reading program designed for middle-school students, but adaptable to multiple levels of learners. It was inspired by the words of Piaget and was designed based on the input from the faculty of a middle school, the information presented in the Secretary's Commission on Achieving Necessary Skills (SCANS) report, and the research available on best teaching practices. The selection of the five basic elements that form the integrated STARR curriculum resulted from conversations among and feedback from the faculty about what students needed to learn, along with the faculty's concern about the lack of time they had to teach all that was required of them. Research to support these elements came from the foundation skills and competencies pre-sented in SCANS (*What Work Requires of Schools* 1991). Integral to this program, SCANS verifies what is termed "workplace know-how."

Why did we elect to build a curriculum using this research as the framework? As educators, we were concerned with the knowledge and skills to which our students were exposed. Our faculty often discussed the general lack of motivation and interest exhibited by the students in our classrooms. We dealt with learners who were frequently bored and turned off to learning. We dealt with state- and district-mandated skills that had to be taught within a required time frame. We asked each other these questions: How could we open doors to new learning environments? How could we motivate students to want to acquire new knowledge? How could we design a curriculum that would teach relevant workplace skills? Where could we find time in our already overloaded day to do this? What did we believe about learning and teaching and how could these new technologies support our beliefs? What motivates today's learners?

A supportive administration listened and a fifth core class—STARR—was added to the seventh-grade curriculum. The process of designing the curriculum began. We first examined ourselves, our beliefs about teaching and learning, and our daily teaching experiences. Next, we looked at SCANS and the available research on best practices in teaching and learning. We wanted to create a dynamic curriculum that turned students on to learning, addressed the issues of how to prepare young people for new work environments, and used the best practices available in education.

WHAT MOTIVATES TODAY'S LEARNERS?

In our classrooms, we watched students intensely involved in research-based projects find answers to pertinent questions and problems. They were using computers and related technologies to access, store, sort, share, and communicate information. Research-based projects, constructivist learning environments, and technology were three successful strategies. Incorporating these elements into the design of the curriculum was based on both experience and solid educational research.

The research-based project was particularly successful. By the time they've reached the seventh grade, unsuccessful readers are very difficult to motivate. After three years of using multiple strategies to engage reluctant readers, one of the authors began to use research-based projects, where students select a question of interest and begin a guided process of finding the answer. As students explore various approaches to accessing, sorting, prioritizing, and organizing information, their reading skills begin to improve. This approach, coupled with computer use, transforms the classroom. As these students naturally build communities of learners, meaningful learning takes place. The project-based method of teaching is one of STARR's cornerstones and it produces significant results.

David Jonassen (1995) presents the seven qualities of meaningful learning and our accomplishments support Jonassen's theories. In Jonassen's model, students are active and responsible for their own learning. They construct their own knowledge and collaborate to gain even more knowledge. Learning in this environment involves social interaction. These learners are focused and have a meaningful cognitive goal. One of the most important aspects is the time the students have to reflect on what they're learning. These qualities are critical to building a learning environment where students may thrive.

Another important piece of research supporting STARR is the Apple Classrooms of Tomorrow Research Project. This decade-long study places technology in the classroom and calls for reforming schools by reemphasizing student problem-solving and higher-order thinking skills. "To facilitate the development of these skills, learning and teaching must shift from a knowledge-transfer process-instructionism to a knowledge-building process-oriented constructivism" (Ringstaff and Yocam 1997).

The final important cornerstone of STARR is constructivist learning. In this environment, children learn by actively expanding their own knowledge. Compared with traditional classrooms, constructivist learning places more responsibility on students. In groups, students work to solve problems or complete projects. The teacher now facilitates the acquisition of new knowledge instead of dispensing it (Healy 1998). Computers play an important role in this environment by providing access to information and support interactive communication.

Technology serves multiple purposes for inquiry-based constructivist learning. We knew that technology could help us reach our goal of turning classrooms into student-centered environments. We were motivated to learn from our own students as they created a HyperStudio® stack or developed a newsletter to share their opinions. Research shows that incorporating technology makes learning more student-centered, encourages cooperative learning, and stimulates increased teacher/student interaction (Sivin-Kachala and Bialo 1996). When used as a learning tool, technology motivates students.

In conclusion, educators can invoke student interest with research-based projects, constructivist learning environments, and technology.

WHAT IS THE SCANS REPORT?

As previously stated, SCANS verifies that workplace know-how defines effective job performance (*What Work Requires of Schools* 1991). Teachers at our school discussed what skills our students needed to enhance learning. In addition to the basic skills, they needed to learn to work collaboratively to know how to access, organize, and communicate information and to learn how to think critically. Their parents were also concerned about preparing them for tomorrow's workplace. As a result, SCANS provided us with a workable framework on which to design the curriculum.

The report presents foundations skills and competencies that lie at the heart of job performance. The foundation skills include basic skills, thinking skills, and personal qualities. The basic skills are reading, writing, arithmetic/mathematics, listening, and speaking. The tools for an expanded intellect include reasoning, creative thinking, decision-making, problem solving, seeing things in the mind's eye, and knowing how to learn. Responsibility, self-esteem, sociability, self-management, and integrity constitute the personal qualities.

The five competencies are resources, interpersonal, information, systems, and technology. The resources category means identifying and organizing needed materials, then planning and allocating them. Interpersonal competencies include working with others, collaborating as a team, acquiring and exercising leadership skills, and valuing diversity. The information competency area encompasses the acquisition, evaluation, organization, interpretation, and processing of information. Systems competencies mean that the learner understands the complexity of our social, organizational, and technological systems. The final competency—technology—includes the appropriate selection and application of technology to the task, as well as the ability to maintain and troubleshoot equipment.

According to SCANS, these foundation skills and competencies are needed in workplaces dedicated to excellence. We analyzed the foundation skills and competencies and used them as the blueprint for the STARR curriculum.

CORRELATING THE SCANS FRAMEWORK TO STANDARDS

Although SCANS provided the setting for STARR, we needed to correlate it with our district proficiencies and the movement toward National Standards. The impetus for developing voluntary National Education Standards started in 1989 when President Bush convened the nation's 50 governors, who agreed that the nation must set ambitious educational goals for our schools. Since that meeting, National Standards have been developed to raise academic achievement and ensure that all students have equal educational opportunities. National Standards, then, define what students should know and be able to do.

Even though National Standards is a controversial concept, its legacy has had an impact. It has given us a sense of what each subject should include, but more importantly, it has revealed that many instructional practices that were once used to teach our students are ineffective. For a thorough discussion of this topic, we suggest you read *Best Practice: New Standards for Teaching and Learning in America's Schools* (Zemelman, Daniels, and Hyde 1998). It is not our purpose here to debate the standards issue, but rather to provide you with a *connection* to standards.

From the beginning, the STARR curriculum was correlated to the district proficiencies where we taught. At this time, many states and districts have written their own standards. In the classroom, teachers are grappling with how to implement standards. We have found that these standards, called proficiencies, correspond well to the National Standards. Each lesson or unit presented in this book is correlated to proficiencies. You can readily adapt them to your own standards.

LEARNING THEORIES

As STARR emerged, we found ourselves drawing from the work of a number of learning theorists and incorporating multiple teaching strategies into our curriculum. This will come as no surprise to seasoned educators who daily draw from a variety of theories and techniques to best meet the myriad learning styles in their classrooms. Among those theories, theorists, and curriculum developers whose collective expertise is integrated into this dynamic process are Howard Gardner, Benjamin Bloom, Jean Piaget, Constructivism, the Apple Classrooms of Tomorrow Research Project, and *Best Practice*. More recent brain research and work in cognition also supports our work. You will surely recognize other influences as you go along.

Howard Gardner's Multiple Intelligences

Howard Gardner, the Harvard University psychologist (Project Zero), states that all normal individuals are not limited to one overall intelligence, but at least eight distinct ones: linguistic, logical-mathematical, spatial, musical, bodily-kinesthetic, interpersonal, intrapersonal, and naturalistic. Although students may possess qualities that exhibit stronger tendencies toward one intelligence more than another, Gardner feels that all eight coexist and students can display some forms of all intelligences. Intelligence is multidimensional and not static or fixed at birth. As we designed STARR and the units and lessons in each of the five core areas, we kept Gardner's intelligences in mind. A variety of intelligences are addressed, so that learners have the opportunity to learn via their strengths. In addition, opportunities to develop those intelligences that are not normally challenged are provided.

Bloom's Taxonomy of Learning

Benjamin Bloom and a group of educational psychologists developed a classification of learning that has come to be known as Bloom's Taxonomy. Bloom and his colleagues identified six levels of cognition ranging from simple recall of facts at the lowest level to evaluation at the highest. The six domains are knowledge, comprehension, application, analysis, synthesis, and evaluation. This taxonomy of learning illustrates the importance of presenting learning at many levels to meet the needs of a variety of learners. We introduce these domains to our students to give them a model of learning for application in their work. For example, they learn to use the taxonomy to develop higher-order research questions. As teachers, we use the taxonomy to form questioning strategies to help students reach higher levels of thinking. Combined with other theoretical perspectives and models, this tool is useful in developing units of learning.

Jean Piaget

As one of the seminal leaders in developmental psychology, Jean Piaget is well known for his studies on how children learn. Although much of his work is questioned today, his understanding of the stages of development has had an impact on education for decades. Piaget's research builds a solid argument for the use of active learning. Piaget believed that people are active information processors and that cognitive development results from interactions of individuals with their physical and social environments. This research supports our belief that learners need an environment where they can be actively involved in the learning process. Piaget's work leads us into the constructivist theory that continues to support our philosophy of creating an active learning environment.

Constructivism

In the constructivist theory, the student is the center of the learning experience. With STARR, we strive to create a student-centered learning environment. Constructivism includes these assumptions: (a) learners are constructors of their own knowledge, (b) learning is a collaborative process, (c) knowledge is a product of the ways in which the student's mind is engaged by the activities and resources in the classroom, and (d) learning involves a continual process of building, interpreting, and modifying experiences (Grabinger and Dunlap 1995; Jonassen, Campbell, and Davidson 1994). Constructivist teaching practices, then, facilitate the learner in the internalization and transformation of new information (Brooks and Brooks 1993).

Brooks and Brooks (1993) present a number of helpful constructivist assumptions. To develop and implement this curriculum, three features stand out. One, teachers facilitate the learning process while the student takes on more and more responsibility for learning. Two, the curriculum is designed in an inquiry-based format. Three, students are encouraged to explore multiple avenues to find and communicate new knowledge.

Constructivist classrooms change the teacher's role to one of facilitator. As you read this book you will see that constructivist learning plays a major role in the students' acquisition of knowledge. Although students are provided with frameworks and foundations, they are expected to seek knowledge and information on their own as well as in collaborative groups.

Apple Classrooms of Tomorrow Research Project

The Apple Classrooms of Tomorrow Project provides educators with rich information on how to integrate information technologies in the classroom. The guidebook, written by Sandholtz, Ringstaff, and Dwyer (1997), furnishes solid evidence for changing teaching practices that use technology as a learning tool. This research supports the placement of computers and peripherals in the classroom for easy access. We drew from this research to set up the physical environment according to this model.

Best Practices

In *Best Practice: New Standards for Teaching and Learning in America's Schools* (Zemelman, Daniels, and Hyde 1998), the term Best Practice is defined as shorthand for serious, thoughtful, informed, responsible, and state-of-the-art teaching. As we developed the STARR curriculum, we were encouraged to find that many experts agreed with our teaching philosophy. We wanted to create a student-centered classroom where the teacher's role shifted from expert to facilitator. We knew that students thrived in an environment where they became researchers themselves. The students ask the questions and the students seek the answers. Moreover, they did not do their research in isolation. The social component is an essential element in learning, especially for middle-level students. So we encourage collaboration. All these philosophies are acknowledged by the current research in *Best Practice: New Standards for Teaching and Learning in America's Schools*.

INSTRUCTIONAL STRATEGIES

STARR is an interdisciplinary program. Each quarter students receive instruction in the five focus areas: speaking, technology, analysis, reading, and research. We implement a variety of instructional strategies, ranging from direct teaching through mini-lectures to student exploration. The underlying philosophy is that of constructivist learning and guiding learners through the process of acquiring new knowledge. Although we wanted to create consistent inquiry-based learning environments, we sometimes had to deliver information in a more straightforward, didactic manner for the sake of expediency.

In this inquiry-based fashion, we begin each quarter by asking our students to make a list of topics they are curious about and things they would like to learn. Sometimes they originate the central motifs, and sometimes we provide the thematic structure. In small group discussions, they share their questions and begin identifying a research question. Peers probe and prod to help the learner create a question that is neither too broad nor too narrow for the quarter-long project. This research question becomes their focus for the quarter as they search for information, sort through their findings, organize the data into manageable chunks, and share their discoveries.

During the discovery and inquiry phase, students are exposed to critical thinking techniques, such as questioning assumptions or information sources. Learners share through speeches, written papers, HyperStudio® stacks, PowerPoint® presentations, Web sites, and more. Of course, they learn how to use technology as they read and research.

Because STARR is developmental in nature, students are provided with additional skills each quarter. By the fourth quarter, students have experienced a wide variety of learning opportunities in all five STARR focus areas. In this book, we have presented each focus area separately, which allows you to use the materials and ideas in your classroom in some sort of sequential method. However, we do not teach the curriculum elements separately. All elements are intertwined and interconnect. In the section on speaking, you will see that students have to read and do research before giving speeches. In the reading section, both units incorporate all five elements. As you read each section, think systemically and create a mental image of a fluid program that provides learners daily connections to all factors.

THE STARR LEARNING ENVIRONMENT

The STARR learning environment neither looks nor sounds like a conventional classroom. Circular tables provide students with space to work collaboratively, while seven computers are clustered in workstations. Students begin each day by checking the white board for messages. One day may begin with a mini-lecture on the elements of an informative speech; another day may see students checking their own progress on the sources they have found on the Internet. The teacher manages the process by scheduling activities and meeting with small groups and individuals. Formal and less formal assessments are ongoing. Learners become increasingly more responsible for their own learning as each quarter progresses. A scaffolding process provides assistance when a student needs it and gently pulls away the teacher's reminders, prompts, and support, as the learner is able to assume more responsibility. Every chapter provides assessment information with each of the five STARR elements. In addition, Chapter 9 provides a more thorough discussion of evaluation and assessment opportunities.

For STARR to work optimally, it is necessary to include the collaborative efforts of the Media Specialist and Technology Specialist. Each chapter contains a section that addresses the role of these two important support people. Media Specialists are critical because they can design instruction with the teacher as well as plan for research skills development. Their expertise in information literacy is pivotal to the successful implementation of STARR. They can teach lessons that draw on their expertise and supplement the classroom teacher. Technology Specialists can also provide support in various ways. They can help to plan access to technologies and offer expertise in how to use the latest available programs. Their support in teaching software programs and how to use the Internet will bolster the quality of the students' work. If your school does not have a Technology Specialist, your Media Specialist can fulfill that role.

STARR can have a major impact on learners. We found that it changed the way we taught and the way we interacted with our colleagues. We frequently taught as teams. While the language arts teacher taught mythology, we designed a mythology newsletter. Learners began to see connections among disciplines. The power of this curriculum is in the connections it makes between what students learn and their growth as well as between schoolwork and future work. We encourage you to use the materials in this book to promote inquiry-based learning for your students and to help them make the connections between their schoolwork and their future work.

STARR AND TECHNOLOGY

You don't have to be a technology guru to use technology as a learning tool. We laugh when we reflect on how little we knew about computers when we began this program. We learned as we went along and used the expertise of students. We took every course the district offered and pestered our own Technology Coordinator to teach us more. Our summers were spent writing material for this program and learning new technology skills. Don't let technology intimidate you. Embrace it and learn to use it as a tool.

You'll find numerous references to computer programs and applications throughout this book. Although our classrooms were designed for Apple systems, the platform is ultimately irrelevant. The computer programs and applications we mention can be purchased at most local computer stores or through your district purchasing system. The word processing program we use is ClarisWorks® and the presentation software is HyperStudio®. Student Writing Center® is a newsletter program. Similar programs from Microsoft include Microsoft Word® and PowerPoint®. The browser you use is also a personal or district preference. We access the Internet through Netscape®, but others may prefer Microsoft Internet Explorer®. Often the computer programs and applications are dictated by district guidelines. Other software we refer to is listed with ordering information in the References and Useful Information section at the end of each chapter.

RESOURCES

Books

Bloom, Benjamin S. *Taxonomy of Educational Objectives: The Classification of Goals: Handbook 1: Cognitive Domain.* New York: Longman Publishing Group, 1956.

Brooks, J. G., and Brooks, M. G. *The Case for Constructivist Classrooms.* Alexandria, Va.: Association for Supervision and Curriculum, 1993.

Gardner, Howard. *Frames of Mind: The Theory of Multiple Intelligences.* New York: Basic Books, 1991.

Gardner, Howard. *Multiple Intelligences: The Theory in Practice.* New York: Basic Books, a Division of Harper Collins Publishers, 1993.

Grabinger, R. Scott, and Dunlap, Joanna C. "Rich Environments for Active Learning: A Definition," *Alternate Learning Technologies Journal,* Vol. 3, No. 2 (1995): 5–34.

Healy, Jane M. *Failure to Connect: How Computers Affect Our Children's Minds—For Better and Worse.* New York: Simon & Schuster, 1998.

Jonassen, David H. "Supporting Communities of Learners with Technology: A Vision for Integrating Technology with Learning in Schools," *Educational Technology,* Vol. 35, No. 4 (1995): 60–63.

Jonassen, David H., Campbell, J. P., and Davidson, M. E. "Learning with Media: Restructuring the Debate," *Educational Technology Research and Development,* Vol. 42, No. 4 (1994): 31–39.

Lazear, David. *Seven Pathways of Learning: Teaching Students and Parents About Multiple Intelligences.* Tucson, AZ: Zephyr Press, 1991.

Lazear, David. *Seven Ways of Knowing: Teaching for Multiple Intelligences.* Palatine, IL: Skylight Publishing, 1991.

Piaget, Jean. *The Origins of Intelligence in Children.* New York: International Universities Press, 1952.

Ringstaff, Cathy, and Yocam, Keith. "Creating an Alternative Context for Teacher Development: The ACOT Teacher Development Centers" in *Apple Computers of Tomorrow Research Report 18*, 1997. Accessed January 1999 at http://www.research.apple.com.

Sandholtz, Judith H., Ringstaff, Cathy, and Dwyer, David C. *Teaching with Technology: Creating Student Centered Classrooms.* New York: Teachers College Press, 1997.

Sivin-Kachala, Jan, and Bialo, Ellen R. *Report on the Effectiveness of Technology in Schools '95 and '96.* Washington, D.C.: Software Publishers Association, 1996.

What Work Requires of Schools: A SCANS Report for America 2000 by the Secretary's Commission on Achieving Necessary Skills. Washington, D.C.: U.S. Department of Labor, 1991.

Zemelman, Steven, Daniels, Harvey, and Hyde, Arthur. *Best Practice: New Standards for Teaching and Learning in America's Schools.* Portsmouth, NH: Heinemann Publishers, 1998.

Proficiency Information

We have elected to use the Cherry Creek School District proficiencies for correlation in this book. The Cherry Creek Schools reading proficiency, referred to most often, is one of the five district Language Arts proficiencies. For more information, contact Cherry Creek Schools, Division of Performance Improvement, 4700 S. Yosemite Street, Englewood, Colorado, 80111. Phone: (303) 485-4316.

Web Sites

Apple Research: This site provides research from the Apple Classrooms of Tomorrow Project that supports the use of technology in the classroom. http://www.apple.com/education/K12/leadership/acot/

Software Publishers Association: This site provides research that supports the use of technology to motivate students. http://www.siia.net

Videos

Learn and Live, The George Lucas Educational Foundation, 1997. http://glef.org. This book and video are invaluable resources for technology staff development.

Software

HyperStudio® is a multimedia presentation software package developed by Roger Wagner. Ordering and product information is available at http://www.hyperstudio.com.

PowerPoint® is presentation software developed by Microsoft. It is available through http://www.microsoft.com.

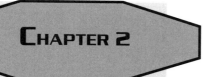

CHAPTER 2

Speaking, Technology, Analysis, and Reading Through Research

"All great speakers were bad speakers at first."
—Ralph Waldo Emerson, "Power," *The Conduct of Life* (1860)

SPEAKING FOUNDATION SKILLS

The Secretary's Commission on Achieving Necessary Skills (SCANS) report lists speaking foundation skills under the basic skills category. Speaking skills are described as the ability to organize ideas and communicate them orally. In addition to this basic definition, we broaden the skill base by including content proficiencies in language arts that specify speaking standards for middle-level learners.

CONTENT PROFICIENCIES IN LANGUAGE ARTS

The learner verbally expresses thoughts clearly and coherently to inform, persuade, and/or entertain an audience about a topic.

- The student is able to gather information from a variety of resources to develop speeches that will inform, explain, demonstrate, and entertain an audience.

- The student can organize a speech to include an appropriate introduction, body, and conclusion with adequate transitions.

- The student is aware of adaptations that need to be made to speeches to meet the needs of the audience.

- The speech is delivered with substantial eye contact, appropriate volume and posture, and adequate enthusiasm.

- Visual aids are adequately presented, incorporated, and supportive of the speech.

- The student is aware of the verbal and nonverbal implications that are a part of the speech.

CONNECTING SPEAKING TO WORKPLACE SKILLS

Speech is oral communication. Interpreting and conveying information are essential skills in the workplace. Students must communicate effectively to get ideas across, justify positions, persuade, and provide feedback. To foster students' understanding of the relevancy of speech skills, we ask them to conduct an informal research project where they ask five adults how they use speaking skills at work. They have one week to report their findings. This activity helps them to make the connection between what they learn and how that knowledge is translated into a work context for use in later life.

UNIT ONE: SPEECHES: INFORMATIVE, DEMONSTRATION, AND PERSUASIVE

Aligning Instructional Practices with Proficiencies and Assessments

The learner verbally expresses thoughts clearly and coherently to inform, persuade, and/or entertain an audience about a topic.

Learning Objectives

The students will:

- Understand and develop improved listening habits.

- Distinguish speech traps.

- Distinguish the main idea, supporting details, and conclusion of a speech.

- Incorporate planning, researching, outlining, and rehearsing into their speech products (demonstration, informative, and persuasive speeches).

- Develop quality visual aids to support their speeches.

- Evaluate speeches using a speech rubric.

Assessments

For many students, giving a speech is one of the most feared activities in a school year. By offering our students the instruction and opportunity to perform at a younger age than most students, we hopefully help them to overcome their phobias about presenting before a group. We have repeatedly heard from our students that although they still tremble in anticipation of presenting their speeches, "It wasn't so bad, I actually kind of had fun with it." We have been amazed at the progress we have witnessed. Students literally mature before our eyes in their ability to deliver a speech.

Although we offer several formal assessment tools, we would like to stress the importance of videotaping speeches and providing time for self-evaluation. These activities are time intensive, but the feedback for the student speakers is invaluable. We videotape the first informative speech of the new school year. We provide playback time in small groups so that students can critique each other and themselves. We teach them how to provide useful feedback in a constructive manner. Students have the option to schedule a critiquing conference with the teacher in addition to our normal grading rubrics. We then continue to videotape the speeches each quarter. The final video portfolio of the year's work is so much fun to review. The students are always impressed with their progress and proud of their new speaking skills.

> *Teacher Notes:* A list of the assessments provided in this unit follows, and the actual assessments can be found at the end of this unit. Please feel free to modify them to meet your needs. Additional information on assessment and evaluation is presented in Chapter 9.

◆ Speech chapter worksheet (follows informative speech chapter in speech text) properly completed

◆ Group presentation of section in the informative speech chapter in the speech textbook

◆ Two-column notes (Cornell notes) check on speech lectures

◆ Presentation of informative speech (mandala)

◆ Presentation of demonstration speech (self-selected topic)

◆ Presentation of persuasive speech (self-selected topic)

◆ Outlines of speeches

◆ Peer and self-evaluation of speeches

◆ Visual aid development

◆ Teacher evaluations

◆ Videotaping of performed speeches as part of portfolio development

Instructional Strategies

We begin this unit of learning with small group work, including assigned reading from our speech textbook and a worksheet designed to help students organize information. We use the "jigsaw method" as groups read and present assigned sections of the chapter on informative speech to the rest of the class. This involves the worksheet (included at the end of this unit) that the group must complete, which provides answers for the class to write on their worksheets. This becomes part of their informative speech presentation. Because the entire group is presenting, it becomes less formidable for the individuals. The students move from small groups to individual presentations in the mandala assignment. This section includes the mandala unit, which is the individual informative speech presentation. Later in the school year, students will use the basic knowledge gained from this unit to present informative speeches in conjunction with their research projects.

The following is a list of mini-lectures and student worksheets included in this chapter. Please feel free to modify them to meet the needs of your learners.

- Mini-lecture on listening skills

- Mini-lecture and two-column note taking on listening for the main idea

- Mini-lecture and two-column note taking on listening for speech traps

- Mini-lecture and two-column note taking on building a speech

- Worksheet on how to outline a basic speech format

- Worksheet on format of a demonstration speech, including basic expectations

- Presentation of demonstration speech (preparation includes practicing with a group and videotaping practice speeches for peer and self-evaluation)

- Mini-lecture and two-column note taking on persuasive speech: "Methods of Persuasion"

- Mini-lecture and two-column note taking on persuasive speech: "The Art of Persuasive Speech"

- Worksheet on building a persuasive speech outline

- Presentation on visual aids: What works and what doesn't work using the previous year's examples to demonstrate each

Remediation Strategies

Adaptations for this speech unit can vary widely depending on the learners' needs. For example, taking notes can be quite difficult for some students. We suggest providing notes to those students so that they can follow along and highlight key points. Restricting the length of written speech requirements, delivery requirements, evaluation expectations, and so forth are also possible. Occasionally, some students balk at presenting before their classmates. In those few instances, we allow students to present speeches individually before the teacher in an after-school setting. Although this defeats the intent of presenting before a group, it gives the student a sense of accomplishment and a belief that he or she can deliver a speech.

Enrichment Strategies

In the speech curriculum, enrichment strategies are limitless. We give students who show great promise the opportunities to perform in speech contests, such as the local annual speech contests (e.g., 4-H, Rotary Club, Lion's Club). Our students do well in these contests, and in a few instances they have gone on to state and regional competitions. When time permits, interested students are encouraged to participate in classroom debates. Further, interdisciplinary opportunities abound in this area. Aligning with a social studies or science teacher to debate relevant and topical issues brings the development of speech skills into everyday life.

Additionally, computer literate students may develop visual aids using presentational software such as KidPix® slide show, Power Point®, or HyperStudio®. Creating a Web page is another superb way to encourage super achievers.

Notes to Users of This Unit

Classroom Teachers: Speeches demand quite a bit of time. We usually plan for a full week of presentations. Preparing for the presentations also involves considerable time, from introducing students to the type of speech (informative, demonstration, persuasive, debate), up to the culminating event. Videotaping takes time, but we find that once the students learn the basics of operating the camera, they are quite adept at it and seem to enjoy videotaping each other. A section of our hallway is reserved for students who wish to rehearse their presentations and enhance their videotaping skills.

Media Specialists: The students will need assistance in researching and developing information for informative and persuasive speeches. You can best support this research with a rich supply of print materials and available databases. Assisting students in bookmarking Internet sites appropriate to their topics also helps. Further, when developing visual aids, students need access to materials such as die cuts, paper cutters, and scissors.

Technology Specialists: Technology Specialists may guide students to research databases, such as Newsbank® and EBSCO®, as well as showing them how to locate and bookmark Internet sites. Help with Web page design, or providing instruction in other presentational software, such as PowerPoint®, HyperStudio®, or KidPix®, assists students who take visual aids a step beyond the expectation. If your school does not have a Technology Specialist, the Media Specialist can assist with technology issues.

Specific Knowledge

The student will need to:

♦ Work individually and within a group to achieve learning.

♦ Read, take notes, and review learning to achieve proficiency in speech performance.

♦ Use technology to research and create visual aids.

♦ Do research, organize notes, and develop outlining skills.

♦ Practice speech delivery.

♦ Deliver speeches as assigned.

♦ Evaluate self and peer speeches.

♦ Operate a video camera.

Environmental Considerations

The following features help students to achieve their goals in public speaking:

♦ Access to an instructional resource center (library) for research

- Assistance with research databases, the Internet, or computerized encyclopedias
- Art materials for visual aid creation
- Space to rehearse and videotape speeches

Assignments and Intelligences Addressed

Assignment	Intelligence
Reading and two-column note taking	Intrapersonal, Linguistic
Listening skills participation	Auditory, Interpersonal
Group presentation of informative speech section	Interpersonal, Linguistic
Speech presentations	Linguistic, Interpersonal
Visual aids	Spatial, Visual, Kinesthetic

> *Teacher Notes:* This unit involves the student in learning about how we communicate, including how we listen, and how we receive and convey messages. Specifically, students learn to listen for main ideas, supporting details, and conclusions. They learn the basics of informative, demonstration, and persuasive speeches. Research, note taking, and outlining are also incorporated into this unit. Self-evaluation is an extremely valuable part of this unit, because students can view their efforts on videotape. Formal speech was once a dreaded part of the educational experience. Now, students are thrilled at the end of the school year to view their progress on individual videotape portfolios.

Mini-Lectures on Giving Speeches

Mini-Lecture: Reasons for Being Poor Listeners

> *Teacher Notes:* The following is a warm-up or prompt. This leads into a mini-lecture on the ten worst listening habits, and a discussion of why we should be better listeners. If we spend 63 percent of each waking day just listening, why aren't we better listeners? Most people remember only about 25 percent of what they hear. What are the reasons?

Prior to this mini-lecture, we have students brainstorm a list of what they consider to be the worst listening habits. Then, using a previously prepared transparency, we display the following list on an overhead projector.

Ten worst listening habits:

1. Calling the subject boring and uninteresting because it sets up a mental attitude that prevents information from getting in
2. Criticizing the speaker's delivery

3. Listening only for facts

4. Trying to make an outline out of everything heard

5. Faking attention to the speaker

6. Tolerating or creating distractions in the audience

7. Evading attentiveness toward difficult material

8. Letting emotion-filled words throw us out of tune with the speaker

9. Wasting the difference between speech-speed and thought-speed

10. Thinking we "know it already" and closing our minds to new twists or information

Withhold your evaluation until you completely comprehend what is being said. Do not judge until you know the whole story or until you have truly assimilated the speaker's experience.

Mini-Lecture: Why Listen?

1. Listen for information.

2. Listen for facts and ideas.

3. Listen to analyze or compare. For example, if you hear two vocalists sing the same song, do they sound identical? Have you compared their styles? Do you like one better than the other? Perhaps you differentiate word emphasis, rhythm, voice inflection, or verbal messages.

4. Listen to judge or evaluate.

5. Listen to music or television for relaxation and enjoyment.

> ➤ *Teacher Notes:* This mini-lecture focuses student attention on the speech as it is delivered.

Mini-Lecture: How to Focus Your Concentration

1. Anticipate the speaker's next point.

2. Identify the speaker's supporting evidence with testimony, analogy, illustration, and specific instances.

3. Silently summarize every four or five minutes.

> ➤ *Teacher Notes:* Students often have a difficult time pinpointing the main idea. This mini-lecture helps them perceive what is important when they listen.

Mini-Lecture: Communicating the Main Idea

Communication occurs only when correct meanings are received!
Listen for main ideas, stated in different ways as follows:

Main Idea

Topic Sentence: "I believe that solar power will soon be the world's main energy source."

Axiom: "Honey draws more flies than vinegar."

Quotation: "H. G. Wells once said, "The past is but the beginning of a beginning.""

Question: "Do you enjoy scary movies?"

Analogy: "Young children are like tennis shoes. They are always underfoot, constantly dirty, but very comfortable when you want them."

Personal Example: "This morning I saw five cans, three bottles, and four candy wrappers on the school grounds."

> ➤ *Teacher Notes:* Now that your students know types of main ideas to listen for, the next step is to have them create one for a speech. This leads into development of an informative speech on a chosen topic.

In-Class Assignment

Student Instructions: Using one of these statement types, write a main idea for a familiar topic. For example, I know a little about 4-H clubs, because I was a member of 4-H for eight years. I could start out my speech with, "Do you know what organization's letters mean Head, Heart, Hands, and Health?" What type of main idea example did I use? Now you choose a topic you know about to write a main idea sentence using one of the above examples.

Have the students take turns reading their main ideas aloud. Instruct them to keep their ideas for a future topic.

Mini-Lecture: Developing Supporting Details

> ➤ *Teacher Notes:* This lesson introduces students to developing supporting details, and includes the in-class assignment begun during the previous mini-lecture on main ideas.

In this assignment, students create supporting details in their outlines.

How to Listen for Supporting Details

These are points that further explain main ideas, and can be anything from facts to beliefs. Supporting details usually have transitional words such as moreover, yet, furthermore, for example, or for instance. The speaker may also use transitional words such as first, second, third, and finally to signal supplementary items.

> ➤ *Teacher Notes:* The following information is best provided as a handout or on an overhead transparency for students to copy.

Supporting details can be anything from facts to beliefs. They usually have transitional words such as:

- ◆ Moreover

- ◆ For example

- ◆ Yet

- ◆ Furthermore

- ◆ For instance

The speaker may also use words such as:

- ◆ First, second, third

- ◆ Finally

- ◆ In conclusion

- ◆ In summation

In-Class Assignment

Instructions to Students: Take out your main idea sentence from yesterday and add supporting details.

Instructions to the Teacher: Show the overhead or handout and offer expanded examples. Use the transitions provided above and have students submit main idea sentences with newly added supporting evidence.

Link Introductions with Conclusions

Students usually have great difficulty with conclusions. They often write "The End" when they think they are finished. Teaching that their writing is not complete until they end with a conclusion brings them to a new level. A good speech is like a birthday present. The box is the introduction, the contents are the body of the speech and the gift-wrapping and bow are the conclusion.

> *Teacher Notes:* Students now create their conclusions. The main idea is often repeated or rephrased at the end. For example, a speaker might begin with a question and conclude with its answer. The speaker might first ask, "Have you ever wondered what causes . . .?" Then in the summation, he or she might say, "The things that cause . . . are . . ." Listen to the conclusion. It should be similar to the main idea. If comparable, the main idea was successfully conveyed.

In-Class Assignment

Students now create conclusions.

Instructions to Students: With your main idea sentence in mind, create a conclusion. Make certain you link the conclusion to your introduction. Hand in your sentences when you have done this step.

Mini-Lecture: Speech Traps

> ➤ *Teacher Notes:* We include this lecture because novice listeners are often misled by speakers, including friends at the lunchroom table. This lecture helps them distinguish between fact and opinion. They also should recognize generalizations, half-truths, misleading comparisons, personal attacks, and faulty reasoning.

1. *Distinguish Between Fact and Opinion.* An opinion is a statement that has not been proven true or false. We have problems when people state opinions as facts. So your job is to decide whether a statement is fact or opinion. For example, "The basketball team lost every game this season" is a FACT. However, "The team didn't try very hard this season" is an OPINION. Qualifying words provide clues to opinions, such as said, said that, suggested, and think. They signal that an opinion is coming. Which of the following are facts, and which are opinions?

   Elvis Presley was the most popular singer of the 1960s. (Opinion)

   My mother thinks that Elvis Presley was the greatest singer in the world. (Opinion)

   People who ride bicycles are fighting air pollution. (Fact)

   More people ride bicycles today than ever before. (Opinion unless backed by a statistic)

2. *Generalizations,* e.g., "Teenagers today are lazy." (Opinion) A generalization is a statement that lumps a whole group of people or things together. Then it condemns all for the qualities of some, as follows:

   Teenagers are unreliable.

   All men like football.

   All college students have rich families.

3. *Half-Truths.* Statements that tell only half the story. They are correct as far as they go, but they do not go far enough. For example, a student tells everyone that her drawing of a horse came in third in a statewide contest. However, she fails to mention that this category attracted only three submissions.

4. *Misleading comparisons.* They do not compare equal things. They compare the best thing in one group with the worst in another.

5. *Personal attacks (ad hominem arguments).* They try to discredit a person's ideas by attacking the person who holds them. Politicians play this game all the time.

6. *Faulty Reasoning.* Analyze what you hear. Don't believe everything you hear. Be especially alert when listening to persuasive messages.

Mini-Lecture: Building a Speech

> ➤ *Teacher Notes:* Students have developed a rough outline of a speech in the mini-lectures prior to this lecture presentation. This lesson

delves more deeply into the creation of a quality speech, and ends with an outline format to help students build a good speech. The basic outline has worked very well to help students apply knowledge. In addition, a basic speech requirement list is provided at the end of the outline to guide students.

Building a speech means you carefully plan, outline, and rehearse, but you never memorize wording. You will memorize only three things: the first one or two sentences, the concluding statements, and the order of the main ideas. However, it is important that you not memorize specific words. Wording may change with each presentation as you think of more exacting terms. You need to adapt to each audience and occasion. When you are assigned a speech, progressively do each of the following:

1. Determine the general purpose of, or general reaction you want from your audience.

   - Are you informing?
   - Are you persuading?
   - Are you entertaining?
   - Did you analyze your audience and occasion?
   - Did you select and narrow your subject?
   - Did you determine what you can adequately discuss in the time allotted and focus on what interests the audience? Most students choose too broad a topic for the time limits. Rather than "animals," narrow the subject down to "dogs," and then narrow it further to one of the following:

     Bathing a dog properly
     Teaching a dog three basic commands
     Training your dog to hunt
     Grooming of house dogs
     Dogs and their diets
     Traits of the French poodle
     My dog Rover

2. Gather material.

3. Analyze what you already know about the subject.

4. Determine if you can observe the subject.

5. Talk to authorities on the subject.

6. Read.

7. Use the *Reader's Guide* (index to periodicals).

8. Outline the speech (see the format sheet).

9. Practice aloud.

Students find the following outlines easy to adapt. With a format sheet to complete, students can design their speeches.

> *Teacher Notes:* You need to instruct students in the use of attention getters, the difference between general and specific purposes, and how to establish credibility. We define attention getters as quotes, illustrations, a descriptive incident, a startling statement, humor, questions, or in general, a method the speaker uses to grab the audience's attention. An example of a general purpose is "To inform the audience about dogs." The specific purpose might be "How I teach my dog new commands." To establish credibility, the speakers must inform the audience of how they have knowledge of the topic. What makes them an expert? It might be research or direct experience like, "I have been teaching my dog Rover new tricks and commands for three years and he's still learning."

OUTLINE FOR INFORMATIVE SPEECH

Speaker's Name _____

Topic _____

General Purpose _____

Specific Purpose _____

_____

_____

Outline

I. Introduction

    A. Attention Getter

    B. Establish Credibility

        1. Purpose for the speech

        2. Preview what you will discuss

II. Body (two or three major points)

    A.

        1.

        2.

    (Internal Summary and Transition)

    B.

        1.

        2.

    (Internal Summary and Transition)

    C.

        1.

        2.

III. Conclusion

    A. Attention getter (rephrase the one used in the introduction)

    B. Wrap up

IV. Bibliography

DEMONSTRATION SPEECH

>*Teacher Notes*: One type of informative speech is a demonstration speech. We found this the best speech to begin the curriculum because the students enjoy showing off for their classmates. Basically, this format is identical to the outline above, but includes elements specific to the demonstration speech.

I.   Introduction

    A.   Attention getter

    B.   Purpose of speech

    C.   Preview

II. Body of Speech

    A.   Main points

    B.   List materials required

    C.   Details

    D.   Review what you said

III. Conclusion

    Wrap up

    Restate the main idea

    Leave the audience with something to think about

    Speech requirements

        1.   Three minutes in length

        2.   Note cards

        3.   Eye contact

        4.   Loud voice

        5.   Good posture

        6.   Smile

We have come to the end of informative speech basics. The next section discusses persuasive speech.

> ➤ *Teacher Notes:* Generally we put our warm-up or day's prompt on the overhead or chalkboard. The prompt is intended to help students "warm up" to the day's lesson.

Warm-up or prompt: What is persuasion? Discussion on student responses follows.

Mini-Lecture: The Art of Persuasive Speaking

> ➤ *Teacher Notes:* At this point, students can take notes or an outline can be provided to complete during the lecture.

"The truth is always the strongest argument."

Persuasion is a communication process designed to change the listener's beliefs or behavior.

Two approaches to persuasion:

- ◆ Coactive—show how your ideas relate to the listeners' and lead them to agreement. Example: Persuade someone to buy raffle tickets because it helps an important cause.

- ◆ Coercive—get listeners to do things against their will. Example: Persuade someone to buy raffle tickets or trouble will follow.

Try to focus your methods on the coactive approach because threats are an undesirable means of communication. Successful persuaders present conflict and force listeners to resolve it. By effectively asserting ideas, speakers encourage listeners to view the topic the same way they do.

The Process of Persuasion

I. Decide your goal.

"I want my audience to . . ." Therefore you:

II. Analyze your audience.

III. Decide how you approach the members of the audience.

IV. Develop credibility. Establish credibility because listeners:

 A. Respond to persuaders with expertise.

 B. Are concerned with your overall image.

 C. Must perceive effective persuaders as honest.

V. Create the persuasive message.

VI.   Gather evidence.

VII.   Select correct channel for message.

VIII.   Organize message.

    A.   Inform first.

    B.   Persuade second.

Monroe Method

> *Teacher Notes:* The "Monroe Method" provides a way to organize a persuasive speech. Demonstrating the method is the most beneficial way for students to understand the elements.

Attention—get the audience's attention.

Need—convey your need to the audience.

Satisfaction—identify what can be done to meet these needs.

Visualization—see advantages of relieving the problem. Look to the future either positively or negatively. What will resolving the situation achieve? What will result from neglecting to act?

Action—decide what steps to take.

Example of Monroe Method

"Hey, listen to me."

"You need to hear what I am saying."

"See what it can do for you."

"So what are you going to do about it?"

Mini-Lecture: Code of Ethics

> *Teacher Notes:* All speeches need to follow a basic code of ethics. Include this as a part of your expectations. Students must understand that the quality of the speech is built on the integrity it contains.

* Don't falsify or make up evidence.

* Don't deceive the audience about your purpose.

* Don't manipulate reasoning to reach invalid conclusions.

* Don't distort evidence so it no longer makes the same point.

* Respect the decision of each audience member.

Mini-Lecture: Methods of Persuasion

> ➤ *Teacher Notes:* This next mini-lecture discusses a variety of persuasive methods. It is fun to use television commercials and/or political ads to demonstrate these techniques. The students enjoy seeing examples from real life.

1. *Card Stacking.* Card stacking presents all the evidence, but really tells only those facts that support the point the speaker is trying to make. A listener should suspect card stacking when a speaker is strongly in favor of something, mentions no drawbacks and makes no positive points about alternatives.

2. *Bandwagon.* The speaker asks you to "get on the bandwagon" by joining an overwhelmingly large group of people already in favor of the idea.

3. *Glittering Generality.* This is an idea so broad and encompassing that everybody agrees on its value, but no one is really sure what it means. For example, a politician might say that he or she favors "law and order."

4. *Non Sequitur.* Non sequitur is Latin for "it does not follow." For example, a student says she is running for class president and that you should vote for her because she did a great job running on the track team last year. Running sprints does not necessarily make her a good class president.

5. *Cause–Effect Relationships.* If I drop the vase on the floor (cause), it will break (effect). Listen for faulty cause–effect relationships. For example, if Bob reads the *Wall Street Journal* and makes the honor roll, is it because he reads the *Wall Street Journal?*

> ➤ *Teacher Notes:* The following outline is similar to the informative speech outline presented earlier. The basic differences are only the request in the introduction of what listeners can do when the speech is finished, followed in the conclusion with appeal to action.

PERSUASIVE SPEECH OUTLINE

Introduction

Attention Getter

Establish credibility: What makes you knowledgeable about this topic? Research? Experience?

Purpose: State why you want the audience to pay attention to your message. Do you want them to join you in some activity? Get them to give you money for a campaign? Why should they care? What do you want them to do when you are done?

Preview: TELL 'EM WHAT YOU'RE GOING TO TELL 'EM. What two or three things will you talk about and in what order?

Body

I. First main point

    A. Subdetail

        1. Supporting details (statistics, quotes, etc.*)

    B. Subdetail (internal summary and transition**)

    C. TELL 'EM!!!!

II. Second main point

    A. Subdetail

        1. Supporting details (statistics, quotes, etc.*)

    B. Subdetail (internal summary and transition**)

III. Continue with as many main points as you have (internal summary and transition**)

IV. Outlook for the future (internal summary and transition**)

V. Conclusion

    A. Steps that we can take

    B. TELL 'EM WHAT YOU TOLD 'EM

    C. Return to or reflect on attention getter (quotes, illustrations, incidents, appeals)

    D. Wrap up with final thought—try to tie to introductory main point; leave audience in proper state of mind. Present ideas slightly differently from what was said in the beginning.

VI. Bibliography

    A. Students must have at least two sources.

---

*Types of support include personal experience, humor, definitions, examples, descriptions, quotes, statistics, and compare/contrast.

**Briefly review what you just said and lead into the next main point using transitions.

Mini-Lecture: Visual Aids

> ➤ *Teacher Notes:* This is another fun mini-lecture presentation. We use the previous years' visual aids to demonstrate quality versus poor visual aids. We cover the student names so no identification remains. We show only the exemplary ones. We create the poor ones so no one is offended. As the school year unfolds, the portfolio videotapes become key in showing students why visual aids work and why they do not.

- Is a picture really worth a thousand words?
- Studies show that we learn better if we use more than one of our senses.
- What does this suggest to a speaker who wants his listeners to get the most out of his presentation?
- Audiovisual aids enhance the speech with illustrations.
- Audiovisual aids help to support speaker ideas and keep the audience interested.

Examples of audiovisual aids:
- Posters
- Overhead transparencies
- Models and objects
- Slides (no photos unless greatly enlarged)
- Flip charts
- Chalkboard
- Recordings/Video
- Laser disc

Things to keep in mind when preparing visual aids:
- Prepare them neatly and carefully.
- Make them large enough to be seen in the back of the room.
- Keep them very simple.
- Use striking colors and thick lines.
- Organize them.
- Make sure you know how to operate any audiovisual equipment.
- Make sure the aid is relevant to your topic.

Things to keep in mind while using your materials:
- Use the hand closest to the aid to point.
- Make sure everyone can see the aid.

- Allow enough time for all to see.

- Practice using the aid with your speech.

- Talk to the audience, not to the aid.

- Remove the aids when not in use so the audience is not distracted.

Assessment and Evaluation of the Informative, Demonstration, and Persuasive Speeches

In this section you find quizzes, rubrics, and evaluation forms we have developed to assess student work. We use a combination of formal and informal assessments, including the video portfolio.

We have used the first worksheet at the beginning of the speech unit. Students are divided into teams of four and assigned a section of text—*Communication: An Introduction to Speech*, Chapter 14, "The Informative Speech" (Newcombe 1988)—to read and then present to the rest of the class (a jigsaw lesson). As each group discusses their assigned section, they must answer questions from their section of this worksheet so the rest of the class has all the answers for that section. By the time all groups have presented their assigned sections, the worksheet is complete, and the informative speech basics have been covered.

INFORMATIVE SPEECH QUESTIONS

Name _____ Period _____

Directions: Listen carefully as the groups present lessons on informative speech. You should be able to answer these questions as the groups present. A word bank appears at the bottom of the second page for fill-in-the-blank questions.

Chapter Introduction

1. Any talk whose main purpose is giving information to people is a(n) _____.

2. True or False: An informative speech offers useful or interesting facts.

3. True or False: An informative speech can be based on personal experience or research.

4. True or False: The goal of an informative speech is to explain a subject so clearly that listeners easily understand.

5. True or False: More informative speeches are given than any other kind.

Beginning an Informative Speech

6. Each of the following is one of the purposes of the introduction to an informative speech except:
    a. An introduction introduces the speaker and subject.
    b. An introduction sets the tone of a speech.
    c. An introduction presents and supports the speech's main points.
    d. An introduction prepares listeners for the speech's main points.

7. Each of the following is a good attention-getting device for an informative speech except:
    a. Humor
    b. A brief biography of the speaker
    c. A rhetorical question
    d. A quotation

8. Each of the following statements is false except:
    a. A startling statement never makes a good opening for an informative speech.
    b. Listeners have no desire to know what to expect in a speech.
    c. The use of smooth transitions between points helps listeners understand the message.
    d. It is never proper to remind an audience of a speech's purpose in the conclusion.

9. Good attention getters in a speech include the following except:
    a. Humor
    b. Narrative (telling a story)
    c. Shock or startling statement
    d. Quotation
    e. Rhetorical question (asking a question for which you expect no answer)
    f. Throwing rotten fruit at the audience

Worksheet continues on page 32.

10. True or False: One of a speaker's most important jobs is to establish a good feeling with the audience.

The Body

11. True or False: The body is the core of your informative speech.

12. True or False: In the body of a speech, you fulfill your purpose of informing the audience about, or explaining, your topic.

13. True or False: When possible, you should use the same words in the body of your speech that you used in your introduction to refer to each main point. This helps the listeners to understand.

14. The definition for a _____ is "a statement that can be proved as true."

15. The definition for a _____ is "a fact expressed in numbers."

16. The definition for _____ is "pictures or objects that help to explain a point."

17. To be effective, audiovisual aids should be all of the following except:
    a. Small, for easy transportation to the speech site
    b. Neat and attractive
    c. Large enough for your audience to see
    d. Have been practiced with for maximum audience benefit

18. True or False: The speaker has enough to remember without having to watch the audience closely to see if anyone is confused or cannot hear the speaker well.

19. True or False: A good speaker does not need to know how to "read" audience "body language" or adjust the speech as needed.

20. The definition for _____ is "a word or phrase that shows how ideas are related."

The Conclusion

21. True or False: A speaker uses the conclusion to strengthen the main points.

22. True or False: The following are rules for speaking to an audience:

    Tell them what you are going to say (introduction).

    Say it (body).

    Tell them what you just said (conclusion).

23. True or False: In your conclusion, you should briefly summarize your main points to help the listeners learn.

24. True or False: There is no need to remind the audience in the conclusion of the purpose for the speech.

25. If a question and answer period follows an informative speech and the speaker does not know the answer to a question, the speaker should:
    a. Guess at the answer.
    b. Admit that he or she doesn't know.
    c. Answer another question that is somewhat related.
    d. Tell the questioner that he or she will find the answer.

Word Bank for Fill-in-the-Blank Questions

Fact

Statistic

Informative speech

Humor

Narrative

Audiovisual aids

Evaluation

Rhetorical question

Quotation

Transition

Answer Key for Informative Speech Questions

1. Informative speech

2. True

3. True

4. True

5. True

6. An introduction presents and supports the speech's main points.

7. A brief biography of the speaker

8. The use of smooth transitions between the points made in a speech helps listeners understand the speech's message.

9. Throwing rotten fruit at the audience

10. True

11. True

12. True

13. True

14. fact

15. statistic

16. audiovisual aids

17. Small, for easy transportation to the speech site

18. False

19. False

20. transition

21. False

22. True

23. True

24. False

25. Admit that he or she doesn't know

SPEECH EVALUATION FORM

>*Teacher Notes:* We have used the following speech evaluation format to "grade" speeches. However, the best gauge of achievement has been peer evaluations, using these formats during practice speeches. If time permits, we have students practice speeches in a peer group, have the peer group videotape rehearsals, and then have peers evaluate them. The quality of the final presentation rises dramatically using this technique. Usually peer groups are MUCH tougher on one another than the teacher is.

Directions: Please pay close attention to other students' speeches and they will pay close attention to yours. You will grade the elements of the demonstration speech today and give insight as to how the presentation might be improved.

Name _____ Period _____

Who are you grading? _____

Grade everything on a scale of 0–4.

> 0 = Didn't do this or exceptionally poor effort
> 1 = Poor effort
> 2 = Needs improvement, but okay
> 3 = Good effort
> 4 = Excellent effort

What Did You See?

_____ 1. Did the speaker wait until you were ready to listen?

_____ 2. Was the speaker's posture good? (Stands up straight, no leaning, no "dancing" or swaying, no hands in pockets)

_____ 3. Was the speaker's eye contact good?

_____ 4. Did the speaker show enthusiasm for the topic?

What Did You Hear?

_____ 5. Was the volume loud enough?

_____ 6. Were the words pronounced clearly and correctly?

_____ 7. Was the rate of speech appropriate? (Not too slow or too fast?)

Worksheet continues on page 36.

What Was Said?

Introduction

_____ 8. Was there an introduction?

_____ 9. Did you hear a good attention getter?

_____ 10. Did you hear a statement of the purpose of the speech?

_____ 11. Did you hear a preview (what main points will support the purpose)?

_____ 12. Did you hear a transition to the body?

Body

_____ 13. Were there sufficient details to support the topic?

_____ 14. Did the speaker use transitions to link main points?

Conclusion

_____ 15. Did you hear a concluding transition?

_____ 16. Did you hear a review of the main points?

_____ 17. How would you rate the closing thought?

Visual Aid

_____ 18. Was it appropriate to the topic? Did it aid the speech?

_____ 19. Was the lettering large enough to be seen at the back of the room?

_____ 20. Was it neat and attractive?

_____ TOTAL POINTS

Suggestions for Improvement

_____

_____

_____

_____

UNIT TWO: CREATING A MANDALA AS A VISUAL AID

Aligning Instructional Practices with Standards and Assessments

> ➤ *Teachers Notes:* In Eastern cultures the "mandala" is an expression of life. Based on this cultural perspective, this unit provides students with a creative way of sharing their personal backgrounds with peers. The learner expresses thoughts clearly and coherently to inform, persuade, and/or entertain an audience about a topic.

Learning Objectives

- Students will come to understand the cultural significance of the mandala.
- Students will use the artistic method best suited to their own individual intelligence to design and complete the mandala assignment.
- Students will read and follow directions.
- Students will use the mandala design to organize a three-minute speech.
- Students will select the appropriate visuals to support the speech.
- Student will deliver the speech.
- Students will participate in self and peer evaluations using guiding rubrics.

Assessments

Mandala grading rubric: self, peer, and teacher evaluation
Speech grading rubric

Instructional Strategies

The mandala assignment uses a creative approach to preparing students for their first speech. We use this assignment during the first quarter. It allows students to work in a collaborative learning environment, have access to technology and use creativity to share who they are. We intentionally provide only basic directions for the creation of the mandala. Students should be encouraged to add their own inventiveness in the mandala's design and development.

Remediation Strategies

This assignment can be adapted to a variety of needs. The speech's length may be shortened. Students with special adaptive needs may use a variety of methods to assist their presentations, such as a sign language interpreter for hearing impaired students.

Enrichment Strategies

Students may research the history of mandalas on the Internet and prepare background information supporting their creations.

Notes to Users of This Unit

Classroom Teachers: We use this assignment at the beginning of the school year. It provides us with the opportunity to do some informal assessing of student skills in interpersonal communication, as well as developing the first informative speech. Students have created very individualistic mandalas that reflected their artistic abilities. For example, one student created his mandala on a stone, while another used Inspiration® software.

The mandala is a vehicle to teach the first unit. Students follow a step-by-step organizational format. Students practice in teams before the first speech is videotaped. This videotape becomes part of their portfolio for the year. It is a great way for students to literally see their progress.

Media Specialists: The more students know about the history of mandalas and their part in the Eastern culture, the richer the experience. You could teach the history, assist in computer applications and help create artistic elements with library media resources. You can support this unit by gathering print materials on this topic and bookmarking pertinent Internet sites. In addition, you may want to find space in the media center to display some of the mandalas.

Technology Specialists: Students who know graphic software like to use it for mandalas. Because this unit is taught at the beginning of the school year, access to graphics software is often limited. Having graphics software, such as Inspiration®, loaded on a few computers would be most helpful. Internet access to the history of mandalas also supports this unit of study.

Learning Activity

This unit is based on this cultural perspective and provides students with a creative way of sharing their personal backgrounds with their peers. The mandala is used as a vehicle to prepare students for their first speech.

Specific Knowledge

The student will need to:

- Broaden cultural understanding.

- Use technology tools to support learning.

- Read and follow directions.

- Use the mandala design to organize a three-minute speech.

- Select the appropriate visuals to support the speech.

- Deliver a three-minute speech.

Environmental Considerations

Students will need:

- ◆ Computer access with graphics software and the Internet.

- ◆ Floppy disks and/or a file server location to store their works in progress.

- ◆ Art supplies, such as markers, rulers, compasses, glue, construction paper, and poster boards.

Assignments and Intelligences Addressed

Assignment	Intelligence
Design a Mandala	Artistic and Visual/Spatial
Three-Minute Speech	Linguistic

THE MANDALA

A mandala is a circular picture and an Eastern symbol for the expression of life. Your mandala assignment is meant to be a creative way to share information about yourself with the class. Here are the directions for making a mandala.

Materials: White or light-colored drawing paper or poster board, compasses, a ruler, colored fine-point felt markers or colored pencils, and graphics software.

Directions: The following directions are guidelines for you to follow in the creation of your mandala. You may follow these directions to make a poster board mandala, or you may use graphics software. If you have other creative ideas, please discuss them with the instructor prior to beginning work on your mandala.

1. Find the center of your paper by very lightly drawing a diagonal line in pencil from one corner to another corner. Repeat this step by drawing a diagonal line between the two remaining corners. The lines cross at the center.

2. Draw the first (outer) circle so that it is one-quarter inch from the side edges of the poster board.

3. Subsequent circles will move in toward the center point at one-half inch intervals.

4. Continue to draw circles until there is one band for every year of your age (including the center circle)

5. Do this in pencil so you can erase later if necessary.

6. Carefully erase the diagonal pencil lines.

7. In pencil, place a symbol in the center circle for the first year of your life. Some ideas: a baby bottle, a rattle, or your Zodiac sign.

8. List the most important event that happened during each year of your life. Think of a symbol that you could use to show this event and draw the symbol next to the year.

9. In each band or circle, draw enough symbols to fill in the band for that year.

10. Write the year in each band with the symbol.

11. You may place filler designs, such as zigzags, stars, or additional symbols to vary the patterns.

12. Go over each symbol with a fine point black marker.

13. Fill in all the symbols with colored markers or colored pencils.

14. Provide a key with the symbols for each year and attach it to the back of your poster.

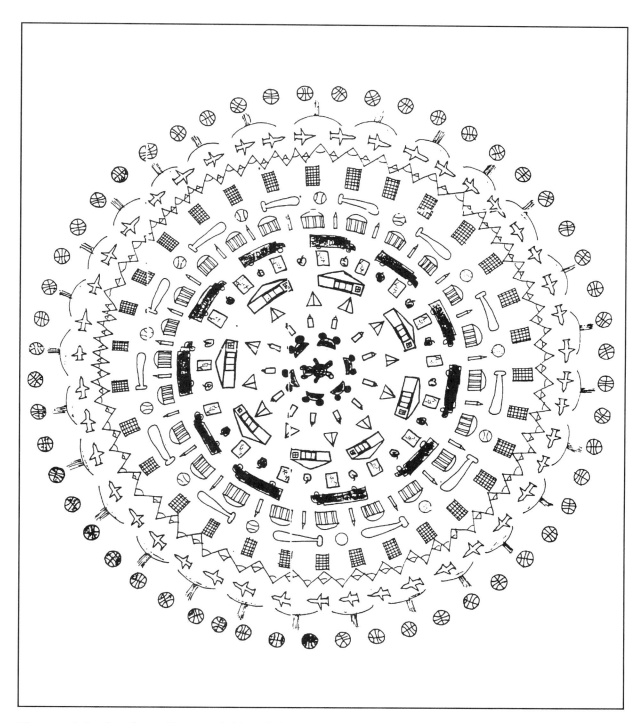

Figure 2.1. Student-Created Mandala

Figure 2.1 continued on next page.

Mandala

Tim Seier
3-15-93
8-6 B

Teddy Bear
    August 17, 1978 I was born

Mickey Hat
    My family and I took a trip to California

Baby bottle
    My little sister was born

Tent
    My family and I took a trip to the Black Hills

House
    Moved to the country in Nebraska

Book and Apple
    Started School

Moving Truck
    Moved to Littleton, Colorado

Memorial
    My family and I took a trip to Washington, D.C.

Baseballs
    My baseball team went to state finals

Hospital
    Went to hospital to get an Ultrasound on my stomach

Mountains
    Went on ski trip with my fifth grade class

Airplane
    My mom and I flew to Georgia

Geyser
    My family and I took a trip to Yellowstone

Basketballs
    My basketball team played almost 70 games

Speech Outline for Mandala Unit

Introduction: The purpose of the initial three-minute speech is to introduce yourself to your classmates via your mandala. Therefore, the mandala will be your visual aid.

Parts of Your Three-Minute Speech

I. Introduction

    A. Begin with a statement or question that focuses the audience's attention.

    B. Give the purpose of your speech.

    C. Tell the audience what you plan to talk about.

II. Body

    A. Deliver the main points.

    B. Use your visual aid (the mandala) as supporting evidence.

    C. Summarize the main points.

III. Conclusion

    A. Wrap up your speech by restating the purpose.

    B. Leave the audience with something to think about.

MANDALA GRADING SHEET

Name _____ Period _____

Due date _____ Turned in _____

Total points available: 48   Your actual points _____

Followed Directions	6	5	4	3	2	1	0
Neatness	6	5	4	3	2	1	0
Colorful	6	5	4	3	2	1	0
Creative	6	5	4	3	2	1	0
Key	6	5	4	3	2	1	0
Symbol for Each Year	6	5	4	3	2	1	0
Used Class Time Wisely	6	5	4	3	2	1	0
Turned in on Time	6	5	4	3	2	1	0

SPEECH EVALUATION CHECKLIST

Name _____ Date _____ Period _____

Time _____   Possible points: 65   Your points _____

5—Exceptional 4—Advanced 3—Proficient 2—Basic 1—Below standard

0—Did not meet minimum standards

Introductory Speech

What was seen:

Speaker waited until the audience was ready.	5	4	3	2	1	0
Speaker was appropriately dressed.	5	4	3	2	1	0
Posture was good.	5	4	3	2	1	0
Eye contact with audience was good.	5	4	3	2	1	0

What was heard:

Voice was loud enough to be heard.	5	4	3	2	1	0
Rate of presentation varied.	5	4	3	2	1	0
Good, clear pronunciation of words.	5	4	3	2	1	0
No "Ums, uhs, likes" or long pauses.	5	4	3	2	1	0

What was said:

Purpose of speech was clearly stated.	5	4	3	2	1	0
Speech was well organized.	5	4	3	2	1	0
Visual aid supported main points.	5	4	3	2	1	0
Introduction got audience's attention.	5	4	3	2	1	0
Conclusion was strong.	5	4	3	2	1	0

RESOURCES

Books

Emerson, Ralph Waldo. "Power," in *The Conduct of Life*. Temecula, CA: Reprint Services Corporation, 1992.

Fincher, Susanne F. *Creating Mandalas*. Boston: Shambhala, 1991.

Newcombe, P. Judson. 1988. *Communication: An Introduction to Speech*. Newton, MA: Allyn & Bacon, Inc., 1988.

Tripp, Rhoda Thomas. *The International Thesaurus of Quotations*. New York: Thomas Y. Crowell, 1970.

What Work Requires of Schools: A SCANS Report for America 2000 by the Secretary's Commission on Achieving Necessary Skills. Washington, D.C.: U.S. Department of Labor, 1991.

Speaking, *Technology,* Analysis, and Reading Through Research

"Technology is about connections—connecting people to each other, to ideas, and to possibilities. Imagine being able to sample the atmosphere of a planet millions of miles away and go hands-on with the universe—this is the stuff that gets kids excited about science! What's there not to love?"

—Shirley Malcolm, American Association
for the Advancement of Science

TECHNOLOGY COMPETENCIES

The Secretary's Commission on Achieving Necessary Skills (SCANS) report lists technology as a competency. Skills include selecting the appropriate computer and peripherals, applying technology to the task, and maintaining and troubleshooting equipment. In addition to these competencies, the information, systems, and interpersonal and resources competencies apply to technology use. Information involves the acquisition, evaluation, organization, interpretation, and communication of information. The computer is used specifically to process information. Understanding how technology works effectively is listed under the systems competency. The identification, organization, planning, and allocation of resources are all pertinent under the resources competency. And finally, using technology as a member of a team and introducing new skills are critical to interpersonal development. In addition to these SCANS competencies, the International Society for Technology in Education has created technology standards.

NATIONAL EDUCATIONAL TECHNOLOGY STANDARDS FOR STUDENTS

The National Educational Technology Standards (NETS) project is an International Society for Technology in Education (ISTE) initiative funded by the National Aeronautics and Space Administration (NASA) in consultation with the U.S. Department of Education, the Milken Exchange on Education Technology, and Apple Computer, Inc. These standards are reprinted with permission from *National Educational Technology Standards for Students* (June 1998), published by the International Society for Technology in Education (ISTE), NETS Project. The full document is available from ISTE at 800-336-5191 and at http://cnets.iste.org. The student standards are a part of the document.

The Technology Foundation Standards for Students are:

- Basic operations and concepts

    Students demonstrate a sound understanding of the nature and operation of technology.

    Students are proficient in the use of technology.

- Social, ethical, and human issues

    Students understand the ethical, cultural, and societal issues related to technology.

    Students practice responsible use of technology systems, information, and software.

    Students develop positive attitudes toward technology that support life-long learning, collaboration, personal pursuits, and productivity.

- Technology Productivity Tools

    Students use technology to enhance learning, increase productivity, and promote creativity.

    Students use productivity tools to collaborate in constructing technology-enhanced models, preparing publications, and producing other creative works.

- Technology Communications Tools

    Students use telecommunications to collaborate, publish, and interact with peers, experts, and other audiences.

    Students use a variety of media and formats to communicate information and ideas effectively to multiple audiences.

- Technology Research Tools

    Students use technology to locate, evaluate, and collect information from a variety of sources.

    Students use technology to process data and report results.

    Students evaluate and select new information resources and technological innovations based on a task's demands.

♦ Technology Problem-Solving Tools

Students use technology to solve problems and make informed decisions.

Students employ technology to develop problem-solving strategies in the real world.

Connecting Technology to Workplace Skills

Technology helps students make the connection between what they are learning in school and what is happening in the workplace. We invite parents to come into the classroom to talk about how their use of technology enhances their jobs. We have had demonstrations on software development, the computerized systems in F-14 fighter planes, and ACT!® software. Field trips to businesses that manufacture or utilize computers also help students to understand how fast the world of technology is moving and the skills that are needed.

Unit One: Friday Assignments

Aligning Instructional Practices with Standards and Assessments

The Friday assignments align with the technology standards listed above.

Learning Objectives

The students are provided with a variety of opportunities to apply software and other technology applications during the year. In this unit students will:

♦ Practice writing skills in each week's writing assignment.

♦ Practice proofreading and editing skills.

♦ Be instructed in computer vocabulary.

♦ Practice word processing skills.

♦ Practice graphic creation and insertion.

♦ Practice new software programs introduced in class.

Assessments

➤ *Teacher Notes:* These assessments include technology and writing. Please feel free to modify them to meet the needs of your students.

♦ Pre- and post-tests of computer vocabulary

♦ Pre- and post-tests of computer manipulation proficiency

- Rough draft of weekly writing assignment
- Evidence of proofreading and editing
- Peer editing
- Final draft following computer instruction
- Observation of hands-on computer proficiency

Instructional Strategies

Literal: These are lessons directly aimed at instructing the student in writing and computer applications, and specifically conform with the curriculum.

- Vocabulary worksheets
- Lab demonstrations
- Examples posted of weekly assignment expectations including sample final products
- In classroom demonstrations of computer applications using projection pad link to computer
- One-on-one instruction in lab

Lateral: Adjuncts to the literal lessons above.

- Web techniques
- Outlining instruction
- Friendly letter format
- Writing skills instruction
- Editing and proofreading instruction

Remediation Strategies

- One-on-one instruction
- Reduced expectations/modified assignments
- Paired learning on the computer
- Additional time for assignment completion
- Additional time on the computer

Enrichment Strategies

♦ Pre- and post-test pass: move directly to Friday assignments.

Satisfactory completion of Friday assignments allows students to contribute to STARR. Under the guidance of the Media or Technology Specialist, students bookmark interesting Web sites.

Notes to Users of This Unit

This unit begins with a pre-test of computer vocabulary. We have found that most students have a limited technology vocabulary, so additional instruction is required. We focus on the vocabulary so that we all have a common language. Students who pass the vocabulary pre-test immediately move to the Friday assignments. The rest of the class is given instruction in technical terms. Instruction in computer vocabulary usually takes about a week. Once all have a common language, we start the Friday writing assignments. Each Friday assignment is designed to provide an element of language arts development. Different language arts concepts are focused upon each week, as well as the previous weeks' lessons remaining a part of writing development. Additionally, elements of word processing are added each week to the computer lab expectations. Our classrooms are equipped with eight Mac computers. Our computer labs have 18 to 24 Macs. Either platform will work with this unit. The entire unit takes twelve weeks to complete. At the end of the unit, students are very familiar with word processing and have been introduced to presentation software.

Classroom Teachers: Availability of a computer lab is not essential, but it is extremely beneficial for this unit. A one-computer classroom is workable. The obvious restriction is time. The twelve-week unit in a computer lab will extend easily to a full year of computer instruction in a one-computer classroom. A portable bank of computers (on movable carts) would be less difficult and much more manageable than the one-computer setting. The initial writing instruction is completed in the classroom, as is peer proofreading, editing, and rewriting. A projection pad linked to a computer is extremely helpful in guiding students through computer instruction. We also use a class set of *WriteSource 2000* books (Sebranek, Meyer, and Kemper 1992) for instruction in writing techniques.

Media Specialists: In our school, very bright students are occasionally directed to work with the Media Specialist to develop advanced assignments. The teacher creates the lesson and provides minimal instruction. The student is then released to an independent study under the watchful eye of the Media Specialist. This unit includes an enrichment lesson on creating a Web page from bookmarked links to the Internet. The independent student relies on the Media Specialist strictly as a guide on the side.

Technology Specialists: We work collaboratively with our Technology Specialist in the first three weeks of computer lab instruction. As you might guess, novice computer users present interesting challenges. Additionally, our class sizes dictate that up to 30 students share 18 to 24 computers, so juggling time is necessary.

Unit Overview

Our technology component includes a basic introduction to computer hardware, software, and general terminology. Most of our students are fairly computer literate, but this was not always the case. As much as computers have changed over the past ten years, so has our curriculum and the background knowledge students have brought to the classroom. We continue to develop and change lessons, incorporating newer hardware and software as they become available. We continue to teach basics, though, just to be certain that all students have the same foundation of technology knowledge. A computer pre-test is given at the beginning of the technology unit. Students who test well do not need to sit through basic lessons. We immediately move them into Friday assignments.

Each Friday assignment is a separate instructional tool. We find that we have a much improved turn-in rate on these assignments, because students LOVE going to the computer lab, and they know they cannot use the computer on Friday if their Friday assignment is not completed. We have included ten Friday assignments for your perusal.

> *Teacher Notes:* The Friday assignments were adapted from an Internet source that has become lost in antiquity. An English instructor originally created the assignments to cover an entire year of language arts. We adapted selected assignments to use similar language arts instruction with our students, as well as weekly components of word processing, graphics, and presentational software. Also, at the bottom of each Friday assignment, a reading summary paragraph along with a parent's signature are required. Thus, the Friday assignment has several components.

Language Arts Curriculum Development

- Proofreading and editing

- Reading summary paragraphs

- Parent involvement

- Computer applications

As the name implies, writing assignments are to be completed prior to word processing in the computer lab on Fridays. The lessons are designed so that the paragraph, assigned on Monday, is due on Wednesday, peer edited in class, and rewritten with corrections made during the class period, or as homework. To gain access to the lab, the student has to present the peer-edited rough draft and second draft on Friday.

Friday Assignment #1

The first item included in this unit is the cover letter to parents explaining the program. Friday Assignment #1, about a relative, focuses on writing the paragraph and specifically, the topic sentence. In-class lessons develop the concepts of parts of a paragraph and writing a topic sentence. The computer lab assignment for this first week is a general introduction to Writing Center®, a simple word processing program that includes a graphic component. The intent is to familiarize the student with what the program can do, and allow him or her to key the paragraph. Minimal expectations include:

- Saving the document to a disk

- Double spacing the text

- Indenting the paragraph (use of tab)

◆ Placement of title (center alignment)

◆ Placement of student heading (right alignment)

Friday Assignment #2

The second Friday assignment, "Signs of Winter," involves brainstorming and list creation. The same features of paragraph and topic sentence development are used. You will note that a weekly checklist helps students think about the completion of the assignment. Also wrapped in these assignments is the idea of following directions. The checklist helps students to consider whether they have finished the expectations. The computer application for Friday Assignment #2 is the same as Friday Assignment #1, except we add a computer graphic to the final draft.

Friday Assignment #3

Occasionally in our work we try to incorporate components of character building. This Friday Assignment, "Being Treated Nicely," reflects that. Further, the lesson endeavors to aid the student in word choice. Thus, the word "nice" is restricted. The use of brainstorming and list making is used. In-class lessons focus on development of a conclusion. The computer application continues with keyboarding, alignment, and use of styles, fonts, and point size.

Friday Assignment #4

"Popularity" introduces the organization of thoughts through a "concept web." Several questions are first asked of the students to begin consideration of the topic of popularity. In-class lessons this week include the development of supporting sentences and details, as well as a continuing focus on writing conclusions. Word processing functions are continued, except that this week we move on to a new word processing program, ClarisWorks®. Students are usually hesitant to venture into a new program, but they quickly learn that there are more similarities than differences between the two programs.

Friday Assignment #5

The topic of "Water" introduces Friday Assignment #5. This is the fifth week of paragraph development, and we expect students to be able to write a quality eight-sentence paragraph at this point. Proofreading and editing techniques have further developed, and the final drafts are much improved. In the computer lab, this week introduces importing graphics from another application. This takes time, but becomes very valuable later on. We also might add that students who previously did not know how to save to a floppy disk or file server are by now quite proficient at it. We always require a double save, meaning save to the floppy, and also save to the file server folder for the particular class period. This also becomes critical when we move on to working in presentation software such as HyperStudio®. We have included an instruction sheet used in the computer lab for this Friday assignment to give you an idea of typical lab instructions. We do not always have a hard copy document of lab instructions for student reference. Most often the instructions are verbal and demonstrated via a projection pad linked to a computer. Note that students are instructed to use the tool bar to add or change graphics. Students learn to draw a box around their titles and use a fill to complete the background.

Friday Assignment #6

The next assignment, "Invitation to Dinner," has two parts. The first part is to write a paragraph describing whom a student would invite to dinner and why, and the second part is to write a letter inviting that person. In-class lessons develop the ability to compose a friendly letter. During this lesson, we use *WriteSource 2000*, which is an outstanding resource for middle-school students. It demonstrates how to write a friendly letter and a business letter, as well as how to address an envelope. Students must also access an address for their invitee. This week is very busy in the computer lab, because two items must be word processed, the paragraph and the letter. From this point on, lab time generally takes two days.

Friday Assignment #7

This assignment, "Snowstorm," introduces the outline. Students who have previously used a simple web graphic to organize their thoughts move fairly easily to outlining. Again, the *WriteSource 2000* handbook is used to develop outlining skills. We also have worked diligently at writing sentences that have both a subject and a verb. Peer editing and conferencing is fun at this point, because students are questioning one another about what is right or wrong. This week in computer lab is simply a word processing week, except the students are shown the function of making two columns out of their paragraphs. Graphics may be imported if time allows. Also, use of drawing tools is introduced.

Friday Assignment #8

This assignment, "A Good Sub," is always a fun one to read. Students will write anything! This assignment takes two weeks to develop in the classroom and lab. The assignment introduces the use of two paragraphs. Because it is a "Good Sub" versus "Bad Sub" type of comparison and contrast, the in-class writing assignment uses a Venn diagram. Students are encouraged in the computer lab to use the drawing tools to complete their Venn diagrams.

Friday Assignment #9

Transitions, oh, transitions! Now that we are into writing more than one paragraph, we begin to use transitions to link the paragraphs together. This writing assignment, "How to Tie a Shoe," Friday Assignment #9, is one of the most difficult to write. For most students, it is the first attempt made at technical writing, and transition words are critical to the step-by-step process. In the lab, ClarisWorks® slide show is introduced. Each step is placed on a slide. Each slide receives either an imported graphic or a drawn graphic. This lab process takes two to three weeks. When the slide shows are complete, students present them to their classmates. We have them follow one another's directions. This results in a couple of days of laughter.

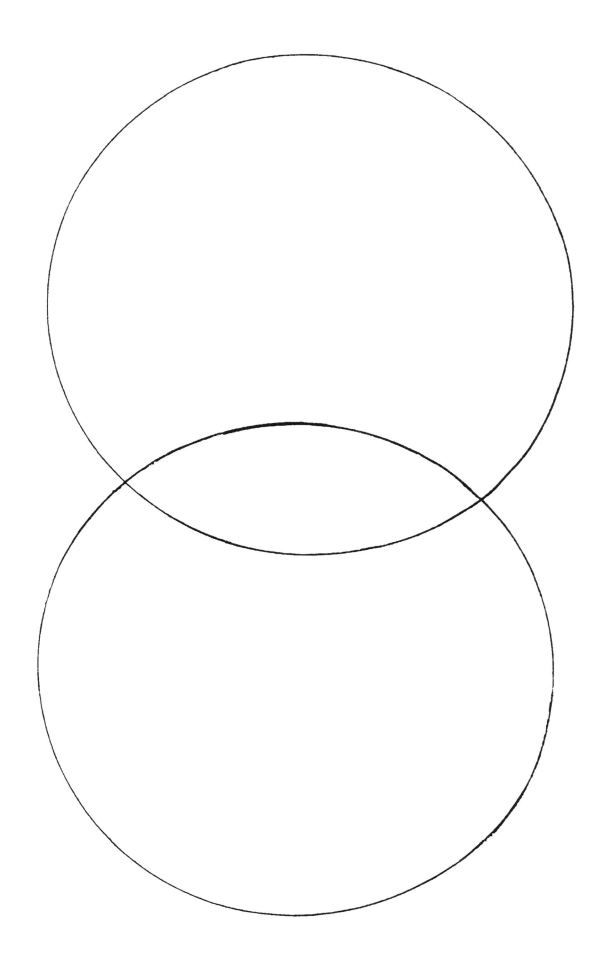

Figure 3.1. Venn Diagram for Friday Assignment #8.

Friday Assignment #10

This Friday assignment, "Television," is an editorial. We discuss editorials in class, bring in newspaper editorials, brainstorm ideas about what types of things students could write editorials about and explore how editorializing is different from creative writing. We discuss what we have learned previously from our research units about documenting with facts. If we have completed our persuasive speech unit, students often note the similar kinds of thinking in both the persuasive speech and editorials. Students are permitted to work in pairs. It takes time and considerable discussion for two students to write an editorial because of the diverse ideas that are generated. We also use a thesaurus to select better words. Students have become familiar with the thesaurus in software. It is news to some that a BOOK has the same information.

We have many more weeks of Friday assignments, but this gives you a good idea of what we are trying to accomplish. During the course of the Friday assignments, we also move into HyperStudio® or other presentation software. Students are well versed in word processing at the end of the Friday assignments, but the presentation software is just introduced. We develop HyperStudio® further when we complete the final research unit.

Friday Assignment #11

We have one final assignment, "Flat Farley," included in this chapter (in other locales, we have heard Flat Farley called Flat Angela). This is truly one of the most enjoyable assignments we offer. It's enjoyable for the students, and it involves their families or friends. The grading matrix for Flat Farley is included. Letter composition, envelope addressing, artwork, and a speech element of reading responses to the class are all parts of this lesson. We hope you enjoy it as much as we have.

Environmental Considerations

This unit is conducted 75 to 80 percent of the time in the classroom. Instruction in writing, proofreading, editing, and rewriting all takes place in the regular classroom. We are privileged to have eight computers in our STARR classrooms, along with an LCD projection pad, which allows us to provide instruction in computer applications on a projection screen. Because our lab is heavily booked, we are somewhat restricted in whole class use of the computer lab. The Friday assignments also involve great student interaction in the peer-editing phases. It is delightful to hear a student ask another if a comma belongs there, or if a better word might be "considerate" instead of "nice." Learning is happening!

> ➤ *Teacher Notes:* The Friday assignments are designed to encourage interaction with the family at home. We send the following letter home at the beginning of the unit so parents or guardians will understand the focus of Friday's assignments. Please modify this letter to meet your needs. In addition, the Friday assignments are designed to introduce students to computer software and their applications to learning. Students read, research, write, edit, and create for these assignments.

LETTER TO PARENTS

Date

Dear Parents,

For STARR this semester each student will have a homework assignment, given on Friday and due the following Friday. The assignment will be described in detail and brought home. Usually it will be a short composition that covers various reading and writing skills.

The cumulative grades of the homework papers will count as a part of the student's STARR grade. The student must hand in the direction sheet and an edited rough draft copy on Fridays. Students will be given time in class to type the final draft.

The first assignment, due Friday _____ is attached to this sheet. Will you please sign below and have your student return it to class by_____ ?

These are the criteria on which each paper will be graded:

1. Heading: Name, STARR Period, Date

2. Title of assignment included

3. Topic sentence (thesis or main point) provided

4. Supporting sentences (at least three) present

5. Concluding sentence present

6. Paragraphs indented correctly

7. Interesting to the reader?

8. Neatness?

9. Spelling is correct

10. Punctuation is correct

11. Grammar is correct

12. No run-on or incomplete sentences

13. Evidence of editing effort

Points possible for rough draft and assignment sheet = 10
Bonus points possible for parent edit and signature on Friday assignment and weekly reading summary = 5
Total possible weekly grade = 15/10

Additionally, the assignment will include a weekly summary paragraph of the outside reading book or designated material.

Summary points possible = 10

Thank you.

I have read and understand the responsibility my child has in completing his/her Friday STARR assignments.

Signed _____ Date _____

FRIDAY ASSIGNMENT #1

Name _____ Date _____ Period _____

Please hand in this sheet with your rough draft!

My Relative

A paragraph is a group of sentences telling about a single idea or topic. The beginning sentence or topic sentence should get the paragraph started. It should tell something important about the subject. It should also make the reader become interested in what will be discussed.

Write one paragraph about a relative. It can be a description of a favorite or not so favorite relative. Be sure to follow each step below. Check off each one as you complete it. Your grade will be based on the successful completion of each step, with special attention to step 1.

1. The first sentence must be a topic sentence. This sentence must express the paragraph topic or central thought.

2. The paragraph must be your original work (no plagiarism!).

3. Each sentence must stick to the topic and relate to the topic sentence.

4. Indent the first word of the paragraph.

5. Begin and end each sentence correctly. Make sure each word is spelled correctly.

6. Edit the paragraph, making certain you have followed the format below.

....

Name _____

STARR period _____

Date _____

Title _____

Be sure to indent. The first line should be 1/2 inch (or TAB on the computer = five spaces) from the left margin. Don't forget to skip a line between the title and first paragraph.

Signature of the person who checked your original rough draft for completeness. This signature is also for the weekly reading summary paragraph below.

READING SUMMARY PARAGRAPH

Name of material read _____

Author _____

Summary (five-sentence summary minimum) _____

_____

_____

....

FRIDAY ASSIGNMENT #2

Name _____ Date _____ Period _____

Please hand in this sheet with your rough draft!

Signs of Winter

For STARR this week you are to spend some time outside all alone. Be sure no one is around to disturb you. Listen carefully, smell deeply, and touch objects. Slowly look around you. Look up, down, and to each side. Next, make a list of all signs of winter on the BACK of this paper.

Now choose one sign of winter that you would like to write about. Describe it very carefully so that I will have a vivid mental picture.

Be sure to develop a strong topic sentence with three or four supporting sentences and a good concluding sentence. Check yourself:

- I took plenty of time to think.

- I wrote one rough draft and reworked it.

- I used complete sentences.

- I began each sentence with a capital letter and ended with the correct punctuation.

- I have handed in the direction sheet with my list on the back, and my edited rough draft.

Signature of the person who checked your original rough draft for completeness. This signature is also for the weekly reading summary paragraph below.

READING SUMMARY PARAGRAPH

Name of material read _____

Author _____

Summary (five-sentence summary minimum) _____

_____

_____

_____

_____

_____

FRIDAY ASSIGNMENT #3

Name _____ Date _____ Period _____

Please hand in this sheet with your rough draft!

Being Treated Nicely

All of us like to have special things done for us. What types of action do you consider pleasing? What do you like to have people do for you? Do not use the word "nice" in your paragraph.

List ten ideas of considerate things people do for one another.

1. _____

2. _____

3. _____

4. _____

5. _____

6. _____

7. _____

8. _____

9. _____

10. _____

What do you do that is really thoughtful? Do you have to think about your behavior, or is it automatic? This week, not only will you write a paragraph about something you consider gracious, but you are to do something agreeable for at least three people. What will these actions be, and who will you choose? List your three good deeds on the bottom of your rough draft.

Remember:

1. Name, STARR period, date

2. Indent

3. Check spelling

4. Title?

5. Use five or six sentences in your paragraph (including topic and concluding sentences).

6. List three good deeds at the bottom of your rough draft.

Signature of the person who checked your original rough draft for completeness. This signature is also for the weekly reading summary paragraph below.

READING SUMMARY PARAGRAPH

Name of material read _____

Author _____

Summary (five-sentence summary minimum) _____

_____

_____

_____

_____

_____

FRIDAY ASSIGNMENT #4

Name _____ Date _____ Period _____

Please hand in this sheet with your rough draft!

Popularity

For this week's Friday assignment, you will write about popularity. Think about the following ideas:

- Do you think someone has to be good-looking to be popular?

- Does popularity depend on your personality; your looks; where you live; how much money your parents have; how good you are at sports; how smart you are in school; if you are kind, polite, or honest; the freedom your parents give you?

- If you think popularity depends on any of the ideas above, explain why.

- Are some people popular at one time and not at another?

- What behaviors could you change or improve about yourself that would make you more popular?

After thinking about some of these questions, choose one topic about popularity, web your ideas on the back of this paper, and write a good paragraph about that topic. Do not try to include all these ideas in one paragraph!

Needed:

1. A good topic sentence

2. Three or four supporting sentences

3. A good concluding sentence

4. No spelling errors

5. A title

6. Web of ideas on the back

Signature of the person who checked your original rough draft for completeness. This signature is also for the weekly reading summary paragraph below.

READING SUMMARY PARAGRAPH

Name of material read _____

Author _____

Summary (five-sentence summary minimum) _____

_____

_____

_____

FRIDAY ASSIGNMENT #5

Name _____ Date _____ Period _____

Please hand in this sheet with your rough draft!

Water

Your Friday assignment this week is to write a paragraph about water. You may choose a drop of rain, a river, a tear, a storm, the ocean, or any type of water. On the back of this paper, list at least ten more types of water. Choose one type of water and web ideas also on the back of this paper.

You may want to discuss how water is used, where you find it, what it looks like, feels like, tastes like, etc. Whatever you choose, be sure to stick to the chosen topic.

Remember:

1. A good topic sentence

2. A concluding sentence to pull the paragraph together

3. Heading

4. Spelling checked?

5. No run-on or incomplete sentences?

6. Punctuation checked?

7. Title

8. Neatness

Signature of the person who checked your original rough draft for completeness. This signature is also for the weekly reading summary paragraph below.

READING SUMMARY PARAGRAPH

Name of material read _____

Author _____

Summary (five-sentence summary minimum) _____

_____

_____

_____

_____

LAB INSTRUCTION SHEET

Name _____ Date _____ Period _____

ClarisWorks Practice Assignment

This is the last ClarisWorks® word processing *practice* assignment. Future work will be in HyperStudio®, or will be assignments that require you to word process documents with no written or verbal instructions. By the end of the day, you will have successfully completed the unit on ClarisWorks®, unless you have not turned in previous work. In today's assignment, you need to:

- Right justify your heading in 12 point Helvetica font and plain text style.

- Subscript your class period number in your heading.

- Increase the point size to 18 in your title, boldface and underline once and center justify.

- Return point size to 12-point type for your paragraph and select the Times font.

- Change margins to two-inches on all sides.

- Indent your paragraph.

- Check spelling.

- Proofread out loud and have another student read it to you out loud to catch errors.

- Choose clip art from any source and center it beneath your paragraph.

You should know how to do all of the above without asking for assistance.

New instructions: Under VIEW in the menu, select "Show Tools." A tool bar will now appear down the left side of your document.

- The top left arrow tool or pointer, moves any art you create.

- The "A" is the text tool for word processing and must be selected to type words.

- Play with the line, box, rounded rectangle, oval, arcs, polygon, freehand, bezigon tool, regular polygon, and eyedropper.

- Notice the handles when a graphic is selected. Handles let you move, resize or delete. You cannot do anything with a design unless it has handles.

- Click and hold on the multicolored box (fill color) to see a palette of colors.

- If you click and hold on the boxes to the right of the color palette (the fill pattern and fill gradient), you'll see patterns they create.

- You'll notice a tool that looks like a pen and a box with four squares next to it (the pen indicator).

- Beneath the pen is another color box (pen color), pen pattern, pen width, and arrows.

- Play with all tools in the tool bar for a few minutes until you feel comfortable with each one.

- Place a box, rounded rectangle, oval, or polygon around your title. Fill with color (your choice) and change the fill pattern. You may want to play with the fill gradient, but at a minimum you must have a boxed and filled title.

- Did your title disappear when you created the box? Not to worry!! Click on the arrow tool (the menu bar changes). Click on the box to select it. Handles appear. Select "Arrange" from the menu bar and then "Move to Back." Now your title is in the foreground and the box is in the background!

FRIDAY ASSIGNMENT #6

Name _____ Date _____ Period _____

Please hand in this sheet with your rough draft!

Invitation to Dinner

This week's Friday assignment has two parts. They are to be handed in on two separate pages.

You may invite anyone in the world as your dinner guest. For the first part of the assignment, write a paragraph about your guest. Who will you invite? Why have you chosen this particular guest? Try to write a creative, interesting paragraph with a good topic sentence that gets the reader's interest and attention.

Now, for part two, write the letter inviting your guest. First look at the *WriteSource 2000* handbook to format your letter correctly. It must be set up in a friendly letter style. Be sure your letter is interesting enough to make the guest want to come. Why should he/she come? What do you plan to do to make it worth his/her time?

Check:

1. Did you write the paragraph on one paper and your letter on another?

2. Did you include a title for your paragraph?

3. Is your letter in the correct *WriteSource 2000* format?

4. Is the guest's name spelled correctly? Where can you check?

5. Did you check spelling, punctuation, capitalization?

Signature of the person who checked your original rough draft for completeness. This signature is also for the weekly reading summary paragraph below.

READING SUMMARY PARAGRAPH

Name of material read _____

Author _____

Summary (five-sentence summary minimum) _____

_____

_____

_____

_____

FRIDAY ASSIGNMENT #7

Name _____ Date _____ Period _____

Please hand in this sheet with your rough draft!

Snowstorm

Take a minute and think of all the things a person can do in the snow. Make a list of as many things as you can:

1. _____

2. _____

3. _____

4. _____

5. _____

6. _____

7. _____

8. _____

9. _____

10. _____

Choose one snow activity to write a paragraph about. You may find that two or three ideas will go together to make one good paragraph. Develop a rough outline on the back of this paper. If you are uncertain about outline format, check the *WriteSource 2000* handbook. A web format will not count. Next, develop a paragraph with at least five quality sentences.

Make sure you have an interesting topic sentence! I will check for a strong topic sentence before I read the rest of the paragraph. The paper will not be accepted if it does not have an interesting, attention-grabbing topic sentence. Also, check spelling. Any spelling error will result in your paper being ungraded and returned to you.

Worksheet continues on page 68.

Check:

1. Outline on reverse side

2. Terrific topic sentence

3. No run-on or incomplete sentences

4. Spelling

5. Punctuation and capitalization

6. Concluding sentence

7. Title

Signature of the person who checked your original rough draft for completeness. This signature is also for the weekly reading summary paragraph below.

READING SUMMARY PARAGRAPH

Name of material read _____

Author _____

Summary (five-sentence summary minimum) _____

_____

_____

_____

_____

_____

FRIDAY ASSIGNMENT #8

Name _____ Period _____ Date _____

Please hand in this sheet with your rough draft!

A Good Sub

When your teacher is ill or has to be out of the classroom, a substitute teacher is called in. Some substitutes are very good. Why? What makes someone a good substitute or regular teacher?

Write one paragraph describing what good substitutes do and what they are like. What do they do to be successful? I do not want to read that the substitute was nice. Be more specific. Write about what they did or said that made you conclude they were nice.

Add a second paragraph describing the WORST substitute you have ever had. What made him or her so poor? What good teaching qualities were missing? What would you have done differently if you had been that day's substitute? We will develop a Venn diagram comparing and contrasting good and poor substitutes. You will include a Venn diagram with your final draft.

Focus on interesting sentences. Don't settle for simple third-grade writing. Support your ideas with reasons of who, what, when, where, why, and how types of thinking.

Check:

1. Two paragraphs with interesting sentences

2. Spelling

3. Capitalization, punctuation, indentation

4. Appropriate word choices. Remember, no "stuff," "cuz," or similar slang.

Adult signature for editing of rough draft _____

READING SUMMARY PARAGRAPH

Title of reading material _____

Author _____

Summary (five-sentence summary minimum) _____

_____

_____

_____

_____

FRIDAY ASSIGNMENT #9

Name _____ Period _____ Date _____

Please hand in this sheet with your rough draft!

How to Tie a Shoe

A paragraph with five or six sentences usually includes all problems of a longer composition. It requires practice to organize and shape a single topic. Each paragraph offers a clear and orderly thought.

This week you will write a paragraph about how to tie a shoe. You are to physically go through each step and write them down as you proceed. Use these steps to help build a paragraph.

List the steps to tying a shoe on the back of this sheet prior to composing your paragraph. Use transition words or phrases, such as first, second, next, in addition, further, and also to illustrate the sequence of steps in tying a shoe.

Check:

1. Did you use capital letters for each word in the title?

2. Did you indent the paragraph?

3. Is your paragraph interesting?

4. Did you remember your heading on the rough draft?

5. Did you remember to physically go through your steps just as you have them written?

6. Did you check spelling, capitalization, and punctuation?

7. Word choice

READING SUMMARY PARAGRAPH

Title of reading material _____

Author _____

Summary (five-sentence summary minimum) _____

_____

_____

_____

_____

FRIDAY ASSIGNMENT #10

Name _____ Period _____ Date _____

Please hand in this sheet with your rough draft!

Television

> *Teacher Notes: Channel One* is referenced in this assignment. *Channel One* is a daily news program available to schools by satellite. Daily lesson plans that link the news to classroom planning are also available.

For this Friday assignment, you will write two paragraphs about television. You need a topic sentence for each paragraph. The first paragraph needs to have a transition sentence or "lead-in" sentence that will introduce the second paragraph. The second paragraph needs a concluding sentence for the whole paper.
Ideas to consider:

- How is television useful?
- What are the drawbacks of television?
- Are commercials effective? Why?
- Why are some programs more popular than others?
- What would you want to know if a TV producer came to talk to you?
- Do you have any knowledge or questions about live broadcasts?
- Are live broadcasts more effective than tape-delayed ones?
- Does news coverage interest you? Why?
- Can you think of improved uses for television?
- What do you think of the age-appropriate rating scale?
- What is good or bad about watching *Channel One*? Why?

Each paragraph needs a topic sentence and three or four supporting sentences. Push your brain! Do some good thinking before you begin. Create a web on the back of this paper first to sketch out ideas. Write a paper worth handing in. *Do not describe your favorite program.*
Do:

- Have a title and heading.
- Edit for spelling, punctuation, and capitalization.
- Work hard for good word choices. Remember, a thesaurus is helpful.
- Use clear handwriting so your editor and I can easily read the rough draft.
- Check for quality writing in BOTH paragraphs.

Adult editor signature _____

READING SUMMARY PARAGRAPH

Title of reading material _____

Author _____

Summary (five-sentence summary minimum) _____

FRIDAY ASSIGNMENT #11

Name_____ Period _____ Date _____

Please hand in this sheet with your rough draft!

Flat Farley

This week you will learn the proper way to write a friendly letter. This is something you have surely done before, but this time we are going to type it in Writing Center®.

First, however, we must design Flat Farley. Alas and woe is me, Flat Farley was flattened by a semitrailer on I-25 and then run over by a steamroller. Flat Farley needs a vacation and desires to visit as much of the world as he can before the flatness condemns him or her to lifelessness. Please design a female or male Flat Farley using your wonderful imagination. Your Flat Farley graphic will be sent in your letter. All artwork entries will receive ten points extra credit. The best Flat Farley selected by students to represent that period will receive 20 points extra credit. The winning Flat Farley will be posted on the school's Web site and placed on a hallway bulletin board.

Your mission is to send Flat Farley to a faraway place to visit someone you know. Ask the friend/relative in your cover letter to take Flat Farley somewhere, to a movie, store, museum, sports event, or wherever they wish. Then the friend/relative writes a letter back to tell you of their adventure. If we send the letters now, we may have Flat Farley's escapades completed by winter break. We just want to know where and how Flat Farley is. You will need to explain all this in your letter.

Remember, you must use the checklist below to edit your letter. A parental edit of your rough draft is worth five extra points.

1. My letter is properly set up in a friendly letter format.

2. I have no spelling errors.

3. I have no punctuation or capitalization errors.

4. I have no incomplete sentences.

5. I have two peer edits.

6. I have handed in this sheet with my edited rough draft.

_____

PARENTAL EDIT SIGNATURE LINE

Assessments

Name _____ Period _____

Water Grade Matrix

    ____ Heading right justified (1)

    ____ First name superscript (1)

    ____ Period # subscript (1)

    ____ Title centered and boxed (4)

    ____ Picture added (3)

    ____ Paragraph left justified (1)

    ____ Computer proof and spell check (3)

    ____ Content—final draft (10)

    ____ Peer editing x 4 (8)

    ____ Checklist (3)

    ____ Web (5)

    ____ Rough draft (5)

    ____ Corrected draft (5)

    ____ Parent edit bonus (5 extra)

        ____ TOTAL of 55 possible

Flat Farley Grade Sheet

    _____ Friendly letter format (10)

    _____ Content (12)

    _____ Grammar, punctuation, and capitalization (5)

    _____ Spelling (5)

    _____ Peer edit and two corrected rough drafts (10)

    _____ Checklist (3)

    _____ Parent edit (2 extra)

    _____ Flat Farley (10 extra)

➤*Teacher Notes:* We hope you have enjoyed the Friday Assignments. It is one of the finest units we have used to teach both writing skills and technology applications.

UNIT TWO: STAFF DEVELOPMENT—LEARNING ABOUT TECHNOLOGY INTEGRATION

> *Teacher Notes:* This unit deviates a bit from the others, because it is a unit for teachers. We share some thoughts on technology staff development and some information on how to integrate technology. This information is used with real teachers in real classrooms as one of the authors works with educators on incorporating technology.

Staff Development

According to research, staff development works best when it is ongoing and situated in the classroom. This model helps teachers as they journey from a beginner through mastering technology skills. Novices who have not embraced technology are initially overwhelmed. If technology use is a requirement, they send students to the computer lab because they simply have not acquired the skills to create lessons integrating technology. Alan November, a seminal leader in educational technology, terms this the automating phase. Technology is used at this stage to carry out class assignments. At this point, teachers use their familiar curriculum and pin technology on top of old assignments. Adherence to well-worn material seems to be a natural part of the evolutionary process and forms a bridge to the next stage.

Teachers who use technology to save time or as a personal productivity tool are ready to explore other technology options. They probably use computerized grade books or electronically record attendance.

In the integration stage, teachers rethink the curriculum. This is what STARR is about. New activities are created using technology as a tool. Students access the Internet to find new information. They create multimedia presentations. In the final stage, a new curriculum emerges. The classroom is now a new learning environment where technology is integrated into learning. This stage is sometimes referred to as the innovation or "informating" (November 1998) stage.

To facilitate movement from the beginning level to the informating level, staff development must be designed to meet teachers where they are in their acceptance of technology. Often teachers need to see technology in use before they can begin to implement it. Begin by offering workshops in hardware and software use. At the beginning, teachers need a foundation in technology basics. Most preliminary training is offered in a lab. The educators are learning how to operate the computer, scanner, or video camera. They learn to troubleshoot hardware. Their comfort level rises. In the classroom, they frequently teach technology, especially word processing software. At the next step, educators integrate technology. They create project-based lessons. Teachers as learners are using the Internet to access information. Multimedia presentations are used to convey and communicate lessons. At this point, the training is a combination of lab presentations to the educator as well as in-class sessions. In this information stage, the teacher is tossing aside old lesson plans and creating new ones that integrate technology.

At the true integration stage, the classroom transforms into a new learning environment. Technology is a seamless tool used for accessing and sharing information. Students talk with experts via e-mail and video conferencing. Their products are often Web sites with chat rooms. Staff development is situated in the learning environment and comes from team members and Technology Specialists who coach and mentor. As we move through this process, the learning environment changes. Teachers become facilitators. They no longer provide all the answers. The inquiry-based environment is leaner. It is at the informating and integration stages that the greatest increase in student achievement can be seen. At these levels, we see the technology use for STARR. We encourage you to move through the technology learning process to create the kinds of environments we support in STARR. It is vitally important to remember that this process takes time. Honor your own learning style and give yourself the time you need to explore and practice new skills.

> *Teacher Notes:* The following Technology Competency Checklist is based on the ISTE standards referenced earlier in this chapter.

Technology Competency Checklist: Tracking My Own Progress
Basic Computer/Technology Operations and Concepts Achieved/Date

1. Start up and shut down computer system.

2. Navigate and use icons, windows, and menus.

3. Start a software program and create a document.

4. Name and save a document.

5. Change font size and styles and format a document.

6. Insert and eject a floppy disk and a CD ROM.

7. Copy a document from hard disk to floppy disk and vice versa.

8. Save, open, and place documents inside subdirectories/folders.

9. Understand how to move documents to and from multiple platforms.

10. Initialize and name/rename a floppy disk and a hard disk.

11. Run programs from CD ROMs and a network.

Using the Internet with Students

> *Teacher Notes:* This information was created for teachers who want to use the Internet on a small scale and in a controlled environment.

First, go to http://www.concentric.net/~mongeau/. This Web site was the final project for IT 5160 at the University of Colorado at Denver. Denise Mongeau is a Technology Staff Developer for the Public Education and Business Coalition located in Denver, Colorado.

For those who don't want to do that right now, here is the short version:

1. Preparing lessons using the Internet takes both *time* and *patience.*

2. Decide on your purpose for using the Internet. Students love it; it frustrates teachers, but the bottom line is: *What is the educational objective for using the Internet?*

3. So, you have an educational objective. You want your students to complete research on the rainforest. You must first take time to access, sort, and select appropriate sites. Remember those words: access, sort, and select. (Also known as information and knowledge management.)

4. Yahoo and Yahooligans. Educators evaluate this site, so the sites have the good educational sites' seal of approval. Begin sorting and selecting there.

5. Some hints: The more specific the search, the better your information. Typing in rainforest brings up a zillion sites. Quotation marks narrow the topic, like "Rainforests of Brazil". Quotation marks tell the search engine you only want articles with the entire phrase in it. Omitting quotation marks instructs the search engine to look for every article with rainforest and Brazil.

6. Read the search engine's help section. Each one uses different techniques to narrow the search. One uses quotation marks, while another uses and/+ and other unique devices.

7. Preview the sites.

8. *Beware.* Teachers can get into big trouble for directing students to inappropriate Web sites. Just as you have to preview a video, preview the Web sites.

9. Hint: If pressed for time, bookmark the sites that look good and go back and pick the ones you want. A few well-selected sites are better than a whole slew of mediocre ones. Once you have bookmarked the Web sites, your students are ready to begin their Internet research experience.

10. Teach your students how to access, sort, and select within your bookmarked sites. This is essential to them as information managers.

11. *Never* waste instructional time by printing out sites, because it is an incredible waste of paper and energy. TEACH them to select articles that support their research. They can print out some or take notes from the screen.

12. Be patient with yourself and your students. Using the Internet is fun and motivating. Kids love it and learn so much. Just remember that the Internet is one more tool that can help students learn. Use it appropriately.

13. Finally, take the time to go to Denise's site. It is really worth it.

Creating Online Scavenger Hunts

> *Teacher Notes:* The Online Scavenger Hunt was designed to help teachers overcome obstacles to using Internet resources in the classroom. By bookmarking Web sites, some teachers feel safer in using the Internet. It also can be a time saver.

1. Determine the purpose of your hunt. Goal(s)? Objective(s)?

2. Follow this example.

WOMEN OF THE AMERICAN CIVIL WAR SCAVENGER HUNT

Name _____ Date _____ Period_____

Directions: You may work alone or in teams to complete this scavenger hunt.

Read and complete the information in each step.

Step 1. Click on the Netscape® browser icon.

Step 2. Go to Bookmarks.

Step 3. Open the Civil War folder in Bookmarks.

Step 4. Open The American Civil War folder.

Step 5. Look for Women in the War.

Step 6. Click on Harriet Beecher Stowe.

Step 7. Read and answer these questions about Harriet Beecher Stowe:

a. What was her position concerning slavery?

b. How did she communicate the slaves' views?

Step 8. Go back to the Women of the American Civil War screen.

Step 9. Select two other women. Read about them and describe their contributions to the American Civil War.

Step 10. Be ready to share what you have learned with the class.

➤*Teacher Notes:* Web site: http://www.americancivilwar.com. Remember that the integration of technology is a developmental process for both you and your students. Allow yourself to experiment and take risks. Customize the materials we have provided to fit your teaching style.

RESOURCES

Books

Burness, Patty. *Learn & Live*. Nicasico, CA: The George Lucas Educational Foundation, 1997.

Sebranek, Patrick, Meyer, Verne, Kemper, Dave, and Krenzke, Chris. *WriteSource 2000*. Burlington, WI: Write Source Educational Publishing House, 1992.

What Work Requires of Schools: A SCANS Report for America 2000 by the Secretary's Commission on Achieving Necessary Skills. Washington, D.C.: U.S. Department of Labor, 1991.

Software

ClarisWorks®. A multifaceted program, including word processing, spreadsheet, database, painting, and graphics. It is available at http://www.claris.com or through Apple Computer, Inc. at 1-800-325-2747.

Web Sites

Alan November, Educational Renaissance Planners. http://edrenplanners.com

Apple Research: This site provides research from the Apple Classrooms of Tomorrow Project which supports the use of technology in the classroom. http://www.apple.com/education/K12/leadership/acot/

Channel One: http://www.channelone.com

The International Society for Technology in Education (ISTE), NETS Project. *National Educational Technology Standards for Students*. The full document is available from ISTE at 800-336-5191 and at http://cnets.iste.org.

teachworld.com: This site is part of the Channel One Network. http://www.teach1.com

Yahoo!: http://www.yahoo.com. This site is a search engine that allows you to explore the Internet via subject areas.

Yahooligans: http://www.yahooligans.com. This site within Yahoo is designed for kids. All the Web sites listed are considered safe and have been reviewed and selected for educational use.

Speaking, Technology, *Analysis*, and Reading Through Research

---

"We do not live to think, but, on the contrary, we think in order that we may succeed in surviving."

—Jose Ortega Y Gasset

ANALYSIS FOUNDATION SKILLS

The Secretary's Commission on Achieving Necessary Skills (SCANS) report lists thinking skills under the three-part foundation. We purposefully selected the term "analysis" because we wanted to focus learning on the processes included in this term: analyzing, appraising, calculating, categorizing, comparing, contrasting, criticizing, differentiating, discriminating, distinguishing, examining, experimenting, questioning, and testing (Bloom 1956). Within this context, students are indeed thinking. The thinking skills listed in the Foundation Skills include creative thinking, decision-making, problem solving, seeing things in the mind's eye, knowing how to learn, and reasoning. These thinking skills correlate to and support the third component of STARR—analysis.

CONTENT PROFICIENCIES IN ANALYSIS

The student demonstrates an understanding of information gathering, problem solving, critical thinking, and decision-making. With instruction in these thinking skills, students will be able to:

* Generate interesting questions to be answered while reading.

* Establish and adjust purposes for reading (e.g., to solve problems, answer specific questions, and form opinions).

* Generate new ideas through creative thinking.

- Learn to apply decision-making skills.

- Recognize problems and devise ways to solve them.

- Use efficient learning techniques to acquire and apply new knowledge and information.

- See relationships and make connections among curricular areas.

The student expresses thoughts clearly and coherently to inform, persuade, and/or entertain an audience about a topic. Students will:

- Ask questions in class.

- Organize ideas for oral presentations.

> *Teacher Notes:* The analysis component of STARR is an integral part of the students' daily learning. Analysis cannot be taught as a discrete skill, but is woven into the learning process. Our goal in including analysis as one of the five components in STARR was to underline the importance of producing students who are thinkers capable of asking important questions about what and why they are learning.

UNIT ONE: PROBLEM SOLVING

Learning Objectives

In this unit students think about problems and how they might approach solving them in a variety of ways. The graphic organizer we introduce is used throughout the year. In this unit students will:

- Define problem solving.

- Learn to identify the cause of a problem.

- Become aware of a variety of methods for solving problems.

- Apply methods to solving real-life problems.

Notes to Users of This Unit

Classroom Teachers: The ability to use a variety of methods to solve life's problems is not inherent to one's learning. Students need to be taught how to identify a problem, the cause, and possible solutions. This process is one that works well when all the teachers in a team use the problem-solving model with their students. Our science teacher likes to connect it to the scientific method. She helps students see how we cause ecosystem problems and solve them. Our other content teachers use the process in similar ways.

Media Specialists: This area offers the classroom teacher the opportunity to use a variety of wordless books that introduce the concept of how a fictional story creates a problem and how characters solve it. You may want to teach concepts in wordless books and follow up with an application activity where students select their own wordless book and present the problem and solution. Students in middle and high school delight in wordless books used to teach a concept. These books are simple, yet effective in conveying the problem-solution idea. Help your teachers locate wordless books that best illustrate this point. Another superb book for teaching problem solving is *Winnie the Pooh on Problem Solving* (Allen and Allen 1995). While it is considerably longer than a wordless book, the idea of a step-by-step problem-solving technique is explained well. Further, once problem solving has been taught and you are aware that the students know the steps, you can help them apply their knowledge in library and electronic research methods.

Technology Specialists: We have successfully used problem solving to walk students through troubleshooting their hardware and application problems. Problem solving, along with practical application, has worked wonders in helping students feel a sense of competency and achievement when they learn they can solve the problem themselves rather than waiting for the teacher to solve it. We encourage you to assist the teacher in applying this strategy when working with students in the computer lab or individually in classroom settings.

> *Teacher Notes:* The following mini-lecture is designed to present a process for identifying and solving problems. We have students select an authentic problem to solve. The two worksheets are used to help students work through the process.

Mini-Lecture: Problem Solving

    I.   Define the problem (hypothesis)

        A.   What is problem solving?

        B.   How do we determine what a problem is?

        C.   How do you know it is a problem?

        D.   What happens when we are not able to determine what the problem is?

        E.   What happens if we define the problem incorrectly?

Student Activity: State a problem clearly in a sentence or two.

    II. What is the cause of the problem?

        A.   Once we have defined a particular problem, what is the next step?

        B.   What do you need to determine a problem's cause?

           1.   What have you observed? What are the facts? Gather evidence.

           2.   How reliable is the information concerning the problem?

3. What can you predict will happen if the problem is not solved?

4. Can you compare this problem to others that have surfaced in the past?

III. What methods can you use to find possible solutions to the problem?

A. If one thing happens, then what? This is called an if/then relationship.

B. Imagine every possible solution or alternative. Brainstorm.

C. What can you predict will happen if you select a particular solution?

D. What will be the effect if you select one solution over another? (This is inference and drawing a conclusion.)

E. Make a two-column visual of the positive and negative aspects of the solution.

F. Form a statement of solution to the problem.

G. Test the solution. Act on your decision.

H. Evaluate the solution. Did your desired result materialize? Why or why not?

➤ *Teacher Notes:* The following graphic organizer is one we designed and continue to use with our students as they work through the problem-solving process. The Parent-Student Analysis is used to make a connection with the home to promote problem solving and communication.

PROBLEM-SOLVING GRAPHIC ORGANIZER

What is the problem? Write a clear sentence stating the problem:

_____

_____

_____

What caused the problem? List evidence here:

_____

_____

_____

Predict what will happen if the problem is not resolved:

_____

_____

_____

Brainstorm possible solutions:

_____

_____

_____

What are the positive and negative aspects of your solutions? List them here:

_____

_____

_____

Select the best solution and write it here:

_____

_____

_____

Test your solution by putting it into action.

_____

_____

_____

Evaluation: How did the solution work? _____

_____

PARENT-STUDENT ANALYSIS

Name _____

Date _____

Period _____

1. Print your current grade in STARR (This is the effect.) _____

2. Why have you earned this grade? (This is the cause.)

   _____

   _____

   _____

   _____

   _____

   _____

3. Yes or No. Are you satisfied with this grade? (Reflection.) If your answer is yes, skip to question number 7 to continue. If your answer is no, continue with question number 4. _____

4. Brainstorm three ways you can achieve a better grade.

   a. _____

   b. _____

   c. _____

5. From the three brainstormed ideas above, select the one that will most likely help you to achieve a better grade and write it in sentence form as a statement of commitment (e.g., I will ...).

_____

_____

6. What evidence do you have to support this choice as the best of the three? Why did you choose this idea over the other two?

_____

_____

7. How is your behavior in this class? Is it contributing to your grade in a positive or negative way?

_____

_____

8. How is your participation in class discussions or question and answer sessions in this class? How does this affect your grade?

_____

_____

Parent comments about portfolio, grade sheet, and/or student responses:

_____

_____

_____

_____

Parent/Guardian Signature _____

You may use the back of this sheet for additional space for responses.

➤ *Teacher Notes:* One of the most rewarding experiences in one author's teaching career relates to the problem-solving lesson. In a journal, a student wrote that she had been trying to determine a way to discuss a family problem with her parents when along came this lesson at school on problem solving. She wrote that her parents were receptive to discussing the problem and were amazed at how well thought out her thinking was. She continued to write that for the first time in her young life, she felt that her parents listened to her worries. She was relieved, even joyous, that they seriously considered her opinions.

UNIT TWO: LEARNING TO CREATE RESEARCH QUESTIONS

Learning Objectives

In this unit students are exposed to metacognitive skills and provided with opportunities to reflect on their learning. The students will:

- ◆ Understand how to frame a good research question.

- ◆ Use Bloom's Taxonomy to identify levels of learning.

- ◆ Understand the connection between Bloom's Taxonomy and the learning levels of research questions.

- ◆ Write a good research question based on a grading rubric.

Notes to Users of This Unit

Classroom Teachers: Framing good research questions is essential to facilitating analytical thinking in students. To move away from topical research projects and toward analytical thinking research questions, we use modeling of good questioning strategies. Sharing these with your colleagues will help to encourage their use of higher-order thinking with students.

Media Specialists: You may support the classroom teacher in this unit by teaching students how to frame good research questions. Obviously, they will need more resources than ever. Rather than one good book on the country of Africa, students will need atlases, magazines, videos, and online resources. As they compare and contrast resources, they learn invaluable skills. You can facilitate learning during this time. Once the students have framed their research questions, the classroom teacher will schedule a meeting with you. At this time you can help identify and list the appropriate resources. You may want to collaborate with the teacher on communicating the content of the research process.

Technology Specialist: The Internet and online resources are essential for students as they begin to gather information for research. You can demonstrate the variety of online resources and show students how to use search engines. You may want to get a list of research questions from the teacher to help expedite the process.

> ➤ *Teacher Notes:* One of the most difficult skills for our students to master is the creation of their original research questions. The ability to frame good questions is essential because the question guides the learning process. A poorly framed question may produce a shallow answer. During the first quarter of the year, we carefully teach students how to frame good questions. This continues for the rest of the year.

Bloom's Taxonomy

Benjamin Bloom and a group of educational psychologists developed a classification of levels of intellectual behavior that became known as Bloom's Taxonomy of Learning (Bloom 1956). We use Bloom's Taxonomy to help learners understand different levels of learning.

Lesson: Brainstorming Research Questions

We begin this part of the unit with a brainstorming session. Each student generates a list of five questions they might want to spend a quarter researching. We put the first question from each student on chart paper and display the questions around the room. We then categorize the questions into groups such as sports, environmental issues, and political issues.

Then, we ask the students, "What kinds of research questions do we have?" This usually generates a blank stare. "What do you mean, what kinds of questions?" This is when we introduce Bloom's Taxonomy. We discuss the kinds of questions that might generate knowledge, comprehension, application, analysis, synthesis, and evaluation learning. We use this handout to help students in their thinking.

APPLYING BLOOM'S TAXONOMY

Name _____ Date _____ Period _____

       Now that we have discussed the six levels of learning in Bloom's Taxonomy, it is your turn to decide to which levels of learning these research questions belong. Match each research question with one of Bloom's levels and describe why they match.

Bloom's Taxonomy

1. Knowledge

2. Comprehension

3. Application

4. Analysis

5. Synthesis

6. Evaluation

Research Questions

1. You have been hired as a consultant to determine which computer platform your school will use, PC or Mac. Use the Internet, as well as books, newspapers, and other appropriate resources to build your case.

2. Present your case for selection of the player who is the better quarterback (select two current outstanding quarterbacks).

3. Who was Harriet Tubman and what contributions did she make to society?

4. You and other students at your school schedule a meeting with the principal. You propose a new six-period day that would allow more time in each class period. Prepare your presentation. Use the Internet, interviews, books, and whatever resources you feel are appropriate.

Students next meet in small groups to discuss their research questions and what learning level these questions meet. This advances research questions from knowledge and comprehension to analysis, synthesis, and evaluation. Students rewrite their research question for the quarter and list pertinent subquestions. The teacher meets with students to discuss their questions. When both the teacher and students are comfortable with the research question, the data collection process begins.

Throughout the year, teachers seize every opportunity to continue framing good questions. The old-fashioned method of asking students to do topical research does not stretch their analytical and thinking abilities. Asking them to gather information about three countries in Africa to determine which would be the best place for a family to live provides them with a broadened research question that has a purpose. As students become more proficient in using the Internet, they begin to understand how digital resources can be used appropriately. Our students are required to use multiple resources such as books, encyclopedias, letters, newspapers, magazines, videos, interviews, and the Internet. We want them to understand how each resource can contribute to a well-rounded presentation.

SCORING RUBRIC

Questioning Skills

Exceeds Standards

1. Independently selects and uses Bloom's Taxonomy

2. Communicates questions to extend thinking beyond what is previously known

Meets Standards

1. With some guidance, selects and uses Bloom's Taxonomy

2. Needs some guidance to communicate questions to obtain information

Developing Toward Standards

1. Needs significant guidance to select and use Bloom's Taxonomy

2. Needs significant guidance to communicate questions to obtain information

UNIT THREE: JOURNAL PROMPTS

> *Teacher Notes:* At the beginning of each day, students check the chalkboards for the day's journal prompt. We use this activity to generate metacognition. Here is a selection of prompts we have used over the years.

What makes you unique and special?

You have done poorly on a test, but feel that the grading is unfair. How do you handle this problem?

The best day of my life was when . . .

How are you preparing yourself for tomorrow's workplace?

Write down every major decision you have to make within the next 24 hours.

We have also developed a research unit that capitalizes on the problem-solving method described earlier. The enigma research unit follows.

UNIT FOUR: ENIGMA RESEARCH

> *Teacher Notes:* Problem solving and mysteries go hand in hand. We took mystery reading a step further. Working with our language arts teacher, who helped with the reading element, we developed an enigma research unit. Our Media Specialist taught students mini-units on the variety of real-life enigmas. This was a wonderful resource for developing investigative skills.

Students are offered a variety of past and present real-life enigmas to research. Our students learn that real life can sometimes be a mystery, and that humankind may not always be able to solve the unknown. Our students learn that thinking and analyzing applied to their research of enigmas do not necessarily produce a solution, but certainly offer a puzzle worth considering.

Learning Objectives

In the enigma research unit, students are offered a variety of real-life enigmas. They also have the opportunity to plan a research project on an enigma they wish to research that may not be on the teacher-prepared list. In this unit, students will:

- Use collaborative partner work.
- Use technical or expository reading skills.
- Read for comprehension.
- Read to interpret information.
- Use library research skills.

◆ Use computer technology for research.

◆ Organize and outline notes.

◆ Write and edit rough drafts.

◆ Create a bibliography.

◆ Demonstrate informative speech skills.

◆ Create quality visual aids.

Notes to Users of This Unit

Classroom Teachers: This is a terrific conclusion to the literature study of mysteries. Students may not know the word enigma. When they realize that there are real-life mysteries for which there are no answers, they experience an awakening of sorts. We have often linked this research unit with our science teacher's curriculum to help students explain natural mysteries. For example, black holes provide a wonderful starting point that truly amazes students.

Media Specialists: This area offers the classroom teacher the opportunity to use a variety of wordless books that introduce the concept of how a fictional story creates a problem and how characters solve it. Students in middle and high school delight in wordless books. These children's books are simple, yet effective in conveying the problem/solution idea.

You can assist students and teachers in locating wordless books that best show this concept. Another superb book for teaching problem solving is *Winnie the Pooh on Problem Solving* (Allen and Allen 1995). Although considerably longer than a wordless book, it explains step-by-step problem solving well. Further, once students fully comprehend problem solving, you can help them to apply their knowledge in library and electronic research methods.

You may wish to collaborate in teaching research skills, organizing and outlining notes, using computer technology for research, and teaching students how to develop bibliographies.

Technology Specialists: We have successfully used problem solving to walk students through troubleshooting their hardware and application problems. The problem-solving methods, along with practical application, have worked wonders in helping students feel a sense of competency and achievement when they learn they can solve problems themselves rather than waiting for the teacher to solve them. We encourage you to assist teachers in applying this strategy when working with students in the computer lab or individually in the classroom.

> *Teacher Notes:* The list of enigmas in the student instructions is by no means all-inclusive of life's mysteries. These are topics we have developed over the years. We hope it assists in helping students to understand the enigmas around us. We have not included all of the research worksheets we use for this project, because they are more or less duplicated in the research chapter. However, you can probably get the feel for this unit and understand why students love to research the unknown. We include a list of enigmas, examples of daily commentary on research progress checks from the teacher to the partners involved in the research, the grading worksheet, and an evaluation that the students perform on their partner's efforts.

ENIGMAS

The following is a list of enigmas to consider for your research. Remember, you may suggest another real-life enigma, but be sure to have my okay before beginning.

Bermuda Triangle	Atlantis
The lost squadron	Pillars of Hercules
The pyramids	Mesa Verde
What killed King Tut?	Anasazi Indians
How was the Sphinx constructed?	Chupacabras
Black holes	Goatsucker
Project Blue Book	Stonehenge
Bigfoot or Sasquatch	Vampires
Yeti	Amelia Earhart
Hsing Hsing	Roanoke Island
Abominable snowman	Loch Ness Monster

Examples of Teacher Commentary on Research Progress Checks

Student Names: Sung, Marcus   Date: 10/30   Period: 7
Research Topic: Black Holes   Today's Grade: 17/20 (B)

Hit words: (These are topic words you might use to assist your research): black holes; singularity; supernova; Wheeler, John; Cygnus X-1; white dwarfs; super stars; space; galaxy; universe

Additional ideas: Look at the end of your encyclopedia article for the "see also" list of other places in which to look for information.

Comments: Be sure you document correctly; follow the format information given. I don't see any note taking in your packet.

Student Names: Chuck, Derrick, Randy   Date: 10/30   Period: 1
Research Topic: Bermuda Triangle   Today's Grade: 14/20 (C-)

Hit words: Bermuda Triangle, Devil's Triangle, Lost Squadron, Limbo of the Lost, Flight 19

Additional ideas: Also look up the additional hit words above. Use EBSCO®, the encyclopedia indexes, *Compton's Encyclopedia*, and Newsfile® on the computer, too.

What is the name of the area on the other side of the world?

Ask me if you need more help.

Comments: I don't see any source information—remember you need to accurately record your information sources.

Student Names: Mikara, Audrey   Date: 10/30   Period: 1
Research Topic: The Pyramids   Today's Grade: 16/20 (B)

Hit words: pyramids; tombs; mummies; temples; Amon-Re; Re; Osiris; Isis; Horus; Ptah; Egyptians; King Tutankhamen; Valley of the Tombs of the Kings; pharaohs; archaeology; Carter, Howard

Additional ideas: Look at the end of the encyclopedia article for indications of additional information. It will say, "See Also . . ."

Comments: What religion required burial of the rulers in pyramids? What else was buried with the mummies? You also need the copyright date for John Week's book.

> *Teacher Notes:* Partners are given a manila envelope to contain their research materials, notes, list of resources, and so on. The outside of the envelope is marked in the upper right corner (nonflap side) with the students' names, period, and their research topic. This system facilitates easy storage of research materials. We stacked the manila envelopes in a plastic milk crate until the next day's class. Students stapled the grade sheet that follows to the flap side of their manila envelope.

ENIGMA RESEARCH GRADE

Outline

Introduction (10)

    ___   1.   Uses attention getter

    ___   2.   States thesis of paper

    ___   3.   Previews main ideas to support thesis

    ___   4.   Includes transition

    Total introduction: _____

Body (20)

    ___   1.   Four major topical statements (paragraph main ideas)

    ___   2.   Adequate details for main ideas

    ___   3.   Transitions between main ideas

    Total body: _____

Conclusion (10)

    ___   1.   Restates thesis

    ___   2.   Restates main ideas to support thesis

    ___   3.   Ends with strong closing thought

    Total conclusion: _____

Rough draft (50)

    ___   1.   Follows outline format

    ___   2.   Converts outline to sentences/paragraphs

    Total rough draft: _____

Worksheet continues on page 96.

Peer edit

1. Minimum two peer edits   _____ (5)

2. Parental edit bonus   _____ (5)

   Title page   _____ (5)

   Bibliography   _____ (15)

Total edits: _____

Final draft	excellent	good	fair	poor
Overall content quality	70	56	49	42
Total content: _____				
Editing	4	3	2	1

a. Spelling _____

b. Punctuation _____

c. Capitalization _____

d. Grammar _____

e. Run-on or incomplete sentences _____

Total editing: _____

Total points: _____

Total possible: 210

Your grade: _____

Partner(s) Grade + Your Grade = _____ /50

> *Teacher Notes:* The following warm-up culminates the enigma research project. Partners are asked to grade their own and one another's efforts. As noted above, this grade is added to the overall grade for the project.

Warm-up

Consider your effort and the effort of your partner(s) on the enigma research project. Give yourself a score out of 30 possible points:

My name: _____

My point score: _____

30	29	28	27		26	25	24		23	22	21		20	19	18
A+	A	A	A-		B+	B	B-		C+	C	C-		D+	D	D-

Consider the efforts of your partner(s). Give him or her a score out of 20 possible points.

Partner name: _____

Partner score: _____

Partner name: _____

Partner score: _____

20	19	18	17	16	15	14	13	12
A+	A	A-	B	B-	C	C-	D	D-

RESOURCES

Books

Allen, Roger E., and Allen, Stephen D. *Winnie-the-Pooh on Problem Solving.* New York: Dutton Book, 1995.

Arbetter, Sandra R. (M.S.W.), "Learning with Style, (Your Own, That Is)," *Current Health,* September 1990.

Bloom, Benjamin S. *Taxonomy of Educational Objectives: The Classification of Goals: Handbook 1: Cognitive Domain.* New York: Longman Publishing Group, 1956.

Campbell, L., Campbell, R. B., and Dickenson, D. *Teaching and Learning Through Multiple Intelligences,* 1992.

Knox, Richard A. "Brainchild Harvard Professor Howard's Theory of 'Multiple Intelligences' May Be Controversial, but Some Educators are Calling It the Most Profound New Idea in Teaching Since John Dewey Promoted 'Learning by Doing.'" *Boston Globe,* November 5, 1995, p. 23.

Pennar, Karen, "How Many Smarts Do You Have?" *Business Week,* September 16, 1996. p. 104.

Tripp, Rhoda Thomas. *The International Thesaurus of Quotations.* New York: Thomas Y. Crowell, 1970.

What Work Requires of Schools: A SCANS Report for America 2000 by the Secretary's Commission on Achieving Necessary Skills. Washington, D.C.: U.S. Department of Labor, 1991.

Lesson Plans and Supporting Materials

Ruggiero, Vincent Ryan. *Lesson Pack for Creative and Critical Thinking. A Collection of Teaching Materials.* Available through Mindbuilding, P.O. Box 1919, Dunedin, FL 34697.

Speaking, Technology, Analysis, and *Reading* Through Research

---

"What's a book? Everything or nothing. The eye that sees it all."
—Emerson, *Journals*, 1834.

READING FOUNDATION SKILLS

The Secretary's Commission on Achieving Necessary Skills (SCANS) report lists reading foundation skills under the Basic Skills category. Reading skills include locating, understanding, and interpreting written information in prose and in documents, such as manuals, graphs, and schedules. In addition, we broaden the skill base by including the National Content Standards in Language Arts that specify reading standards for middle-level learners.

CONTENT PROFICIENCIES IN LANGUAGE ARTS

The student reads to construct meaning by interacting with the text, by recognizing the different requirements of a variety of printed materials, and by using appropriate strategies to increase comprehension. The student:

- Reads a variety of materials including literature, textbooks, and reference materials.

- Comprehends and draws inferences beyond the literal level.

- Recalls and builds background knowledge by exploring information related to the text.

- Identifies the author's intent, main idea, and supporting details.

◆ Applies appropriate strategies to increase fluency and adjusts rate when reading various materials.

The student produces writing that conveys purpose and meaning, uses effective writing strategies, and incorporates the conventions of written language to communicate clearly. The student:

◆ Produces creative, expository, technical, or personal writing on an assigned or self-selected topic.

◆ Indicates understanding of the topic through specific, accurate, and sufficient details.

◆ Organizes clearly and logically sequences ideas.

◆ Uses appropriate writer's voice and word choice.

◆ Applies a variety of sentence structures.

◆ Edits and eliminates errors.

CONNECTING READING TO WORKPLACE SKILLS

In her book, *The School-to-Work Revolution,* Lynn Olson states that, "Today's economy has little room for those who cannot read, write, compute, frame and solve problems, use technology, manage resources, work in teams, and continue to learn. Well-paying jobs for unskilled labor are disappearing at an alarming rate." (Olson 1997, vii) To help students become more aware of how important reading skills are in the workplace, we place this quote on a transparency and ask students to respond to it in small group discussions. We then create a chart of their responses, including questions they have. Next we have them conduct research to find out what kinds of reading skills are required in the workplace. Students interview their own parents, local business owners, and managers, and find data and information that present viewpoints on this issue. A lively discussion ensues from their findings. They bring in a variety of materials from the workplace, ranging from technical manuals that workers need to interpret, to directions for completing tasks and memos. One student brought in a flight manual. Their need of high-level reading skills becomes clearer through these contacts.

In this chapter you will find two units that promote reading in the classroom. As we discussed earlier in chapter 1, while this unit is placed in the reading section of the book, you will find speaking, analysis, technology, and research assignments and activities integrated in the reading units. The facilitation of the acquisition of these skills is an ongoing part of STARR.

The following two units are ones that students have found success in and that engage their interest. The first unit on dragons always creates an atmosphere of excitement and fun. Middle-level learners are fascinated with the medieval period and especially dragons. The second unit on mysteries provides us with an opportunity to expand reading past Nancy Drew and the Hardy Boys. Although they love these books, students are ready for a more in-depth understanding of the elements of mystery stories. As they learn about the eight elements of a mystery, discussed later in this chapter, they become familiar with some great mystery writers. As a result of their new knowledge, they create some pretty intriguing detective characters and twisted mystery plots of their own.

UNIT ONE: INCREDIBLE EXPLORATION OF DRAGONS

Aligning Instructional Practices with Proficiencies and Assessments

Students read to construct meaning by interacting with the text. They recognize different requirements of a variety of printed materials and use appropriate strategies to increase comprehension.

Students produce writing that conveys purpose and meaning, use effective writing strategies, and incorporate conventions of written language to communicate clearly.

Learning Objectives

In this unit students are presented with opportunities to meet a broad range of learning objectives. The student:

- Reads a wide variety of materials for information, for pleasure, and to enrich experience.

- Implements reading comprehension skills to complete assignments.

- Constructs meaning by interacting with the reading materials, recognizes the requirements of different types of readings, and uses appropriate strategies to increase comprehension.

- Follows directions individually and collaboratively in a HyperStudio® stack prepared by the teacher.

- Discusses as a part of the group readings and participates in group answers to questions in the stack.

- Uses methods best suited to individual intelligences and completes a final project.

Assessments

> *Teacher Notes:* The assessments included in this assignment are both formal and informal. We suggest that you provide multiple opportunities for students to reflect on what they have learned through small group and individual discussions. Please feel free to modify the material to meet the needs of your learners. Chapter 9 provides more information on creating assessment and evaluation opportunities.

Student Assessments for the Dragon Unit

- Daily log of group participation

- HyperStudio® stack activities for reading comprehension using Gardner's Multiple Intelligences

- Final individual project and presentation to class

- Self-evaluation and group evaluation

- Dragon map worksheet

Instructional Strategies

Literal: These strategies include those skills directly targeted by the teacher's curriculum. For example, the overriding focus of this unit is reading development, an element of STARR.

- Reading strategies

- Audio interpretation

- Video interpretation

- Computer application

- Collaborative group participation and responsibilities

- Decision-making and problem-solving skills

Lateral: Please note that these strategies are associated with, but are not a direct element or focus of the teacher's curriculum.

- Gardner's Multiple Intelligences integration

- Social Studies map

- Speech presentation

- Research skills

- Art

- Music

Remediation Strategies

- Adapted reading materials by reading level

- Video- or audiotaped stories to view or listen to

- Creation of artistic drawings, collages, and/or paintings

Enrichment Strategies

- Research dragons in history or mythology

- Write one scene of a play based on individual research of dragons; use multimedia slide show or presentation software such as HyperStudio® or PowerPoint® to illustrate and convey information.

- Create a HyperStudio® stack of art/artists who have incorporated dragons in their work.

- Create an original drawing, sculpture, or art piece that includes dragons.

- Design a computer-based dragon game.

Notes to Users of This Unit

Classroom Teachers: We found this to be one of the most exciting and motivating units our students experienced. In this unit you will find a list of considerations for your environmental arrangement in the classroom, the resources you need to gather before you begin, an overview of the unit, and student instructions. Because this is a multicultural, cross-curricular unit, it is fun to collaborate with other teachers on your team. In particular, the social studies teacher could work with the students on the mapping assignment. In addition, the Technology Specialist may teach the presentation software available at your school and facilitate delivery of the student's final product. Please use this as a guide and feel free to add or delete elements that work best for your situation.

Media Specialists: We include a resources list, but your expertise in recommending and locating additional materials will greatly enhance the learning experience. We urge you to work as a collaborative team in customizing this unit. In addition, because of the size of this unit, you may want to teach only a part of it. Presenting a book talk on resources dealing with the medieval period and dragons would be a great way to entice students to read more. Locating resources is an ongoing skill that students need to develop. Finding appropriate Internet sites on dragons and bookmarking them would also be helpful.

Technology Specialists: HyperStudio® is the chosen software for this unit. Other presentation software lends itself well to the design and development of these materials and student presentations. Your recommendations to the teacher about what applications and technology are available and appropriate would be most helpful. In addition, you may want to teach students how to use software to create dynamic presentations. Students will also want to access the Internet to gather more information about dragons.

> *Teacher Notes:* Middle-level learners are fascinated with the medieval period, especially dragon legends. This unit on dragons capitalizes on this curiosity. Although it is included in the reading section of this book, it is a cross-curricular unit that lends itself well to collaboration with teachers from other disciplines.

Specific Knowledge

The student will need to:

- Use reading strategies to follow the HyperStudio® Stack and complete reading assignments.

- Show comprehension of the readings through completion of writing assignments.

- Develop proficiency with presentation software.

◆ Access specific information via the Internet.

◆ Actively participate and contribute in group work.

◆ Complete a notebook and final presentation piece.

Environmental Considerations

Students must have access to computers with presentation software and the Internet, as well as floppy disks and/or a file server location to store their works-in-progress. Students need to rearrange the classroom for group discussions. Notebooks to complete written assignments are also required.

Assignments and Intelligences Addressed

Assignment	Intelligence
Dragon story	Linguistic
Dragon game	Mathematical/Logical
Produce scene	Bodily/Kinesthetic
Dance	Bodily/Kinesthetic
Ballad	Musical
Caricature	Artistic
Collage	Intrapersonal

Why a Dragon Unit?

Simply put, students are intrigued by dragons and enjoy reading about them. Dragons were fabulous, fire-breathing serpents with wings like those of a great bat. These fictitious creatures could swallow boats and men in one delicious gulp. Maps from early times show the parts of the world not yet explored as homes for these mythical beasts. In this unit, students read about some dragons that were considered to be evil and destructive, and others that were thought to be protective and honorable. In literature and in tales handed down for centuries, every country had dragons. In Greece, Hercules, Perseus, and Apollo destroyed dragons. As a symbol of sin in early Christian times, the dragon was abhorred. But the Chinese honored dragons, considered them to be royalty and even thought of them as gods. Students complete this unit with a new view of dragons and their cultural significance.

Disclaimer

This reading unit is a study of dragons as a mythological/historical aspect of literature. The students read short stories and poems, and view videos that support the reading materials. This study implies no connotations with respect to religious or cultural beliefs. It is a unit intended strictly for reading pleasure, comprehension skills, and group interaction. With signed parental requests, students may opt out and receive alternative reading assignments.

IMPORTANT FACTS TO KNOW

Group Question

Dragons were the first scary monsters people believed in. Where did the first ideas of dragons come from? Write your answers in your dragon notes. Have your group leader initial your dragon notes showing that you have listed two or three ideas you discussed in your group.

Student Instructions, Discussion, and Writing Activity

Stop now and discuss your ideas. Write your answers in your journals.

Notebook Assignment 1: Writing and Thinking Activity

Write about where you think dragons originated. Think beyond what your group has discussed. Be creative. Dragons came about to explain phenomena such as rain, lightning, and thunder. As a group, read the poem, *Thunder Dragon*.

Notebook Assignment 2: Writing and Thinking Activity

Questions to answer in your Dragon Notebook:

1. In *Thunder Dragon*, the poet tells us about a dragon. What besides a dragon is the poet describing? Give reasons for your answer. *Answer:* The poet is describing a thunderstorm. *Reasons:* The reader can visualize the building storm; lightning; dark, ominous clouds; whistling winds.

2. Where does this poem take place? Describe the surrounding area by providing details from the poem. *Answer:* The thunderstorm comes over the mountains, rains over a town, then recedes to the mountains.

3. Other things can be compared to a dragon. Think of a dragon as a speeding train, a steam shovel, or a volcano. Write a short poem of six to eight lines in which you compare a dragon either to one of the above images, or to something of your own choice.

Group Assignment 1

Listen to *Puff the Magic Dragon*. Then select one of your group member's poems to work with. With a familiar song or one you made up, put the poem's words to music. Be prepared to present your musical arrangement to the class!

Worksheet continues on page 106.

Group Assignment 2

The Reluctant Dragon

Read *The Reluctant Dragon* in your group. *Synopsis:* The *Reluctant Dragon* is a play. The story takes place a long time ago in the English countryside. The characters include Father; Mother; Boy; the Reluctant Dragon; Villagers; and St. George, the hero. The dragon is a friendly and quiet soul who does not wish to frighten anyone or fight like other dragons.

Act out the parts of the play. Some members of your group will have to read more than one part. After you have read all the way through, choose one section of the play to act out in front of the class. You may need to practice before or after school, or at someone's home to be well prepared. Perhaps you will need a narrator to tell the class where/when the play takes place and to fill in missing details since you will act out only a part of the play. Plan on a three- to four-minute performance. We will videotape each performance, so do your best!

Notebook Assignment 3: Reading, Writing, and Thinking

The Reluctant Dragon Questions

Answer these questions in your Dragon Notebook:

1. Why did Father first become suspicious of the cave? *Answer:* He never liked it to begin with, and his sheep also do not like the cave. Noises have been coming from the cave.

2. Do you think the villagers were more interested in eliminating the dragon or in watching a good fight? Give two reasons for your opinion. *Answer:* They wanted to watch a good fight between St. George, their hero, and the dragon. However, this would mean the death of the dragon. So actually, they are interested in both.

3. Do you think the Boy always kept the dragon's best interests in mind? Why or why not? *Answer:* The boy does not care very much about the Dragon's interests. He tells the dragon that his opinion about fighting does not count. However, he does care enough about the Dragon to take St. George to the cave to talk to the Dragon to arrange a mock fight.

4. What do you think the Villagers learned from St. George's lecture? Do you think it had any effect? What was the effect? *Answers will vary.*

5. Did you ever want someone to fight for you? Tell about the situation.

Group Assignment 3

View the video *St. George and the Dragon.* In your group, discuss the similarities and differences between *The Reluctant Dragon* and *Saint George and the Dragon.* List at least three similarities and three differences in your Dragon Notebooks. Have your group leader initial your lists.

More History to Read About

➤*Teacher Notes:* The following history of dragons is adapted from a wonderful book by Birdie Stallman, *Learning About Dragons.* We suggest that you access this resource. A map of the world should also be provided. We use the students' atlas to make enough copies of the political map and then elicit help from our social studies teacher to assist students in locating dragons.

Notebook Assignment 4: Reading and Mapping Skills

You need to mark all locations noted below on a map of the world. Place the name of the dragon as well as the name of the country in the proper locations.

In Babylonia, the first lady of dragons was Tiamut. She was too big to measure. She had a scaly snake's body with horns on her head. Her children were also very bad. Her son, Marduk fought Tiamut in a long battle. Marduk sent a flash of lightning to Tiamut's heart, killing her. This legend says that Marduk used half of Tiamut's body to make the heavens and the other half to make earth.

In Egypt, Apep looked like a serpent and lived in the dark. Apep hated the sun and tried to kill it. The sun's helper, Seth, was as fierce as the dragon. When Apep attacked the sun, Seth killed the dragon and saved the day. But Apep did not stay dead. Seth had to kill the slimy serpent every night so the sun could rise.

In Scandinavia, the dragon known as Nidhoggr, or the Dread Biter, hated everything and everybody. In his cave, he gnawed at the root of the universal tree. If he killed the tree, the universe would be destroyed. Workmen repaired the tree every day. Every night the Dread Biter gnawed more. The Norsemen believed this battle would last forever.

In Germany, Fafnir was a greedy giant. He cheated his father and brother out of a great treasure. He guarded the wealth so well that he turned into a dragon. That is what happens to greedy giants. Siegfried, a friend of the family, worked out a way to get the riches back. He hid in a pit. When Fafnir crawled across the pit, Siegfried killed the dragon by piercing his body.

In North America, Cherokee Indians believed in the King of Rattlesnakes. This dragon snake lived in the mountains of North America. He wore a prize magical stone on his head. Many braves died trying to kill the dragon. A warrior made a suit of armor out of leather. Because the dragon had never seen leather before, he was confused. The warrior killed the dragon and got the stone.

In Ethiopia, the Big Mouth Dragons live. They are tricky dragons. These tricky creatures sleep with their mouths open. Birds fly by thinking they are safe from sleeping dragons, but dragons can eat while they sleep. Poor birdies! Another trick that dragons have is boat making. If a dragon wants to cross the sea, it finds four or five friends to twist together to make a boat. With their heads up, they sail across the sea.

In Greece, a young boy took a dragon home for a pet and let it sleep next to his bed. One morning he found a baby dragon by his bed. The boy's parents didn't like the tiny dragon, so the father took him to the desert and left him there. The boy grew to be a man and went on a long journey to a faraway country. When thieves attacked him, a great dragon appeared and helped the boy (now a man) fight the thieves. The boy and his dragon were reunited.

Still More Dragon History

Western dragons lurk in caves. Eastern dragons live in water, the source of their power. People from the East believe in dragon-gods called Nagas. They think the rain, lakes, and oceans were ruled by these dragons. No one would kill a monster in control of all the water. (Continue your map locations with this additional dragon history.)

In India, rain comes from Vritra, a dragon-shaped cloud. Vritra stores water in its stomach. To make it rain, the god Indra shot thunderbolts at Vritra. When he hit the dragon, down came the rain.

In China, most dragons are like the Black Dragon. A Chinese emperor went to visit the Black Dragon near Peking. At the Black Dragon Pool he called to the monster. After a while, the emperor saw a Black Dragon about six inches long swim up to him. The emperor laughed. "Is this the great Black Dragon? You would be invisible in my goldfish pond!" The dragon did not answer. He lifted one claw from the water. The claw began to grow. First it overshadowed the pool. Finally the dragon's single claw covered the mountain tops. Dragons are not always what they appear to be.

Today in China everybody waits for the Dragons on Parade. The dragons are made of bamboo. The head is bright red, blue, gold, and green. The body is covered in cloth. Men hide under the cloth to help the dragon walk.

Worksheet continues on page 108.

In Japan, children make long-tailed kites that look like a dragon that is supposed to live in Japan's inland sea.

In England, there is a day named after St. George, a soldier, who one day rode through a bleak and bare land because he knew a dragon lived there. The people of the land were very sad. At first they had fed sheep to the dragon to keep him happy. Soon the sheep were gone, and the dragon asked for children. Finally the dragon demanded the king's daughter.

Notebook Assignment 5: Viewing, Listening, Writing

How did the video *St. George and the Dragon* compare to this story about St. George?
(Be specific—answer this question in complete sentences in your Dragon Notebook.)
Teacher Notes: Answers to this question will vary. We are always fascinated by the variety of answers the groups generate. In the past we have given each group chart paper to list similarities and differences. Lively discussions follow as groups argue points with their classmates.

Dragons are born every day. They usually appear in stories. Bilbo Baggins, a hobbit (*The Hobbit*, J. R. R. Tolkien), knows about storybook dragons. He met a bad one named Smaug. Smaug's teeth were swords and his claws were horrifying spears. His breath was the most feared death. But the dragon had a soft spot over his heart. When Bilbo saw the soft spot, he felt more confident. Then the dragon spouted scorching flames at the hobbit. The hobbit learned his lesson. Never be too confident around a dragon!

Real Life Dragons

The largest lizard living today is the Komodo Dragon. Its long tail is covered with small, dull-colored scales; its mouth has rows of teeth like the edge of a saw. It lives on the island of Komodo in Indonesia. (Locate Indonesia on your dragon map.) The Komodo Dragon is really a lizard. It hunts for food during the day, sometimes even killing a deer. It digs a cave at night and hides in it.

Notebook Assignment 6: Reading, Discussion, Writing

Read *The Smallest Dragonboy. Synopsis:* Set on the planet Pern, where descendants of Earth space colonists live. They are mutually dependent on telepathic dragons. These dragons pick human riders at hatching time in a process termed Impression. Keevan, the smallest dragonboy, hopes to gain acceptance by a dragon on Hatching Day.

Discuss the seven questions below in your group, then write your answers to the questions in your Dragon Notebook.

1. What kind of story is this? Your choices include: historical fiction, science fiction, biography, or mystery?

2. What took place on hatching day?

3. What happened to prevent Keevan from attending the hatching?

4. Why did Berterli pick on Keevan all the time?

5. Why did the bronze dragon try to leave the Hatching Ground without impressing? (Remember that impression occurs during hatching time when dragons pick riders for lifelong companionship.)

6. Why do you think Berterli had been through eight Hatchings without impressing?

7. In your group, list at least ten qualities you would look for in a dragon rider if you were the dragon.

Answers

1. Science fiction

2. Hatched from eggs, dragons choose humans to become companions for life.

3. He was in a fight with Berterli and sustained a fractured skull and a broken leg.

4. Keevan is an easy target as he is very small. Berterli apparently feels insecure about having been rejected at eight impressions. He is almost at the age where he can no longer select a dragon. Berterli is taking out his frustration on Keevan.

5. The bronze dragon had selected Keevan while it was still inside the shell. Keevan was not present on Hatching Day.

6. Berterli is a bully who would not be chosen by the telepathic dragons.

7. Responses will vary, but generally include honesty, decency, kindness, generosity, and other honorable traits.

Group Assignment 4

What Is Impression?

Anne McCaffrey, who wrote *The Smallest Dragonboy*, may have been inspired by newly hatched birds, such as chickens, ducks, and geese. Impression for these tiny birds means treating the first thing they see when they hatch as their mother. Scientists call this imprinting and have found themselves playing mother duck to a flock of young ducklings.

Select one or two team members to prepare a short report on imprinting (three or four paragraphs). Try to find examples of imprinting to share with the class. Other team members will draw pictures to demonstrate imprinting. Prepare this on a poster board and make it large enough for everyone to see.

Group Assignment 5

The final reading assignment is *Beowulf and Grendel*. First written in the eighth century, this poem is 3200 lines long. The poem's sources are found in the history and myth of sixth-century Denmark. This poem deals with the movements of good and evil, courage, and its hero's supernatural strength. Although tragic, it does not look on the dark side of life. Beowulf uses his moral strength and gift of goodness to fight the powers of darkness.

This poem contains many words that you probably do not know. Be sure everyone writes the definitions in their Dragon Notebooks. The group leader should initial everyone's notebook when the list is complete. Please define words according to the way they are used in the poem. In your group, define the following words:

Buffet	Trophy	Distorted
Shingle	Asunder	Puny
Valiance	Moor	Ravening
Runes	Groveling	Brine
Raftered	Spent	Score
Havoc	Misbegotten	Mead
Fens	Wallowed	Gross
Exulted	Gorged	Revelry

> *Teacher Notes:* Definitions for the words above follow.

Buffet: blow or shock

Shingle: a beach of water-worn pebbles

Valiance: bravery or courage

Runes: mystical sayings or poems written in runes (Scandinavian alphabets)

Raftered: supported by timbers, usually steeply sloping

Havoc: devastation; ruinous damage

Fens: low, marshy land

Exulted: felt triumphant joy

Trophy: anything taken in battle, hunting, or competition and kept as a memento of victory

Asunder: into pieces

Moor: a heath; an open, peaty wasteland

Groveling: cringing, servile

Spent: exhausted, consumed

Misbegotten: unlawfully conceived

Wallowed: floundered about; rolled about in water, snow, dust, etc.

Gorged: grossly stuffed with food

Distorted: twisted, deformed, misshapen

Puny: insignificant

Ravening: voracious; wildly hungry

Brine: saltwater

Score: twenty

Mead: liquor made by fermenting honey and water

Gross: large and ugly

Revelry: boisterous festivity

INDIVIDUAL FINAL ASSIGNMENTS

Individually select one of the following projects to conclude this unit.

1. Using characters listed in the history of dragons, create a dragon story. You may use one or several different dragons. Your story MUST be at least three full word-processed pages long, double-spaced. Add graphics, either hand drawn or computer generated to complete this assignment.

2. Make up a dragon game and write directions for how the game is to be played. Have at least two of your friends play the game and have each give a WRITTEN critique about the quality of the game. With graphic illustrations, your game should include the power of good over evil. It can be either print-based or a computer game.

3. Write and produce one scene of a play about dragons. Use the historical information you learned in this written assignment to give your story authenticity. Ask your friends to help you act out your scene. A videotape or live presentation is required. Your scene will also be posted on the Intranet.

4. Create a dragon dance. Your dance must be set to appropriate music and include elements described so far. A videotape or live performance is required. The videotape of your dance will be posted on the Intranet.

5. Write and perform a ballad about what you have learned about dragons. You must include elements described so far. You may have classmates or friends help you. Turn in the word processed lyrics to your ballad. A videotape or live performance of your ballad is required. This will also be posted on the Intranet.

➤ *Technology Note:* Most school districts have release forms for students and parents to sign to agree to the posting of student work on electronic media. The COPPA law requires this.

6. Draw caricatures of at least ten dragons described in either your reading assignments or other readings. On a separate sheet of paper, word process one paragraph about each caricature, describing the dragon's personality and the role it played. Place all drawings and paragraphs in a binder to hand in.

7. Using good and evil as a theme, create a collage of modern-day dragons. What is evil in our lives? (These are the "dragons.") How will good overcome evil? Display this theme in your poster-sized collage. Modern evils and the power of good over evil must be clearly shown. Write a one-page, double-spaced, word-processed report that explains your collage. Attach this to the back of your poster. You will explain your collage to the class.

8. Design and develop a dragon trivia game for the computer. Include material you have learned in class to stump your players.

RUBRICS FOR "THE INCREDIBLE EXPLORATION OF DRAGONS"

Assessment and Evaluation of the Dragon Unit

> *Teacher Notes:* In this section you will find the rubrics, the individual project grading form, and the Dragon History Quiz used to evaluate students.

I. The student uses reading strategies in the HyperStudio® stack.

4 The student completes a notebook answering all questions in the HyperStudio® stack very effectively. Student shows creativity and "goes above and beyond" expectations. All independent and group assignments are completed. The student produces quality work and actively participates in group interactions.

3 The student completes most questions in the HyperStudio® stack adequately. The student produces acceptable work and participates in group interactions. Some direction from the teacher is necessary.

2 The student completes questions in the HyperStudio® stack ineffectively. Answers are not always accurate or complete. Group interaction is weak. Much direction from the teacher is required.

1 The student's HyperStudio® stack notebook is mostly incomplete and not acceptable. The student has difficulty completing assignments and working within his/her group. Group work is very poor. Constant guidance from the teacher is required.

0 No effort made.

II. The student participates in group work.

4 The student actively participates and offers valued discussion elements to the group. Student independently works within the group structure.

3 The student participates frequently and offers good discussion elements to the group. Needs some guidance from teacher.

2 The student is distracted and offers few discussion elements to the group. Needs significant guidance from the teacher.

1 The student is frequently off task and needs constant redirection to focus on group discussion.

0 No effort made.

III. The student selects and produces a final presentation piece.

4 The final product meets assignment criteria. It is visually well prepared, authentic to the purpose of the lesson, and creative. The student has worked independently to produce the final product.

3 The final product meets most assignment criteria, but may lack in quality of presentation, authenticity, and/or creativity. Occasional teacher input is required in the completion of the final product.

2   The final product is missing assignment criteria. One or more elements of quality, authenticity, or creativity are missing. The student has required much teacher supervision.

1   The final product is missing assignment criteria. Two or more elements of quality, authenticity, or creativity are missing. Little effort is made. Student requires constant teacher supervision.

0   No effort made.

DRAGON INDIVIDUAL PROJECT GRADING

1. Dragon Story

Originality/Creativity	40
Typewritten or Neatly Handwritten in Ink Double-spaced and a Minimum of Three Pages	15
Graphics	15
Followed Directions	5

2. Dragon Play

Originality/Creativity	40
Used Dragon History	10
Play Performance	10
Videotape	10
Followed Directions	5

3. Dragon Game

Originality/Creativity	40
Clear Directions	10
Written Critique by Friends	10
Graphics	10
Followed Directions	5

4. Dragon Dance

Originality/Creativity	40
Music Appropriate	10
Dragon Elements Clear in Performance	10
Videotape	10
Followed Directions	5

5. Ballad

Originality/Creativity	40
Dragon Elements Included	10
Typewritten Lyrics	10
Videotape	10
Followed Directions	5

6. Caricatures

Originality/Creativity	40
Ten Dragons Minimum	10
Ten Paragraphs Describing Dragons	20
Followed Directions	5

7. Collage

Originality/Creativity	40
Theme of Good versus Evil Present	10
Typewritten/Ink (One-page, Double-spaced)	15
Neatness	5
Followed Directions	5

8. Presentation Score

Posture	4	3	2	1
Voice Projection	4	3	2	1
Eye Contact	4	3	2	1
Gestures	4	3	2	1
General Impression	4	3	2	1
Conveyed Dragon Reading Comprehension in Project	4	3	2	1

Dragon History Quiz

1. Babylon is located in what present-day country?

   a. Iran

   b. Turkey

   c. Finland

   d. Iraq

2. Who was Tiamut's son?

   a. Vritra

   b. Apep

   c. Marduk

   d. Grondorf

3. What did Tiamut's son use her body for?

   a. To feed his young

   b. To create great wealth

   c. To create the heavens and Earth

   d. To create mountains and hills

4. What did Apep hate?

   a. The moon

   b. The stars

   c. The Earth

   d. The sun

5. What did Nidhoggr gnaw at?

   a. The root of the Universal Tree

   b. Houses built on his land

   c. Ships upon the sea

   d. Fences built across his land

6. What happens to greedy giants in Germany?

   a. They die.

   b. They have to leave their homes and live in another country.

   c. They turn into dragons.

   d. They turn into thunder and lightning.

7. What was the Cherokee Indian's armor made out of?

   a. Nothing—bare skin frightens dragons

   b. Leather

   c. Gold

   d. The bark of the eucalyptus tree

8. Western Dragons lurk in caves. Where do eastern dragons live?

   a. In water

   b. In trees

   c. In mountains

   d. In caves

9. What lesson did the hobbit Bilbo Baggins learn from the dragon Smaug?

   a. Never be too confident around a dragon.

   b. Dragons can be tamed.

   c. A good dragon is hard to find.

   d. Dragons should be given lambs and children for food.

10. Where was Smaug's soft spot?

   a. Under his arm.

   b. At the base of his skull

   c. Over his heart

   d. In the small of his back

Answers

1. a

2. c

3. c

4. d

5. a

6. c

7. b

8. a

9. a

10. c

UNIT TWO: MYSTERY READING UNIT— CURIOSITY AND INTRIGUE

Learning Objectives

In this mystery unit the student will have the opportunity to:

◆ Read a wide variety of materials from the mystery genre for information pleasure and to enrich experience.

◆ Implement reading comprehension skills to complete assignments.

◆ Construct meaning by interacting with the reading materials, recognize the requirements of different types of readings, and use appropriate strategies to increase comprehension.

◆ Produce writing that conveys purpose and meaning, uses effective writing strategies, and incorporates the conventions of written language to communicate clearly.

◆ Compare and contrast the eight elements of a mystery between two or more stories. (See details later in this chapter.)

◆ Participate in a discussion of the questions in the stack as part of the group readings.

◆ Use methods best suited to individual intelligences. Select and complete learning activities from a variety of choices.

Assessments

> *Teacher Notes:* The assessments for this unit are in the form of learning activities and quizzes. Students take the quizzes and turn them into mystery pursuit games. The students will:

• Complete research on mystery authors and apply information in designing a Web site.

• Analyze a contemporary mystery story or novel using the eight elements of a mystery.

• Create a detective character after determining characteristics from stories they have read.

• Design and develop a radio mystery scene from a story completed in class.

• Prepare a closing argument in a murder case focusing on motives.

Instructional Strategies

Literal: Literal strategies are those skills directly targeted by the teacher's curriculum. For example, the overriding focus of this unit is reading development, an element of STARR.

- Reading strategies

- Audio interpretation

- Video interpretation

- Computer application

- Collaborative group participation and responsibilities

- Decision-making and problem-solving skills

Lateral: These strategies are associated with, but not a direct element or focus of the teacher's curriculum.

- Gardner's Multiple Intelligences integration

- Speech presentation

- Research skills

- Drama

Remediation Strategies

- Adapted reading materials by reading level

- Video- or audiotaped stories for review

- Drama: Participate in a radio play

Enrichment Strategies

- Read contemporary mystery novels by at least two different authors. Analyze them using the eight elements of a mystery (covered later in this chapter). Present the information using Inspiration® software.

- Script out the story *Four and Twenty Blackbirds* (Christi 1990) for a radio play. Determine the number of fifteen-minute segments needed for presentation of this story, including commercials.

- After you have created a detective character, write and present a three-minute monologue for the character. The monologue will present clues in the case your character is trying to solve.

Notes to Users of This Unit

Classroom Teachers: Mystery stories are a particular favorite of middle-level learners. We encourage you to read the short mystery stories in a group setting. Use before- , during- , and after-reading questioning strategies to encourage predictions, guess motives, and make observations about the characters. Keeping the predictions, observations, and questions on charts will assist students as they select learning activities designed to enrich their reading experience. You may want to collaborate with the language arts teacher on this unit. Multiple opportunities for writing support the language arts curriculum.

Media Specialists: Although we include a resources list for this unit, your expertise in recommending and locating additional materials will greatly enhance the learning experience. We urge you to work as a collaborative team in customizing this unit to meet the needs of the students in your school. Book talks on mystery novels will help introduce readers to new authors. You may want to place mystery novels of interest to students on a separate shelf for easy access. Bookmarking Web sites of mystery novel writers will provide students with additional resources as they work on learning activities. Teaching a mini-lesson on videotaping will support students as they videotape radio plays.

Technology Specialists: Inspiration® software that assists students in creating Thinking-Maps® is recommended for this unit. You may have other suitable presentation software. Your recommendations about what applications and technology are available and appropriate would be most helpful. In addition, you may want to teach the students how to use software to create dynamic presentations. Students will also want to access the Internet to gather more information about mystery writers.

Mystery stories are an engaging genre for middle school learners. Most have read Nancy Drew or the Hardy Boys by this time and are ready for stories with more depth. In this unit we introduce students to four mystery writers through reading short stories and viewing videos. As students get hooked and want more mysteries to read, we send them to our media specialist who supports this unit by giving book talks and placing selected mystery novels on a reserve shelf. This unit also provides us with the opportunity to have students explore the differences among media, print, video, and radio to gain an understanding and appreciation of each form.

Specific Knowledge

The student will need to:

◆ Use reading strategies to complete reading assignments.

◆ Select from a variety of learning activities for assessment of knowledge.

◆ Learn to proficiently use presentation software.

◆ Access specific information via the Internet.

◆ Actively participate in and contribute to group work.

◆ Use analysis skills to compare and contrast authors and elements of a mystery.

Environmental Considerations

Students need access to computers with presentation software, the Internet, floppy disks, and/or a file server where they can store their works-in-progress. Students will need to rearrange the classroom for group discussions.

Assignments and Intelligences Addressed

Assignment	Intelligence
Author Search	Linguistic and Visual/Spatial
Comparison and Analysis	Linguistic and Logical
Create a Detective	Linguistic and Intrapersonal
Radio Play	Musical and Kinesthetic
Suspects and Motives	Interpersonal and Linguistic
Author Search	Linguistic and Logical
Thinking-Map®	Linguistic and Logical

Why a Mystery Unit?

Students like computer and board games that challenge their skills in solving a puzzle. They like deciding what comes next and finding the correct answer. Learning to appreciate the mystery genre can add to this curiosity and fascination with solving problems. Our goal is to enrich their reading experience by exposure to mystery writers they may not know.

> ➤ *Teacher Notes:* This information can be used to establish a purpose for this unit, to create an anticipatory set, or to generate discussion.

Mystery comes from the Greek word mysterion, which means "one who keeps quiet."

Mystery story is a term applied to two related types of fiction:

♦ Mystery of crime and its solution

♦ Mystery of supernatural events

Mystery stories about crime are also known as detective stories. They are carefully plotted schemes of:

♦ Crime and detection

♦ Clues and suspense

♦ Sometimes pursuit and violence

Enjoyment of mysteries comes from:

♦ Trying to outguess the criminal in the story

♦ Figuring out clues to solve the mystery before the detective does

◆ Guessing who the criminal is before the story ends

A few famous mystery authors:

◆ Sir Arthur Conan Doyle

◆ Agatha Christie

◆ Edgar Allan Poe

◆ Ellery Queen

Why Do We Read Mysteries? Secrets!

We love having secrets, whether someone else's or our own. When someone shares a secret, we are pleased with the trust the friend has demonstrated. We keep our own secrets too because we don't want others to know them. For our own reasons we avoid sharing some problems, acts, or our beginnings, and sometimes our thinking and opinions. We like to believe we can control what others know about us and therefore what they think of us.

But secrets are not always hidden successfully. Mystery stories discuss how one person tries to uncover another's secret. For example, a crime is committed and then discovered. This is the normal beginning of all mystery stories. What is the secret? What is the mystery? The crime is not a secret, it has already been discovered. The mystery (and with it the secret) revolves around the criminal and the motive, or why he or she did the crime. So the mystery is about *who did it and why.*

Because of the interest in the motive, mysteries are psychological stories. When we analyze our own behavior, we start to accept motive as an important part of everyday life. There are reasons behind our actions and to analyze them correctly is to understand them, ourselves, and possibly others.

Mysteries have fascinated mankind for years. Humans enjoy unusual things. Puzzles intrigue us. We love to try to solve the unknown—our own mysteries, and those of our friends, family and nation.

Mystery: The Characters

Our involvement may depend on our interest in the character who is solving the mystery. Crime solvers are typically eccentric and individualistic. We love them for being down-and-out or strikingly rich and snobbish. Whatever their description, crime solvers find facts that do not fit the puzzle, observe the obvious, and deduce the truth about what really happened.

Mystery solvers know the wrongness of situations. They seem to have a kind of sixth sense that others cannot tap into. They are the most observant of all heroes. Like Sherlock Holmes, they have a feel for warm teacups and an eye for crumbs and stray hairs. They notice the misplaced vase, the muddy shoeprint on the carpet, and the initialed matchbox left on the dresser. From these clues they reconstruct the truth of what happened. They think about the illogical or puzzling aspects of each mystery, treating them like the pieces of a large jigsaw puzzle.

Mystery: Survival of the Fittest

Usually mystery solvers are called upon to risk their lives. They survive by their wits. Detectives always snoop around too much for their own good. Snooping is both their strength and their curse. What saves them is their cleverness, intuition, and ability to make sense out of seemingly unimportant details. Their shrewd judgment and what to expect from suspects lead them to safely take physical risks, which in turn lead to the capture of the criminal and the solution of the crime.

Elements of a Mystery

> ➤ *Teacher Notes:* Knowledge of the elements of a mystery provides students with a framework as they read. How you introduce these elements is up to you. We orally read one short mystery story and have students play detective to find all the elements.

Element One: The Crime

There must be a crime, or at least a crime-in-the-making. The crime may be against a person, like a murder, mugging, hold-up, blackmail, or kidnapping. Or it may be against an object, usually one that has special value or meaning to its owner, like a jewel, vase, manuscript, good-luck charm, or a car with important documents hidden in the glove compartment. A crime may also be committed against a place, such as a vandalized church or park, a destroyed tennis club, a bombed car or house, or a booby-trapped patch of land or beach.

Element Two: The Discoverer

The crime must be discovered. Without detection, there would be no mystery story. Who discovers the crime, and how does the discovery take place? This witness may be an innocent bystander who later becomes the prime suspect, such as a relative, maid, detective, police officer, child, or the narrator. Any one of them may force open a locked door and find a body hidden inside. He or she typically opens a safe to find a diamond tiara gone, or perhaps takes a dip in the pool to find a fully dressed corpse at the bottom, weighted down by rocks in his pocket.

Element Three: The Detective

After the crime has been discovered, the mystery solver steps onto the scene. He may be a police officer, a detective, a private citizen, a curious neighbor, or a relative. His motive for taking on the case may be personal interest, love, family responsibility, curiosity, money, or kindness.

The mystery solver tries to figure out whether anyone has seen anything that might be important to the case. This is where witnesses become part of the story. Witnesses are accidental or purposeful observers who have seen a crime or a very suspicious occurrence. Witnesses rarely see the crime as it truly happened. Perhaps they saw or heard part of it, such as a shoe as the criminal ran out the door. Perhaps they heard a loud noise and looked at their watches at that moment. What witnesses think they may have seen may not actually have been what they saw. Or perhaps witnesses lie to protect themselves or someone else.

Element Four: The Suspects

Suspects are the possibly guilty characters. All of them have a motive for the crime and the opportunity to commit it. Some suspects are more obvious choices than others are, but there is no way of identifying the real culprit just from the way he or she looks. Characters become suspects because they are found near the scene of the crime, or because they have no alibi. But most importantly, the suspect must have a MOTIVE.

Element Five: The Motive

Because of the motive, the mystery story is very psychological in nature. Motive can be considered a study in human behavior. A character's motives come from her "inner self" and that part of the personality that readers love to see exposed. Readers always want to know more than how a crime was accomplished and by whom—they also want to know WHY it was done. For example: Why did Sam kill his father? He killed his father because he hated his father. WHY did he hate his father? Because he was cut out of his father's will. WHY was he cut out of the will? Because Sam married against the old man's wishes. WHY did Sam marry against his father's wishes? Sam rebelled against the old man. Motives may include revenge, jealousy, lust, greed, altruism (goodness), fear of blackmail, or fear of exposure of one's past.

Element Six: The Clues

The bad guy never succeeds entirely in covering his tracks. The detective finds clues that implicate the criminal. Clues may be objects that belong to the criminal or that are in some way associated with him. A lighter with the criminal's initials may have been left at the scene of the crime. The murder weapon may provide a clue, such as a set of fingerprints, or maybe the murder scene reveals a piece of clothing, a comb, a handkerchief, or a heel of a shoe. Some clues may be in the form of information or statements provided by the suspects, witnesses, or other characters.

Element Seven: The Chase

The crime solver follows all leads and is often placed in harm's way. There is almost always a chase of some sort that moves the story to a high pitch of excitement and adventure. In some novels, the chase lasts the length of the story. A chase is usually physical (running after the bad guy), but also may have the crime solver and the criminal trying to outwit each other.

Element Eight: The Confession

The mystery ends with a confession that the criminal makes either voluntarily or under extreme stress. Through the confession the true story comes out and loose ends are tied up.

Famous Mystery Writers

> ➤ *Teacher Notes:* The instructional strategies you use for this unit will vary. You may wish to create four separate reading circles and have each circle read the stories and work on the learning activities as a group. You may elect to read the first story as an entire class, modeling before-, during-, and after-reading questioning strategies to build interest in this genre. After the first story you may want to create reading circles that investigate the mystery authors and their stories.

Sir Arthur Conan Doyle

Arthur Conan Doyle was an unsuccessful London doctor. Influenced by Edgar Allan Poe's detective stories, he began writing mysteries in 1887 to support himself. By 1891, he had made enough money from writing to quit his medical practice. Doyle based his detective, Sherlock Holmes, on Joseph Bell, a teacher at medical school. Bell swiftly noted details about patients. Then he deduced what their ailments were. Doyle had Sherlock Holmes use the same process to solve mysteries.

Watson has a slow mind, but he is kind and charming with women. In contrast, Holmes is very smart, but cold and moody.

Holmes appears in 56 short stories and four novels. The last was published in 1927, shortly before Doyle's death. After more than half a century, Sir Arthur Conan Doyle's lanky sleuth remains the best-known detective in literature.

Read Sir Arthur Conan Doyle's *The Hound of the Baskervilles* (1996). *Synopsis:* In one of their most mysterious cases, Holmes and Watson look for a beast that prowls the moors. A curse has hung over the Baskerville family for generations. Now another life has been claimed by the terrifying beast. Is it a demon or an animal prowling the desolate moor? Will the new master of the Baskerville home be its next victim? Sherlock Holmes and Dr. Watson attempt to solve a bewildering case.

In class we read "The Boscombe Valley Mystery" (Doyle 1986). This drama is also by Doyle. *Synopsis:* A young man is accused of his father's murder. His beautiful childhood friend, Miss Turner, approaches Sherlock Holmes hoping that the master detective will investigate and prove the young man innocent of his father's murder despite the overwhelming evidence against him.

Learning Activity #1: Detectives in novels are carefully crafted characters. Return to the two mystery stories you read by Doyle. What do you know about Sherlock Holmes from these stories? Reread the stories and list and categorize all the characteristics and behaviors you can find about Holmes. For example, one category might be "Dress" and another one "Relationship with Dr. Watson." Look over your categories. What does Doyle intentionally tell you about his detective? What does he leave out? Using this information, create your own detective. The more depth you add, the more interesting the character. What does he or she read? Does he or she have hobbies? Does the detective exhibit strange behaviors?

Agatha Christie

Agatha Christie (1891–1973) was born in Torquay, England. Her mother taught her at home and awakened Agatha's interest in a wide variety of subjects. During World War I, while working in a hospital dispensary (like a pharmacy), Agatha planned her first detective story as a means of keeping her mind occupied. *The Mysterious Affair at Styles* started her on the way to becoming one of the few detective writers whose books consistently made best-seller lists. Her dashing little Belgian with a mustache, Hercule Poirot, has solved more crimes than Sherlock Holmes.

Read Agatha Christie's short story, *Four and Twenty Blackbirds.*

Learning Activity #2: The Medium Is the Message. Select an Agatha Christie video, like *Four and Twenty Blackbirds* or a book you have not read such as *Murder on the Orient Express* (1934). What makes the video different from the short story? Both print and video lend themselves well to mystery stories. One requires that you create your own visual images as you read and the other provides visuals for you. Radio offers additional elements that neither print nor video offer. How is radio different from film and literature? Your challenge is to create a radio drama based on *Four and Twenty Blackbirds.* You will select a segment from this short story and write a script for a radio production. Include background sounds and music. Your production will be presented to the class and videotaped.

Ellery Queen

Ellery Queen is the pen name used by two cousins, Frederic Dannay (1905–) and Manfred B. Lee (1905–). Together, they wrote more than 50 mystery stories and sold more than 40 million copies of their books. They first wrote together on *The Roman Hat Mystery* (1929). Using the other pen name of Barnaby Ross, they created a second famous detective, Drury Lane. Dannay and Lee were both born in Brooklyn, New York.

Read Ellery Queen's short story "Miracles Do Happen" (Dannay and Lee 1976).

In-Class Activity on Note Taking

> *Teacher Notes:* You will need to teach two-column note taking prior to this assignment.

Read the story once and have students listen. Reread the story and have students take notes about Ellery Queen. Have students use two-column note taking. Discuss how dual coding, listening, and writing help the brain to process and remember information better. What other ways do we dual code information? Here is an example of two-column note taking.

Ellery Queen:	Pen Name
Two Cousins:	Frederic Dannay (1905–1982)
	Manfred B. Lee (1905–1971)
Birthplace for both:	Brooklyn, New York
Wrote:	Mystery stories
	More than 50 stories
Sold:	More than 40 million copies of books
First story:	*The Roman Hat Mystery* 1929
Other Pen Name:	Barnaby Ross
Other Detective:	Drury Lane

Learning Activity #3: Suspects and Motives. In *Miracles Do Happen,* how does Ellery Queen reveal the possible suspects? What are their motives? What evidence does the writer present that leads you to believe that these people may have committed the crime? Using the biographical information you have on Edgar Allan Poe, make him the suspect in the homicide of his foster father. You are the prosecutor in the upcoming trial. Your task is to prepare the closing argument about his guilt. Write your speech and be prepared to present it to the jury (your classmates).

Edgar Allan Poe

Edgar Allan Poe (1809–1849) was an American poet, story writer and literary critic. Born in Boston, Massachusetts, he wrote famous poems such as "The Raven" (1996) and "Annabel Lee" (1987). Much of his work is mysterious and speaks of death. His poems have been translated into many languages and became more popular in France than in the United States. He set the standard for the modern detective story in such tales as "The Purloined Letter" (1977) and "The Murders in the Rue Morgue" (1987).

His grandfather was a Revolutionary War officer from an honored Baltimore family. Both of his parents died when Poe was two years old and he was taken into the home of John Allan, a wealthy tobacco exporter in Richmond, Virginia. Although he was never legally adopted, Poe used his foster father's name as his middle name. After several years in the Richmond Academy, he was sent to the University of Virginia. After a year there, Allan refused to give Poe more money, possibly because of Poe's gambling losses, so Poe had to leave the university. After that he quarreled with his foster father and left home. Next, Poe published a book of poems that made no money and he enlisted in the U.S. Army under an assumed name. After two years, Allan arranged for Poe to be honorably discharged and enter the U.S. Military Academy. Unfortunately, Poe was dismissed after six months because of neglect of duty and disobedience.

Poe's foster father died without mentioning him in his will. Because of his drinking, Poe lost his job at a literary magazine. Poe married the thirteen-year-old daughter of his aunt in 1836. He returned to the magazine but was dismissed again. He next moved to New York City and then to Philadelphia. He became an associate editor to another magazine, but within a short time he lost that position too. He reached the height of his fame in 1845 when "The Raven" was published. That same year he was appointed literary critic of the *New York Mirror.* Virginia Poe loved her husband dearly. Following a long illness, she died in 1847. Her death almost destroyed Poe, and he tried to commit suicide. He died in 1849.

Read Edgar Allan Poe's short story, "The Murders in the Rue Morgue."

Learning Activity #4: The Eight Elements. Go back and review your notes on the Eight Elements of a Mystery. Reread *The Murders in the Rue Morgue* and make notes about how Poe includes each of the eight elements. Make a flowchart of the elements using Inspiration® software.

Learning Activities for Additional Credit:

Learning Activity #5: Author Search. Select two of the mystery writers we have read in class. Do an Internet search to find out more background information on the authors and what they wrote. After you have gathered the facts, design a Web site for the purpose of marketing (advertising and selling) these authors' works.

Learning Activity #6: Thinking Map. Read two different contemporary mystery authors of your choice. As you read, complete an analysis using the eight elements of a mystery for each one. Create flowcharts for each one. Analyze the information you have from the flowcharts and create a visual map using Inspiration® software to show the interrelationship of the two novels.

Assessment and Evaluation for the Mystery Unit

These assessment quizzes are provided as additional tools. You may give them to your students as assessment instruments or have them design and create board and computer games for challenges with other students.

Answers to the quiz questions follow on a separate worksheet.

ELLERY QUEEN QUIZ
"Miracles Do Happen"

Name _____ Date _____ Period _____

Fact-Based Questions

1. Who was killed?

2. What is the detective's name?

3. Who is the primary suspect?

4. Name the three witnesses.

5. Where did the murder take place?

6. What was used to kill the victim?

7. What time did the murder take place?

8. What is a loan shark?

9. What is Ellery's relationship to the police inspector?

10. What was the motive for the murder?

Sequence Question

11. In what order did the witnesses visit Tully's office?

Draw Conclusion Question

12. What meaning does the title have in the story?

Answers

1. The loan shark, Tully

2. Ellery Queen

3. Henry Witter

4. Mrs. Bogan, cleaning lady; Mrs. Lester, the poker player; Mr. Dominini, barber

5. In Tully's office

6. Tully's letter opener

7. Between 8:30 and 9:30 p.m.

8. A moneylender who charges excessive interest on his loans so that people are never able to pay back the original amount. This is illegal and is known as usury.

9. The inspector is Ellery's father.

10. Mrs. Bogan does not want her son to go to prison for life. He took money from the garage where he works. His boss said he would not file charges if the money was repaid. Mrs. Bogan borrowed money from Tully and he was calling the loan.

11. Mrs. Lester (8:30); Mr. Dominini (8:45); Mr. Witter (9:00); Mrs. Bogan (after Witter)

12. Two answers: The story is entitled, "Miracles Do Happen." Witter's child, Jody, is very ill and her medical expenses are very high, but the parents hope for a miracle to cure her—they will not send her to the state hospital. The second "miracle" is that Ellery clears Witter of the murder of Tully.

Extra Credit Mystery Assignment

Choose one of these ideas to help you create a story about a mysterious house.

1. Write a story about someone who lives in this house.

2. Write a story describing your experiences if you had to spend a night in the house:

   a. With a ghost
   b. All alone
   c. With a friend

3. Pretend *you* are the house. Write a story about some events that have happened inside you.

4. Write a story that follows the idea "you wouldn't believe what is in my closet!"

5. Come up with your own mystery idea—see me for approval.

   a. Your story must be no longer than three handwritten (*in ink*) pages or two typed pages (*double-spaced please*).

   b. You may decorate your front cover any way you wish.

   c. Have an adult edit your rough draft.

   d. Attach the rough draft to the back of your final draft.

   e. A parent signature as editor earns extra credit.

➤ *Teacher Notes: Sherlock Holmes: Dressed to Kill* is a video we watch with our students. Sherlock Holmes, along with his ever-ready sidekick, Watson, must solve the mystery of the stolen music box, and the death of one of Watson's old friends. Prisoners make the music boxes to sell at auction to benefit the prison. One prisoner has made three music boxes and arranged for a friend on the outside to purchase all three. But one is sold to Watson's friend. The solution to the mystery revolves around the melodies played by the music boxes, all variations of the same tune. The video was selected for two major reasons. One is because it is an old black and white video. Students generally believe that if a video does not have fabulous special effects and magnificent color, it has no value. With this video, they quickly learn that the story line is far more important than Hollywood magic. The second and most important reason is that Arthur Conan Doyle has crafted a tale that follows the elements of a mystery exceptionally well. Students are directed by the teacher throughout the video to note the elements of mystery as they appear. This next worksheet may be used to direct their attention as they watch the video. You may want to show this 76-minute video in several segments and discuss the questions.

Additionally, time permitting, we use a second video, *Sherlock Holmes and the Secret Weapon*. In this story, Holmes and Watson must protect Dr. Tobel, a Swiss scientist who has created a secret weapon that may help decide who will win World War II.

SHERLOCK HOLMES: DRESSED TO KILL

Name _____ Date _____ Period_____

1. What are the prisoners making?

2. Why are the prisoners making these items?

3. How many were sold at the auction?

4. What is Sherlock Holmes doing when he is first introduced in the story?

5. What does Dr. Watson do with Sherlock Holmes' exploits?

6. What is Julian Emery's nickname?

7. What had happened to Mr. Emery when he visited Dr. Watson?

8. What does Mr. Emery collect?

9. Where do Holmes, Watson, and Emery go together?

10. What is in the music box that Dr. Watson plays?

11. What does Holmes suggest that Emery do with the wooden music box?

12. Why do you think Holmes whistles the melody from the music box?

13. What did Stinky take off as he started to climb the stairs?

14. Who visits Stinky after Holmes and Watson leave?

15. What happened to Stinky?

16. What is the name of the auction house owner?

17. What happened to the little girl whose father purchased the music box?

18. Who do you think the maid (charwoman) really is?

19. What does Watson do to try to cheer up the little girl?

20. What is the name of the shop where the young lady works?

Worksheet continues on page 132.

21. What happened to the music box she had purchased at the auction?

22. Who do you think she sold it to?

23. What does Scotland Yard do with the music box they have?

24. Who made all three music boxes?

25. Why is Mr. Davidson in prison?

Answers

1. Music boxes
2. To be sold at auction to benefit the prison
3. Three
4. Playing a violin
5. He writes about them and sells them
6. Stinky
7. A music box had been stolen after he was hit on the head
8. Music boxes
9. To Mr. Emery's house
10. A rabbit
11. Lock it up
12. This is an opinion question; to memorize or learn the melody
13. A hairpiece
14. Mrs. Courtney
15. The chauffeur kills him by throwing a knife
16. Mr. Crabtree
17. She was bound, gagged, and locked in a closet
18. Mrs. Courtney
19. He quacks like a duck
20. Clifford's Toys
21. She sold it
22. Sherlock Holmes
23. x-ray it
24. John Davidson, a prisoner
25. He stole a complete, duplicate set of plates for printing five-pound notes

DAY TWO—SHERLOCK HOLMES: DRESSED TO KILL

1. What is important about the three music boxes?

2. What is the key to the mystery?

3. Who are all the people in the bar?

4. Why did Holmes go to Joe for help?

5. Where does Joe say the song is from?

6. What does Joe do after playing the song?

7. Why did the prisoner make three music boxes?

8. What is the problem that Sherlock Holmes needs to solve?

9. Where did Holmes hide the music box?

10. The nineteenth key of the keyboard is the _____ letter of the alphabet.

11. Why does Holmes go to a tobacco shop?

12. How did Holmes go about identifying Mrs. Courtney?

13. What did Holmes steal from Cavanaugh?

14. What did Jaime attach to the motor of the car?

15. What does Mrs. Williams put in the cupboard when Watson goes to get her a glass of water?

Answers

1. Together they contain a message that tells where the plates are hidden
2. The tune
3. Actors
4. There is not a song he does not know

Worksheet continues on page 134.

5. Australia
6. He writes it down
7. His message was too long to convey in one variation of the song
8. The secret in the three variations
9. In the biscuit jar
10. Nineteenth
11. To find a special blend of tobacco in the cigarette and who purchased it
12. By the shape of her ear and her cigarette blend
13. Handcuff key
14. A poisonous gas bomb
15. A smoke bomb

Several great quotes are in this movie. Here are two for you to consider:

1. "It's often a mistake to accept something as true merely because it's obvious. The truth is only arrived at by the painstaking process of eliminating the untrue." (Sherlock Holmes) (Answers will vary.)

2. "There is no problem the mind of man can set that the mind of man cannot solve." (Dr. Samuel Johnson) (Answers will vary.)

Choose *one* of these quotes and write a paragraph of not less than five sentences that explains what the quote means. Give an example of how you can apply the statement to your personal experiences. Careful analysis will yield five points. You may staple an additional sheet of paper to this if you need to. *Bonus:* Refer back to your mystery notes to answer the following questions.

1. *Mystery story* is a term applied to two related types of fiction. Which type is the Sherlock Holmes video?

   _____

2. Who wrote the Sherlock Holmes stories? _____

Bonus Questions Answers

1. Mystery of crime and its solution
2. Sir Arthur Conan Doyle

MYSTERY QUIZ

Name _____ Period _____ Date _____

Multiple Choice

Choose one correct answer and circle it.

1. The definition of deduced is:
    a. crumbled
    b. solved
    c. argued
    d. cried

2. The definition of sleuth is:
    a. miner
    b. pilot
    c. detective
    d. doctor

3. The definition of exploits is:
    a. crimes
    b. deeds or acts
    c. languages
    d. explores

4. Who wrote the Sherlock Holmes' mysteries?
    a. Agatha Christie
    b. Ellery Queen
    c. Sally Seier
    d. Sir Arthur Conan Doyle

5. What was the secret weapon in the video?*
    a. nuclear bomb
    b. new tank
    c. bomb site
    d. bomb suit

6. Who is the best-known detective in literature?
    a. Ellery Queen
    b. Hercule Poirot
    c. Stephen King
    d. Sherlock Holmes

7. What message was contained in the secret code Dr. Tobel created?*
    a. The names of the four people to whom he had given the four pieces of his invention
    b. Directions for creating the invention
    c. Directions for escaping from Germany
    d. Directions for putting the four pieces of his invention together

Worksheet continues on page 136.

8. In Switzerland, who was trying to capture Dr. Tobel and his secret weapon?*
   a. Swiss Army police
   b. Nazi Secret Police
   c. Sherlock Holmes
   d. Dr. Watson

9. How did Dr. Tobel sneak the secret weapon out of Switzerland and away from Germany?*
   a. He put it into the secret lining of his coat.
   b. He put it in his wife's suitcase.
   c. He mailed Christmas packages to England.
   d. He placed them in a hollowed-out book.

10. How did Dr. Moriarty try to kill Sherlock Holmes at the end of the video?*
    a. By draining all of the blood out of Sherlock Holmes
    b. By poisoning him
    c. By putting Sherlock Holmes into a room and then removing all of the oxygen in the room
    d. By shooting him

True/False

Following are true/false questions. Circle true or false.

11. The English Air Force is known as the EAF. True or False*

12. The secret weapon in the story was a bomb. True or False*

13. The author of the Sherlock Holmes' mysteries was a lawyer before becoming a writer. True or False

14. When Dr. Moriarty couldn't find the fourth piece of the secret weapon, he decided he would kidnap Dr. Tobel and take him to Germany. True or False*

15. Genocide means to destroy gems. True or False

Bonus: Write three other words that end with *-cide* and give the definition of each word. (e.g., herbicide, pesticide, homicide)

_____

_____

_____

*These questions refer to the video *Sherlock Holmes and the Secret Weapon* (1943).

Answers

Multiple Choice

1. Solved
2. Detective
3. Deeds or acts
4. Sir Arthur Conan Doyle
5. Bomb site
6. Sherlock Holmes
7. The names of the four people to whom he had given the four pieces of his invention
8. Nazi Secret Police
9. He placed them in a hollowed out book
10. By draining all the blood out of Sherlock

True/False

11. False
12. False
13. False
14. True
15. False

AUTHORS QUIZ

Directions: Number your paper from 1–10. For each question, write the author's name. Spell correctly—the authors' names are provided below.

1. This author was an orphan. _____

2. This author was an editor, a poet, an enlisted soldier, and a literary critic.

   _____

3. This author was married to Virginia. _____

4. *The Boscombe Valley Mystery* was written by:

   _____

5. *Miracles Do Happen* was written by:

   _____

6. This author worked in a hospital dispensary. _____

7. This author was an unsuccessful doctor. _____

8. The Queen of England knighted this author. _____

9. Barnaby Ross was another pen name for: _____

BONUS: (two points.) Write a definition for dispensary. (See question 6)

_____

_____

Authors you have studied are:

Sir Arthur Conan Doyle

Agatha Christie

Frederic Dannay and Manfred B. Lee

Edgar Allan Poe

Answers

1. Edgar Allan Poe
2. Edgar Allan Poe
3. Edgar Allan Poe
4. Sir Arthur Conan Doyle
5. Sir Arthur Conan Doyle
6. Agatha Christie
7. Sir Arthur Conan Doyle
8. Sir Arthur Conan Doyle
9. Frederic Dannay and Manfred B. Lee

Bonus: pharmacy

RESOURCES FOR THE DRAGON UNIT

Books

Grahame, Kenneth. "The Reluctant Dragon," in *Freedom's Ground*. New York: Holt, Rinehart and Winston, 1977, pp. 336–359.

Huus, H., Whitehead, R. J., and Bamman, H. A. "Thunder Dragon," in *Fox Eyes*. Menlo Park, CA: Addison-Wesley Publishing Company, 1971, pp. 59–61.

McCaffrey, Anne. "The Smallest Dragonboy," in *Blueprints*. New York: Macmillan Publishing Company, 1987, pp. 428–447.

Saint George and the Dragon. 12 minutes. Random House Media, Rhache Publishers Limited, 1988.

Serraillier, Ian. "Beowulf and Grendel," in *Awake to Worlds Unfolding*. LaSalle, IL: Open Court Publishing Company, 1977, pp. 77–85.

Stallman, Birdie. *Learning About Dragons*. Danbury, CT: Childrens Press, 1981.

Tolkein, J .R. R. *The Hobbit*. Wilmington, MA: Houghton Mifflin Company, 1997.

Yarrow, Peter, and Lipton, Leonard. *Puff the Magic Dragon*. Pepamar Music Corporation, 1963.

RESOURCES FOR THE MYSTERY UNIT

Books

Christie, Agatha. *Four and Twenty Blackbirds*. Audio book read by David Suchet. Durken-Haynes, 1990.

Christie, Agatha. *Murder on the Orient Express*. London: Collins, 1934.

Dannay, Frederic, and Lee, Manfred B. "Miracles Do Happen," in *Queen's Experiments in Detection*. New York: Signet, 1970.

Dannay, Frederic, and Lee, Manfred B. *The Roman Hat Mystery*. Cutchoegue, New York: Buccaneer Books, 1976.

Doyle, Sir Arthur Conan. "The Boscombe Valley Mystery," in *Sherlock Holmes, The Complete Novels and Stories*. New York: Bantam Books, 1986.

Doyle, Sir Arthur Conan. *The Hound of the Baskervilles*, London: Leopard, 1996.

Doyle, Sir Arthur Conan. *Sherlock Holmes and the Secret Weapon* (video). Roy William Neill, director. 68 minutes. Republic Pictures, 1942.

Doyle, Sir Arthur Conan. *Sherlock Holmes: Dressed to Kill* (video). Roy William Neill, director. 76 minutes. 1946. Distributor: Hollywood Home Theater.

Hyerle, David. *Visual Tools for Constructing Knowledge*. Alexandria, VA: Association for Supervision and Curriculum Development, 1996.

Olson, Lynn. *The School to Work Revolution*. Reading, MA: Addison-Wesley, 1997.

Poe, Edgar Allan. "Annabel Lee." Montreal: Tundra Books, 1987.

Poe, Edgar Allan. "The Murders in the Rue Morgue." William R. Sanford, ed. Mankato, MN: Crestwood House, 1987.

Poe, Edgar Allan. "The Purloined Letter," in *American Fiction*. William Allan Neilson, ed. New York: P.F. Collier, 1977.

Poe, Edgar Allan. "The Raven." New York: Dover Publications, 1996.

Tripp, Rhoda Thomas. *The International Thesaurus of Quotations*. New York: Thomas Y. Crowell, 1970.

What Work Requires of Schools: A SCANS Report for America 2000 by the Secretary's Commission on Achieving Necessary Skills. Washington, D.C.: U.S. Department of Labor, 1991.

Software

Inspiration® is designed and developed by Inspiration Software®, 1994. This software allows students to create conceptual maps, thinking webs, graphic organizers, and flowcharts. It is available for either PCs or Macs through Learning Services at 1-800-877-3278 East or 1-800-877-9378 West. A single copy is $65.95. Lab packs are also available.

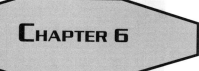

Speaking, Technology, Analysis, and Reading Through *Research*

"The outcome of any serious research can only be to make two questions grow where only one grew before."

—Thorstein Veblen (1857–1929),
The Place of Science in Modern Civilization.

RESEARCH FOUNDATION SKILLS

In the Secretary's Commission on Achieving Necessary Skills (SCANS) report, research skills can be found under the Basic Skills categories of reading, writing, and thinking, and the competency skills of resources and technology. Research incorporates a variety of skills. The reading skills include locating, understanding, and interpreting written information. The writing skills include communicating thoughts, ideas, and information. Learning how to learn as defined in the foundation thinking skills is described as efficiently using techniques to acquire and apply new knowledge. Identifying, selecting, and applying appropriate resources are essential skills in the research process. In addition, knowing which technology to use and how to search, sort, and apply appropriate software and on-line resources are important to the researcher today.

CONTENT PROFICIENCIES

A variety of Content Proficiencies are applicable to the research area.

Language Arts

The student reads to construct meaning by interacting with the text, by recognizing the different requirements of a variety of printed materials, and by using appropriate strategies to increase comprehension.

The student:

- Reads a variety of materials including literature, textbooks, and reference materials.

- Comprehends and draws inferences beyond the literal level.

- Recalls and builds background knowledge by exploring information related to the text.

- Identifies the author's intent, main idea, and supporting details.

- Applies appropriate strategies to increase fluency and adjusts his or her reading rate when reading various materials.

The student produces writing that conveys purpose and meaning, uses effective writing strategies, and incorporates the conventions of written language to communicate clearly.

The student:

- Produces creative, expository, technical, or personal writing on an assigned or self-selected topic.

- Indicates understanding of the topic through specific, accurate, and sufficient details.

- Organizes clearly and sequences ideas logically.

- Uses appropriate voice and word choice.

- Demonstrates a variety of sentence structures.

- Edits and eliminates errors.

Social Studies Proficiencies

The learner demonstrates an understanding of tradition and change by communicating how the past influences the present and the future.

The learner demonstrates an understanding of human diversity by communicating respect for basic human rights and the multicultural nature of societies and the world.

The learner:

- Understands the economic, social, and cultural differences between the North and South.

◆ Understands the development of regional differences and secession prior to the Civil War.

◆ Understands issues other than slavery that led to the Civil War.

◆ Understands the circumstances that produced the Civil War and its outcome.

◆ Understands how different groups of people shaped the Civil War.

CONNECTING RESEARCH TO WORKPLACE SKILLS

One of the first activities in the Civil War Unit is to invite local historians to our classrooms. We are fortunate to have access to people who reenact the Civil War. These men and women bring authentic artifacts from the time and dress in period costumes. Students begin to gain knowledge and a better understanding of what they are reading and researching through this dynamic and interactive program. Union and Confederate uniforms worn by these historians seem to make the students' research come alive. Some students end up accompanying their families to watch local black powder shooting competitions. These activities generate questions from the students. One of the questions is always, "But how do you know all this stuff?" The answer is through research.

UNIT ONE: THE AMERICAN CIVIL WAR

Aligning Instructional Practices with Proficiencies and Assessments

In alignment to the language art proficiencies, the student reads to construct meaning by interacting with the text, by recognizing the different requirements of a variety of printed materials, and by using appropriate strategies to increase comprehension.

The student produces writing that conveys purpose and meaning, uses effective writing strategies, and incorporates the conventions of written language to communicate clearly.

Then, in the social studies proficiencies, the learner demonstrates an understanding of tradition and change by communicating how the past influences the present and the future.

The learner demonstrates an understanding of human diversity by communicating respect for basic human rights and the multicultural nature of societies and the world.

Learning Objectives

Multiple learning objectives are presented in this unit. The student:

- Reads a wide variety of materials for information and pleasure and to enrich experience.

- Implements reading comprehension skills to complete assignments.

- Constructs meaning by interacting with the text and classmates.

- Discusses and asks questions while participating in a literature circle.

- Reflects on reading through journal writing.

- Makes connections to issues through the creation of a thinking map.

- Uses visual literacy skills to create a variety of maps.

- Defines a thoughtful research question.

- Uses a variety of skills to access, organize, and share information and knowledge.

- Selects from a variety of learning activities to create and share new knowledge.

Assessments

> *Teacher Notes:* The assessments for this unit are based on students' journal writing, map activities, and research projects. We have not included formal assessment sheets for the writing, because our assessments are written in the journals. We look for evidence of connections from text-to-self, text-to-text, and text-to-world as described in *Mosaic of Thought* (Keen and Zimmerman 1997). The metacognitive process is the focus of this reading experience. We have groups of students present book discussions to the entire class, since five novels are being read at the same time. These discussions often provide students with a desire to complete additional reading.

We provide feedback on the mapping assignments, thinking maps, and newsletters. The feedback forms are at the end of this section. Please refer to chapter 9 for more information on creating assessments.

Instructional Strategies

Literal

- Reading strategies

- Research strategies

- Analytical thinking skills

- Concept mapping

- Computer application

- Visual literacy skills

Lateral

- Social studies map

- Viewpoint newsletter

- Diaries

- Multimedia presentation

- Art

- Music

- Literature

- Poetry

- Oratory

Remediation Strategies

- Offer reading materials on a broad range of reading levels.

- Provide feedback on journal entries based on ability levels.

- Adjust music, art, and other learning activities to a variety of learners.

Enrichment Strategies

- Adapt learning activities to include higher-level thinking skills.

- Create a thinking map that includes the multiple levels of issues that had an impact on the Civil War.

- Write a speech for President Lincoln that addresses his great concerns about the impact of the war and his hesitation to plunge the nation into war.

Notes to Users of This Unit

Classroom Teachers: This unit is designed to involve several teachers in your school. Our students danced, sang, and created artwork. They gave speeches and dressed like Abe Lincoln and Sojourner Truth in Language Arts classes. They baked corn bread and made apple butter in Consumer Studies. The physical education teacher taught dances of the era. The music teacher introduced students to music and instruments of the period. The art teacher helped students express creativity through painting and drawing. We have provided suggestions for integration across the curriculum.

Media Specialists: This unit of learning presents multiple opportunities for students to express themselves through their own individual learning styles. You can support this unit by finding local resources for classroom use. We invited a group of local history buffs to talk with our students about the life of a typical soldier during the Civil War era. These men came in replica uniforms, from both the North and the South, and painted vivid images of a soldier's life. The women recreated the hardships of living in a war-torn environment. The more resources students have to help them understand this period, the richer this experience becomes. Videos such as *Glory,* which are carefully edited, as well as audiotapes, magazines, and books will help support this unit.

Technology Specialists: We provide a short list of Web sites that supports this unit. Assisting students in locating appropriate sites and bookmarking them for the entire class would be helpful. Students create presentations using a variety of software applications for this unit. Your help in importing video and audio selections would create more depth in these presentations.

In order to help middle-level learners understand significant events in history, it is important to help them make connections to the period of history through art, music, literature, and sociology. In this American Civil War unit we use a multidisciplinary approach, beginning with literature. This unit is one that can easily be taught in a block-scheduling situation or as a collaborative endeavor with other disciplines.

Specific Knowledge

The student will need to:

- Use reading strategies for research and to complete literature assignments.

- Learn to use multimedia software proficiently.

- Access specific information via the Internet.

- Actively contribute to and participate in group work.

- Use analytical thinking skills to support a viewpoint.

Environmental Considerations

Students will need access to computers with presentational software, concept-mapping software, the Internet, floppy disks, and/or a file server location to store their works-in-progress. Space for practicing and presenting speeches and dances would be beneficial.

Assignments and Intelligences Addressed

Assignment	Intelligence
KWL Activity	Linguistic
Novel Selection and Journal	Linguistic
Thinking Map	Visual/Spatial/Intrapersonal
Geographic Map	Visual/Spatial

The American Civil War Newsletter	Linguistic/Interpersonal
Defining a Research Question	Linguistic/Intrapersonal
Research	Linguistic
On-line Scavenger Hunt	Linguistic/Interpersonal

Why the American Civil War?

This important period of history is a critical part of our American past. For students to understand current issues, they must understand the events that affected decisions we make today. In this unit students select a piece of literature to read that becomes the springboard for research into this era. The five books we use span a broad range of reading levels to meet students' needs. You may have other books to add to this unit.

> ➤ *Teacher Notes:* We start this unit with a KWL activity (What I Know, What I Want to Know, and What I Learned) to generate interest. Students then select the novel they will read, and create an ongoing thinking-process map about the causes and effects of events in their novels.

Students are presented with five reading choices for this unit: *Across Five Aprils* by Irene Hunt (1964), *Rifles for Watie* by Harold Keith (1957), *Shades of Gray* by Carolyn Reeder (1989), *Behind Rebel Lines* by Seymour Reit (1988), and *Sojourner Truth Ain't I a Woman?* by Patricia and Fredrick McKissack (1992). All five novels are set during the Civil War era and provide different lenses from which to view this historical period. Synopses are provided in the student handout entitled "Civil War Novels."

Assignment #1: The KWL Activity

Use the KWL activity sheet to complete this assignment. You will start this assignment in class and then keep it in your journal. You will add to this assignment as you read and research. Column one lists everything you already know about the Civil War. Column two lists questions you have about the Civil War. You will add to this list as you read. Make notes in column three about things you learn about the Civil War from reading your novel. This assignment is ongoing and will be checked once a week for updates.

> ➤ *Teacher Notes:* We begin the novel selection process by having students participate in a KWL activity. We use the KWL activity in two ways:
>
> 1. As an individual thinking process
> 2. As a group thinking process

A handout is provided at the end of this unit for duplication. Begin by having students list what they already know about the Civil War on their own notepaper. Then, on a white board, overhead projector, or chart paper, list the things the class knows about the Civil War. Use the "What I Know" list to generate the second part of the KWL—the "What I Would Like to Know" column. Discuss with the class where they might find information they do not already know. List these resource ideas. Of course, one of the main places they find information is in the school media center. The person they work closely with is the Media Specialist. Before you begin work on this unit, meet with your Media Specialist and work together to have him or her prepare a lesson on how to find information that supports this activity.

Assignment #2: Select a Novel and Begin a Journal

> ➤ *Teacher Notes:* Introduce the five novels the students will be reading. We use a HyperStudio® presentation to introduce each one. Students are given the novel overview worksheet so they can make notes. After each novel is presented, provide students with sufficient time to look through books and determine which one each will read for this unit. Once students make a selection, place them in reading circles for their chosen novel.

In the reading circles students keep reading journals. On the second day of the introduction, students are shown excerpts from the *American Heritage Civil War* CD ROM to give them an overview of the period of history. In their journals they write their reflections about what they saw. They list questions about the Civil War.

The reading process we use is the pre-reading, during-reading, and after-reading questioning strategies. Students write questions generated from looking at the front cover of the book and reading the information on the back. As they read each chapter, they stop to reflect on what they read. They list questions about characters, plot, setting, and other areas of interest. These connections become powerful as students continue reading. (This reading strategy is detailed in *Mosaic of Thought* by Ellin Oliver Keene and Susan Zimmermann.)

Assignment #3: Thinking Maps

As you read, one of the questions you gather information on is, "What were the causes of the Civil War?" Using the double thinking map (see student handout titled "Double Thoughts"), you will keep a list of causes of the Civil War. Just fold the handout in half and use it as a bookmark. When you find a cause of the Civil War, write it on the appropriate side of the map. We will use this map to generate discussions and research questions.

Assignment #4: Geographic Map

As you read, keep a list of locations mentioned in your book. When you complete your reading you will make a map of those places. You can create a geographical map of the cities, states, rivers, etc., or you can make a map detailing the places your character visited. Your map is due when you finish your book.

> ➤ *Teacher Notes:* We continue to read, discuss, and reflect to build more knowledge about this period. Students learn about Fort Sumter, the issues of states' rights and slavery, the dilemma of President Lincoln, the Emancipation Proclamation, and some of the battles. As the students read they continue to list questions.

Assignment #5: The American Civil War Newsletter

> ➤ *Teacher Notes:* News of the Civil War came to many people through newspapers of the era. In this assignment, students write two newsletters based on books they read. One newsletter will have a distinctively Northern viewpoint, while the second will support the Southern cause.

You will be assigned to a group to complete this assignment. After you receive your assignment, your group will design and write articles for a newsletter. *Rebel Rag* articles will support the cause of the South. *Northern Star* will let people know about issues from the Union viewpoint. You will begin this project by selecting information about issues and battles from the books you are reading. After your group decides on the issues and battles, each reporter will write an article, an editorial, or an interview piece. The whole team will participate in the selection of art, advertisements, and layout. You will use the computer to create your final copy.

Assignment #6: Defining a Research Question

> *Teacher Notes:* After reading the books and completing the first four assignments, we begin the process of formulating research questions. Using the "What I Learned" column from the KWL activity, we have a round-robin sharing session. Students discuss what they have learned and we use this as a springboard to begin a list of unanswered questions. We put these questions on chart paper around the room and categorize them. The following is a list from one group of students:

- What were the important issues that caused the Civil War?
- Why did the Southern states leave the Union?
- Why did the South want slavery?
- Who were the leaders in the abolitionist movement and what did they do to try to end slavery?
- What kind of leader was President Lincoln?
- What kinds of weapons did soldiers have during that period?
- What were the roles of women during the war?
- What was it like to be a slave in the North? The South?
- How were Native Americans involved in the war?

This process follows the question selection process we discuss in detail in Chapter 4. Students identify the levels (according to Bloom's Taxonomy) of their questions and are facilitated in the process of rewording the question to create an analysis/synthesis question. While they must find knowledge before they can proceed to analysis/synthesis, they learn how to ask good questions. A question posed by one student illustrates this point: "Who were the leaders in the abolitionist movement?" "Who were the leaders . . ." is a knowledge level question. The student who asked this decided she needed to first find out what issues concerned the abolition of slavery. What impact would abolition of slavery have on the economy of the South? Why did the South oppose it? Why did the North want slavery eradicated? She ended up with a reframed research question, "What major issues on both sides concerned the abolition of slavery and how would they impact the economy and people during that era?"

Assignment #7: Research

You have decided on your research question. Now you will use a minimum of five resources to find the answer(s). You may select from books, magazines, on-line resources, videos, CD ROMs, and interviews. You are required to use at least three different types of information sources. For example, your resources must not all be from an encyclopedia. You need to include three different types, such as a video, magazine article, and personal interview.

The final product of your research is the communication of your question and the answer(s) you found. You may present this information through PowerPoint® or HyperStudio®, a formal speech, a video you create, a Web site you design, or artifacts you create. Artifacts can include, but are not limited to diaries, paintings, letters, and models. Complete the American Civil War Research Idea Concept worksheet and meet with your teacher before you proceed.

More Ideas for American Civil War Learning Activities

> ➤ *Teacher Notes:* The following ideas are presented here for your use as you teach this unit. Please select the ones that fit your time frame and student needs.

Oratory

Have students write original speeches defending the major issues of the Civil War. After students have practiced their speeches, invite the community into your classroom to hear the debate. Or have students memorize the Gettysburg Address and have a speech competition.

Apple Butter and Cornbread

Have students find authentic recipes from the Civil War era from a variety of sources. Organize the recipes into categories and prepare a Civil War cookbook. Have students provide information in the cookbook on the background of the food and ingredients. They may even write anecdotes from the novels they read to enhance the recipes. Select and prepare recipes for a food tasting day.

Songs of the American Civil War

Dixie is only one of many songs that came out of the Civil War. Have students who are interested listen to songs of the Civil War and research their backgrounds. The lyrics often tell haunting tales of battles. Create an audiotape and a songbook of favorite songs that the students present. They may also be interested in learning about the musical instruments of the period.

Dances of the American Civil War

Folk and square dancing, as well as waltzes and jigs, were popular during the Civil War. Have students research dances of this period and give a Civil War dance recital.

More Maps

This unit provides students with several options for creating maps. Some ideas are:

1. Statistical map showing the population, number of factories, placement and length of railroad tracks, and capital deposits in banks for the North and South.

2. Alignment maps showing the free Union states, the slave secession states, border states, western territories that supported the Union, and western territories that supported the Confederacy in 1861 and in 1864.

3. Civil War battle maps showing the major battles and who won them for each year from 1861 to 1865. Information about deaths incurred by each side is an interesting feature one student added to his map.

Life on a Southern Plantation

The economic status of the southern plantation was one of the major issues of the war. Have students research a day on a plantation from the viewpoint of the owner and the slaves. Present the findings in a play where the owner and a slave are on the stage and alternate the monologues.

Abolitionists

Students frequently know only the major players in the Civil War who toiled to abolish slavery. Provide them with the opportunity to learn more about the courageous people who often put their own lives in danger to fight for this cause. Richard Allen, Susan B. Anthony, John Brown, Frederick Douglass, William Lloyd Garrison, John Jay, Lucretia Mott, Wendell Phillips, David Ruggles, Dred Scott, Elizabeth Stanton, Sojourner Truth, Lucy Stone, Harriet Beecher Stowe, and Harriet Tubman made major contributions to abolition. As students find information, create a wall mural to depict the people and their contributions.

Abraham Lincoln

In the novels the students read for this unit, Abraham Lincoln is presented through many viewpoints. Have students find out how President Lincoln was perceived by his contemporaries. What were his views on slavery? What was the impact of the Emancipation Proclamation? Students may write letters as if they are from the same family with one son fighting for the North and another for the South and discuss their views about Lincoln from the viewpoints of the mother, father, the sons in the war, and other family members they wish to create. This activity can be one of great depth.

Military Weapons

In the book *Rifles for Watie,* the repeating rifle changed the course of the Civil War. While most soldiers used black powder rifles, a few shot the new lever action rifle. Mention is also made of the ironclads. Military weapons of the period are of great interest to some students. Students may be interested in creating a mini-museum exhibit complete with models and diagrams.

KWL CIVIL WAR ACTIVITY SHEET

Name _____ Date _____ Period _____

Directions: Use this three-column sheet to determine (1) what you already know about the Civil War, (2) what you want to learn, and (3) what you learned. You will need to keep this in your journal and update it each week with your reading circle group.

What I Know   What I Want to Know   What I Learned

CIVIL WAR NOVELS

Name _____ Date _____ Period _____

Directions: This sheet is for your notes. As each of the five novels is presented, make notes so that you can decide which one interests you the most.

1. Book Title: *Across Five Aprils.* Author: Irene Hunt. It is April 1861 and Jethro Creighton, who is nine years old, lives with his family on a farm in southern Illinois. There are rumblings of war, and young Jethro is confused by all the talk. War breaks out, and the Creighton family is torn. A beloved brother, Bill, leaves to fight for the South, while the rest of the family and close neighbors fight for the North. Jethro stays on the farm and learns of the battles. He must make decisions during the next five years as a nation's loyalties, as well his own family's, are divided.

   _____

   _____

   _____

   _____

   _____

   _____

2. Book Title: *Sojourner Truth Ain't I a Woman?* Authors: Patricia McKissack and Fredrick McKissack. Born in 1797, Isabella Van Wagener was a slave for twenty-eight years. She endured the horrors of being sold, beaten, and treated in the most inhumane manner. Through it all, her strength and courage kept growing. When she won her freedom, she began speaking out against the horrors of slavery and dedicated her life to ending this human misery. This riveting story tells the journey of how Isabella became Sojourner Truth, a woman of great honor and integrity who rose from the shackles of slavery to meet with presidents and senators.

   _____

   _____

   _____

   _____

   _____

3. Book Title: *Rifles for Watie.* Author: Harold Keith. Jefferson Davis Bussey is sixteen years old when the Civil War begins. He leaves his family's Kansas farm to defend the Union and quickly learns that the issues surrounding this war are anything but clear. Jeff experiences the exhausting life of an infantryman, the fear of being caught as an enemy spy, the pain of falling in love with a beautiful rebel, and the uncertainty of a critical decision: to stay with the enemy who has befriended him or return to his company.

   _____

   _____

   _____

Worksheet continues on page 156.

_____

_____

_____

4. Book Title: *Behind Rebel Lines.* Author: Seymour Reit. Emma Edmonds decides that she is going to serve her country and enlists in the Union Army. She overcomes the obstacle of being a woman by cutting off her hair and donning men's clothing. She risks great danger when she becomes a spy and infiltrates the enemy camps. This young woman risks her life in suspenseful adventures as she disguises herself as a slave, peddler, and washerwoman to gather information.

_____

_____

_____

_____

5. Book Title: *Shades of Gray.* Author: Carolyn Reeder. Will Page's father and brother were killed by the Yankees during the Civil War and Will was left an orphan. He is forced to live with his uncle, who refused to fight. Raised in the city, Will must learn to live the life of a farmer as well as endure the humiliation of living with a traitor. Can Will ever understand the choice his uncle made?

_____

_____

_____

_____

The book I have chosen is _____ because

_____

_____

Remember: You can read more than one book.

DOUBLE THOUGHTS

Name _____ Date _____ Period _____

Directions: As you know, there are two very different viewpoints about the causes of the American Civil War. Use these graphics to help you keep track of causes you find as you read your novel. These sheets go with Assignment #3.

North

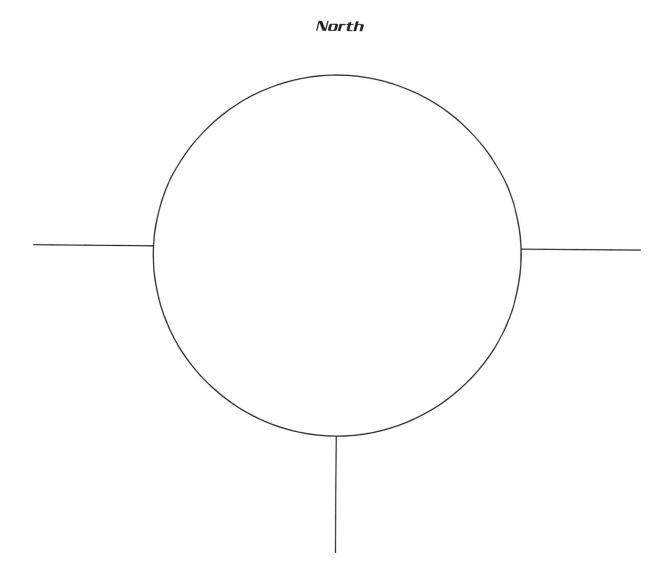

Worksheet continues on page 158.

South

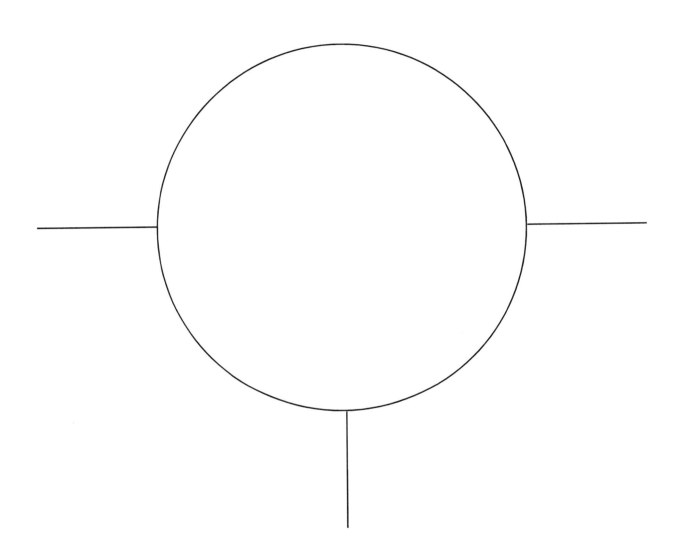

AMERICAN CIVIL WAR CONTRACT AND GRADING RUBRIC

Name _____ Date _____ Period _____

Directions: Assignment #4 asks you to select the kind of map you want to make, and then create it.

Turn this sheet in with your map for assessment.

1. What kind of map did you make?

2. Geographic

3. Battle sites

4. One battle

5. Journey or path the main character traveled in your novel

6. Other (describe)

Grading Rubric for American Civil War Map Assignment

Legend clearly explains map	5	4	3	2	1
Compass included	5	4	3	2	1
Map has a title	5	4	3	2	1
Drawings are neat	5	4	3	2	1
Purpose is clear	5	4	3	2	1
Information is accurate	5	4	3	2	1

Comments

_____

Grade

_____

THE AMERICAN CIVIL WAR NEWSLETTER ASSIGNMENT AND GRADING RUBRIC

Name _____ Date _____ Period_____

Group _____

Name of Newsletter _____

Directions: News of the Civil War came to many people through newspapers. In this assignment, you and your group will write a newsletter based on information from assigned novels. One newsletter will have a distinctively Northern viewpoint; the second will support the Southern cause.

You will be assigned to a group to complete this assignment. After you receive your assignment, your group will design and write articles for a newsletter. *Rebel Rag* articles will support the cause of the South. *Northern Star* will let people know about issues from the Union viewpoint.

You will begin this project by selecting information about issues and battles from the books you are reading. After your group decides on issues and battles, each reporter will write an article, an editorial, or an interview piece. The whole team will participate in the selection of art, advertisements, and layout. You will use the computer to create your final copy.

1. Title of the novel you are reading

    _____

2. Major issues in this novel (divide into northern and southern issues)

    _____

    _____

    _____

    _____

3. Major battles

    _____

    _____

_____

_____

4. Your idea for an article, editorial, or interview

_____

_____

_____

_____

Grading Rubric for the
American Civil War Newsletter

1.	Viewpoint clearly stated	5	4	3	2	1
2.	Writing is free of grammatical errors	5	4	3	2	1
3.	Spell checked	5	4	3	2	1
4.	Content is historically accurate	5	4	3	2	1
5.	Content is persuasive	5	4	3	2	1
6.	Layout and design follow guidelines	5	4	3	2	1
7.	Artwork supports the content	5	4	3	2	1
8.	Creative	5	4	3	2	1

Comments

_____

_____

Final Grade _____

DEFINING A RESEARCH QUESTION FOR THE AMERICAN CIVIL WAR UNIT

Name _____ Date _____ Period _____

Your research question

_____

_____

_____

What level of question are you asking? Defend your answer.

_____

_____

_____

_____

_____

1. Knowledge

2. Comprehension

3. Application

4. Analysis

5. Synthesis

6. Evaluation

Make an appointment with your teacher to discuss your research question and the Bloom's Taxonomy level of your question.

Teacher Sign-off _____ Date _____

AMERICAN CIVIL WAR RESEARCH RUBRIC

Name _____ Date _____ Period_____

Directions: There are three evaluations due for this project. You complete the self-evaluation, have a parent complete the parent evaluation, and I will complete the teacher evaluation.

Research Question_____

1.	Outline	5	4	3	2	1
2.	Title Page	5	4	3	2	1
3.	Introduction	5	4	3	2	1
4.	Body of paper	5	4	3	2	1
5.	Conclusion	5	4	3	2	1
6.	Five sources	5	4	3	2	1
7.	Mechanics, spelling, grammar, and punctuation	5	4	3	2	1
8.	Typed, word processed, or written in black ink	5	4	3	2	1
9.	Research question was answered	5	4	3	2	1
10.	Analysis, synthesis, and evaluation evident	5	4	3	2	1

Comments

_____

_____

_____

Self Evaluation Grade _____

Parent Evaluation Grade _____

Teacher Evaluation Grade _____

PLAN, PLAN, PLAN

Name _____ Date _____ Period_____

Directions: The purpose of this worksheet is to help you organize your work. Use the checklists to help you stay on task and turn work in on time.

Research Question _____

Research Question Approved

1. Outline   Due Date   Turned in   Returned to me

_____

_____

2. Notes Checked   Due Date   Turned in   Returned to me

_____

_____

3. First Draft   Due Date   Turned in   Returned to me

_____

_____

4. Peer Edit #1   Who?   Given to   Returned to me

_____

_____

5. Second Draft   Due Date   Turned in   Returned to me

_____

_____

6. Final Paper   Due Date   Turned in   Returned to me

_____

_____

Research Paper Checklist

_____ 1. Outline

_____ 2. Title page

_____ 3. Introduction

_____ 4. Body of information

_____ 5. Conclusion

_____ 6. Bibliography

_____ 7. Pictures, maps, graphs, charts, etc.

_____ 8. Peer edited

_____ 9. Word processed, typed, or written neatly in black ink

_____ 10. Spell checked

_____ 11. Mechanics, grammar, and punctuation all edited

➤*Teacher Notes:* On-line scavenger hunts can be used to generate interest in a topic, provide additional information, and teach information accessing. The two scavenger hunts here were designed to challenge students to think about the roles that women played in the American Civil War and to help students make a connection between what they read in their novels and the time frame of the Civil War. You can create scavenger hunts to meet your own goals and objectives.

Creating an On-line Scavenger Hunt

1. Determine the purpose of your hunt. Goal(s)? Objective(s)?

2. Look at this example Web site: http://www.americancivilwar.com

WOMEN OF THE AMERICAN CIVIL WAR SCAVENGER HUNT

Name _____ Date _____ Period_____

Directions: You may work alone or in a team to complete this scavenger hunt.

Read and complete the information in each step.

1. Open the Netscape icon (browser).

2. Go to Bookmarks.

3. Open the Civil War folder in Bookmarks.

4. Open the American Civil War folder.

5. Look for Women in the War.

6. Click on Harriet Beecher Stowe.

7. Read and answer these questions about Harriet Beecher Stowe:

   a. What was her position concerning slavery?
   b. How did she communicate her views?

8. Go back to the Women of the American Civil War screen.

9. Select two other women. Read about them and retell what their contributions were to the American Civil War.

10. Be ready to share what you have learned with the class.

➤*Teacher Notes:* The Web site for this sheet is http://www.americancivilwar.com.

THE AMERICAN CIVIL WAR TIME LINE

Name _____ Date _____ Period_____

Directions: You may work alone or in a team to complete this time line.

Read and complete each step.

1. Open the Netscape icon (browser).

2. Go to Bookmarks.

3. Open the Civil War folder in Bookmarks.

4. Open The American Civil War folder.

5. Open 1861.

6. Read and answer the following questions:

    a. What was the first state to secede (leave) the Union?
    b. What were the eleven states that formed the Confederate States of America?
    c. What event occurred on March 4, 1861?
    d. What was President Lincoln's view on slavery in 1861?
    e. Explain the events at Fort Sumter.

7. Select, read, and explain the importance of three battles in 1861.

8. Organize this information and include it in your journal.

UNIT TWO: PLANNING FOR THE RESEARCH PROJECT

> ➤ *Teacher Notes:* This unit is for you, the classroom teacher. We want to provide you with helpful ideas on how to set up the research project assignment. Please feel free to adapt these materials to meet your own needs.

Student Research Notebook

We organized a binder with the materials we wanted students to use during the research mini-lessons. We made copies so our students could use them as resources throughout the year. Use these materials as a starting point and add your own pieces.

What Is a Research Project?

A STARR research project involves a written paper that shares the information you learn and a project that incorporates technology. During the course of this research project you will be required to:

1. Select a topic of interest to you.
2. Locate and use multiple resources on that topic.
3. Prepare a formal or webbed outline.
4. Read and take notes.
5. Create a bibliography of the sources you use.
6. Use your notes and outline to write a first draft.
7. Edit, revise, and rewrite your draft.
8. Turn in an edited final draft using a word processing program.
9. Design and develop a presentation on your topic utilizing technology.

Does this sound complicated? It can be. But if you use this notebook and project planning sheet and stick to deadlines, you can do it.

How to Select a Topic or Research Question

The first step is selecting a topic or research question. As you think about this, keep in mind that you will be researching this topic for six to eight weeks. So Rule One is select a topic you can stick to without getting bored. Rule Two is to select a topic or question you want to learn something about. And Rule Three is to apply Bloom's Taxonomy questions to your topic or question. Remember, if your topic or question is a knowledge only question, it won't get approved. Here are Bloom's categories as a reminder:

1. Knowledge
2. Comprehension

3. Application

4. Analysis

5. Synthesis

6. Evaluation

Locating Resources

Now that you have your approved topic or question, start locating, accessing, sorting, and organizing resources. Where should you start? First, make a list in your notebook with the following headings: books, magazines, newspapers, CD ROMs, on-line resources, and the Internet. You must use five resources for this project. After our Media Specialist has shown you how to locate materials using each of these categories, select one and begin your search. You might want to use different colored note cards to help organize this information. For Internet resources, list the URL so you can go back and access it later.

When you think you have found enough resources, start reading and taking notes. Begin with one resource category, like the Internet. Enter the URLs you found one by one, read the information and take notes. Do this for each category. Read over all your note cards during one reading and compare the gathered information to your outline. Make notes about what is missing. Go back and find resources with this information. Once you have sufficient notes, you are ready to begin writing.

THE RESEARCH PROJECT EVALUATION

Name _____ Date _____ Period_____

Directions: There are three evaluations due for this project. You complete the self-evaluation, have a parent complete their evaluation, and I will complete the teacher evaluation.

Research Question or Topic _____

1.	Outline	5	4	3	2	1
2.	Title Page	5	4	3	2	1
3.	Introduction	5	4	3	2	1
4.	Body of Paper	5	4	3	2	1
5.	Conclusion	5	4	3	2	1
6.	Five sources	5	4	3	2	1
7.	Mechanics, spelling, grammar, and punctuation	5	4	3	2	1
8.	Typed, word processed, or written in black ink	5	4	3	2	1
9.	Research question was answered	5	4	3	2	1
10.	Analysis, synthesis, and evaluation evident	5	4	3	2	1

Comments

_____

_____

Self Evaluation Grade _____

Parent Evaluation Grade _____

Teacher Evaluation Grade _____

PLAN, PLAN, PLAN

Name _____ Date _____ Period_____

Directions: The purpose of this handout is to help you organize your work. Use the checklists to stay on task and turn work in on time.

Research Question or Topic _____

Research Question Approved

_____ 1.	Outline	Due Date	Turned in	Returned to me
_____ 2.	Notes Checked	Due Date	Turned in	Returned to me
_____ 3.	First Draft	Due Date	Turned in	Returned to me
_____ 4.	Peer Edit #1	Who?	Given to	Returned to me
_____ 5.	Second Draft	Due Date	Turned in	Returned to me
_____ 6.	Final Paper	Due Date	Turned in	Returned to me

Research Paper Checklist

_____ 1. Outline

_____ 2. Title page

_____ 3. Introduction

_____ 4. Body of information

_____ 5. Conclusion

_____ 6. Bibliography

Worksheet continues on page 172.

_____ 7.   Pictures, maps, graphs, charts, etc.

_____ 8.   Peer edited

_____ 9.   Word processed, typed, or written neatly in black ink

_____ 10. Spell checked

_____ 11. Mechanics, grammar, and punctuation all edited

Outlining

Outlining provides you with a guide on how to present information you have learned. You have two options for outlining, a formal outline or a web outline. Here is an example of a formal outline:

Topic: Elephants of the World: Their Similarities and Differences

I.   Introduction

   A.   Physical characteristics of the Asian elephant

      1.   Size of male and female

      2.   Color

      3.   Ear size and use

   B.   Development

      1.   Mating habits

      2.   Baby elephant's developmental stages

   C.   Habitat

      1.   Where each lives

      2.   What they eat

      3.   Range for territory and food

   D.   Challenges

      1.   Problems for elephants in today's world

      2.   Solutions to those problems

II. Conclusion

Figure 6.1. Sample Web Outline

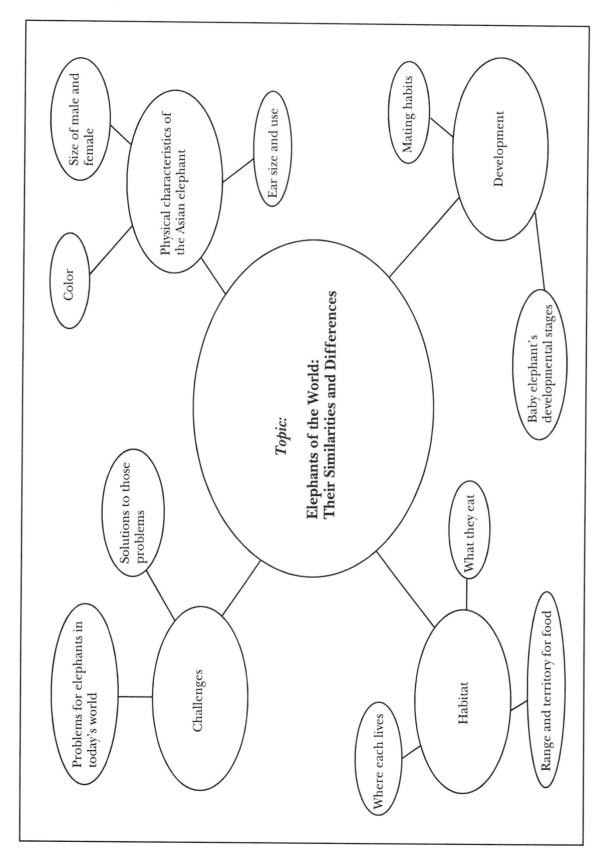

Reading and Note-Taking

This part of the research process is where you find the information, evaluate whether you want to include it, and synthesize it for your report. There are many ways to organize reading and note-taking. I like to gather all my resources in one place and start with one category. Let's say I begin with books. I take my stack of blue note cards with the title, author, publisher, date of publication, and place of publication. I select one information card and read for notes on my topic. I take notes on another card as I read. I do this for each stack of cards by category. When I start reading the same information over again, I discard that resource. When finished with reading and note taking, I compare what I have against my outline. If I need more information, I go back and find additional resources. When I finally have enough, I am ready to start writing.

Bibliography

A bibliography is a list of resources used for your research project. The best way to keep a bibliography list is to write the information required on your note cards when you first find a resource. This saves you time going back to locate a resource later. Here is the information you need to keep:

1. Author's name. Last name first. Example: Rawls, Wilson

2. Title of book, underlined. Example: <u>Where the Red Fern Grows</u>.

3. City of publication. Example: New York:

4. Publisher's name in full. Example: Bantam Books

5. Copyright date. Example: 1961.

All of this is written out like a sentence. Watch out for required punctuation. Here is an example:

Rawls, Wilson. <u>Where the Red Fern Grows</u>. New York: Bantam Books, 1961.

Magazines, encyclopedias, videos, CD ROMs, and the Internet are all cited in different ways. Refer to your bibliography sheet for that information.

Writing the First Rough Draft

You have completed your outline and your notes. Your teacher has signed off on both. Now, you're ready to write your first draft, also called the rough draft. You will need your outline, your notes, and a computer. It would also be helpful to take out the Research Grading Rubric. Read over all these documents. Begin with the introduction. The introduction is like a preview of coming attractions. It should tell your reader what the research is about and it should make them want to read more.

Next use the main topics from your outline and fill in the information from your note cards. Remember to use your own words. Plagiarism will get you into trouble.

End your paper with a strong conclusion. You may summarize major points of your paper in the conclusion and make a statement about what you feel or believe on the topic.

Editing, Revising, and Rewriting

You mean, I have to do that all over again? Yes. It also helps to have a parent or peer edit your paper. Go through the comments made by your teacher, your parents, and your peer. Make changes that make a difference. Check all spelling and grammar. Does your introduction make the reader want more information? Is your conclusion strong? Double-check your bibliography for accuracy. Compare the sections of your paper against the grading rubric. You should be ready to hand in your final draft.

The Final Draft

This is the draft you hand in for your final grade. Remember to use one font, such as Times New Roman, throughout the paper. You may change font size for headings and subheadings. Double-space your paper and insert page numbers in the upper right-hand corner. Check spelling, punctuation, and grammar. Hand in your paper in this order:

- Outline

- Paper

- Diagrams, charts, maps, pictures

- Bibliography

- Grading rubric

- And last, but not least, turn it in on time

RESOURCES

Books

Ehrlich, Eugene and DeBruhl. (eds.) *The International Thesaurus of Quotations.* New York: Harper Perennial, 1996.

Hunt, Irene. *Across Five Aprils.* New York: The Berkeley Publishing Group, 1964.

Keene, Ellin Oliver, and Zimmerman, Susan. *Mosaic of Thought.* Portsmouth, NH: Heinemann, 1997.

Keith, Harold. *Rifles for Watie.* New York: Harper Collins, 1957.

McKissack, Patricia, and McKissack, Fredrick. *Sojourner Truth Ain't I a Woman?* New York: Scholastic, 1992.

Reeder, Carolyn. *Shades of Gray.* New York: Avon Books, 1989.

Reit, Seymour. *Behind Rebel Lines.* Orlando: Harcourt Brace, 1988.

CD ROM

American Heritage Civil War CD ROM. New York: Simon & Schuster, 1995.

What Work Requires of Schools: A SCANS Report for America 2000 by the Secretary's Commission on Achieving Necessary Skills. Washington, D.C.: U.S. Department of Labor, 1991.

Web sites

http://www.americancivilwar.com

http://www.civilwarhome.com

http://www.hist.unt.edu/09w-amw2.htm

Video

Glory. A story of the first black regiment to fight for the North during the American Civil War. 122 minutes. RCA/Columbia Pictures Home Videos, 1990. ISBN 0-8001-0214-2.

CHAPTER 7

Speaking, Technology, Analysis, and Reading Through *Research*
Additional Units

"You will find it a very good practice always to verify your references, sir."
—Martin Routh, *Quarterly Review,* July 1878.

RESEARCH FOUNDATION SKILLS

In the Secretary's Commission on Achieving Necessary Skills (SCANS) report, research skills can be found under the Basic Skills categories of reading, writing, and thinking, and the competency skills of resources and technology. Research incorporates a variety of abilities. Reading skills include locating, understanding, and interpreting written information. Writing skills include communicating thoughts, ideas, and information. Learning how to learn as defined in the foundation thinking skills is described as efficiently using techniques to acquire and apply new knowledge. Identifying, selecting, and applying appropriate resources are essential skills in the research process. In addition, knowing which technology to use and how to search, sort, and apply appropriate software and on-line resources are important to the researcher today.

CONTENT PROFICIENCIES

A variety of Content Proficiencies are applicable to the research area, but reading and writing are the most important.

Language Arts

The student reads to construct meaning by interacting with the text, by recognizing different requirements of a variety of printed materials, and by using appropriate strategies to increase comprehension.

The student:

- ◆ Reads a variety of materials including literature, textbooks, and reference materials.

- ◆ Comprehends and draws inferences beyond the literal level.

- ◆ Recalls and builds background knowledge by exploring information related to the text.

- ◆ Identifies the author's intent, main idea, and supporting details.

- ◆ Applies appropriate strategies to increase fluency and adjusts his or her reading rate when reading various materials.

The student produces writing that conveys purpose and meaning, uses effective writing strategies, and incorporates the conventions of written language to communicate clearly.

The student:

- ◆ Produces creative, expository, technical, or personal writing on an assigned or self-selected topic.

- ◆ Indicates understanding of topic through specific, accurate, and sufficient details.

- ◆ Organizes clearly and sequences ideas logically.

- ◆ Uses appropriate voice and word choice.

- ◆ Demonstrates a variety of sentence structures.

- ◆ Edits and eliminates errors.

CONNECTING RESEARCH TO WORKPLACE SKILLS

Connecting workplace skills to the school environment is sometimes difficult for young learners. They see teachers, administrators, and staff in the workplace, but few other adults who can spark interest in future career goals. This unit in particular showcases the knowledge and skills of one of the central people at school, the Media Specialist. We are very fortunate to have a gifted Media Specialist, who works as a member of our STARR team by teaching lessons, planning with us, and using her vast knowledge and expertise to enrich the learning experiences of both teachers and students. We take the opportunity provided by this unit to share her talents and provide students with insights into a career opportunity.

Some Thoughts

Our research unit would be seriously lacking without this dynamite project. Our Media Specialist, Kathie Jenkins, created this entire unit to help students recognize the many resources available at the school library. We were astounded at the wealth of materials as we helped students delve into the resources contained in this unit. We are aware that your particular library may not have all, or even many of the resources contained in this unit. However, you may select as many as you wish and leave the rest. This unit culminates with students presenting their book or resource to the class, giving the bibliographic information, and detailing what the resource contains. Classmates are expected to keep a record for each resource. An alternative is to have the students scan the cover and title page into a ClarisWorks® document, type answers to specific questions about the contents, and then create a class book of resources available in the library.

UNIT ONE: RESEARCH ROUNDUP

Learning Objectives

The intent of this unit is to have students, through guided learning, instruct themselves with the variety of materials available in their library for research, and to share information with their classmates. In this unit, students will:

◆ Use the Dewey Decimal System to locate research materials.

◆ Answer questions specific to their reference.

◆ Share information about their medium with classmates.

◆ Record information about all shared media for future reference.

Assessments

Assessments in this unit are the individual Reference Roundup worksheets to complete, along with the speech presentation to the class demonstrating what each research source has to offer. Alternatively, the teacher may choose to have the students create a class book using a word processing program or presentational software of your choice.

Instructional Strategies

Literal

◆ Reading strategies

◆ Research strategies

◆ Analytical thinking skills

* Computer application

* Visual literacy skills

Lateral

* Multimedia presentation

* Oratory

Remediation Strategies

* Reading materials are offered on a broad range of reading levels.

* Learning activities can be adjusted to a variety of learners.

* stopped here

Enrichment Strategies

* The learning activities are adapted to include higher-level thinking skills.

* With access to a college or university library, create a multimedia presentation of differences and similarities between the school library and the university or college library materials.

Notes to Users of This Unit

Classroom Teachers: This is a terrific introduction to the library media center and the materials it contains. We are eternally grateful to Kathie Jenkins, our Media Specialist, for creating this dynamite unit. Prior to students delving into their individual assigned references, Kathie also instructed our students in a brief history of libraries, the Dewey Decimal System, and how our library is set up. With this knowledge, our students begin research assignments with greater confidence about locating information. Ask your Media Specialist for similar assistance.

Media Specialists: This unit was created by one of you. Kathie Jenkins, as you will see, has done a creative and unique job of getting students interested in reference materials. It will benefit your classroom teachers if you can pull these materials from the shelves and place them in an area limited to this study. The study lasts only three or four days. We have used a cart in our library to locate materials for this study. All materials are found by the students on the cart at the beginning of each period, and must be returned there before students are dismissed. Your assistance in helping the teacher with this unit is invaluable. Developing a lecture presentation similar to Kathie's regarding library history, the Dewey Decimal System, and location of reference materials is also invaluable.

Technology Specialists: You will note that the Reference Roundup includes research databases. You can best assist this project by ensuring that the databases are up and running properly. If you can, please help students as they study their technology reference. Accessing information on the Internet is an important skill for learners today. You may want to assist the Media Specialist by bookmarking on-line library sites for use in this unit.

If your teacher chooses to have students scan in the cover page and title page of each resource, you can assist them as well as with the word processed document added to the scanned items.

Environmental Considerations

Students will need access to the Learning Resource Center for this unit. Schedule this time with your Media Specialist.

> *Teacher Notes:* Arrange with your Media Specialist in advance to allow students access to the research media for three to five days. If you need your Media Specialist to lecture students on the history, Dewey Decimal System, and location of research materials, you need to also arrange this in advance. Copies of each page of the Reference Roundup—for which you have the corresponding reference—will need to be made in advance. A worksheet for students to follow to present their information to their classmates is also included and will need to be photocopied. Students will need at least two days in the computer lab to work through programs included in the Reference Roundup. Your Technology Specialist and/or Media Specialist may be enlisted to assist you with technology instruction. Further, if you choose to scan the cover and title pages and create a class book of available library references, you should arrange the necessary computer lab time.

REFERENCE #1: *WORLD ALMANAC AND BOOK OF FACTS*

REF 317.3 Wor

➤ *Teacher Notes:* We include several questions pertaining to our geographic region. You will probably want to change these questions to reflect your region.

(Please use newest available year)

Year Used _____

Published annually, an almanac has thousands of very up-to-date facts. You need to think like a detective when you use an almanac. For example, the subjects in the index may not refer to main headings. Think of different headings under which you might find subjects. Do not get discouraged. Just keep thinking.

1. Where is the General Index in this book?

   Pages _____ through _____

2. What is the tallest building in Denver, Colorado?

   _____

3. How many stories does it have? _____

   On what page did you find the answer? _____

4. What is the zip code of Durango, Colorado? _____

   On what page did you find the answer? _____

5. Who was the *first* Pope in the year 827? _____

   On what page did you find the answer? _____

6. What is the address you would use to write to the President of the United States at the White House?

   _____

   _____

   _____

   On what page did you find the answer? _____

REFERENCE #2: *WEBSTER'S BIOGRAPHICAL DICTIONARY*

REF 920.02 Web

A biographical dictionary gives brief information about people. You use biographical dictionaries to check name pronunciation, life dates, and other details; get a quick view of the main events in a person's life; and identify persons whose names occur in reading and conversation.

Look at the table of contents. Notice that explanatory notes and guides are given in the front of the book. Use them when answering these questions:

1. What do the following abbreviations mean when used in this book?

    b _____   c _____

    dau _____   m _____

2. Who was Sir Norman Everard Brookes? _____

    _____ Page _____

3. During what years did Abba Hillel Silver live? _____

    _____ Page _____

4. What kind of work did Isabel Anderson do? _____

    _____ Page _____

5. What was Sir Henry Morton Stanley's original name? _____

    _____ Page _____

6. What book is Gutenberg, the German inventor of printing from movable type, famous for producing?

    _____ Page _____

REFERENCE #3: *BARTLETT'S FAMILIAR QUOTATIONS*

REF 808.88 Bar

This book serves two main purposes. First, you can find out who first said a famous quotation and in what poem or story. Second, you can find a famous quotation on a subject of interest.

Look carefully at the table of contents. Notice that there are *two indexes*. You will use each of them to answer these questions:

1. What was the last command given to the crew of the U.S. Navy dirigible *Akron* by Herbert V. Wiley?

   _____

   _____ Page _____

2. Who said, "Say it Loud, I'm Black and I'm Proud." _____

   _____ Page _____

3. What is the complete quotation that includes this: "Ask not what your country can do for you"?

   _____

   _____

   _____

   Page _____ Who said it? _____

4. What is the famous quotation by Edith Wharton about light? _____

   _____

   _____

   _____ Page _____

REFERENCE #4: *FAMOUS FIRST FACTS*

REF 031.02 Kan

This book contains a record of first happenings, discoveries, and inventions in America from 1007 through 1980. There are four large indexes that allow you to find information in different ways. The body of the book itself is arranged in alphabetical order.

1. Look at the table of contents. List the four indexes:

    _____

    _____

    _____

    _____

2. When and where was toilet paper first made?

    _____ Page _____

3. What kind of animal was flown in an airplane for the first time in 1930?

    _____ Page _____

4. Look up your birthday in the index by days. List one interesting and famous first to happen on your day.

    Date _____ Page _____

    famous first: _____

    _____

5. What is Elizabeth Smith Miller famous for designing?

    _____ Page _____

    _____

    Which index did you use? _____

6. What is the zoo in Denver, Colorado, famous for doing first?

    _____

    _____ Page _____

    Which index did you use? _____

REFERENCE #5: *SIXTH BOOK OF JUNIOR AUTHORS AND ILLUSTRATORS*

REF 809.89282 Six

This book is one of a continuing series of books. It contains 236 biographical sketches of authors and illustrators for young people. It is arranged alphabetically by the name the author most often uses. It also indexes the first five volumes in the series.

1. Explain what each of the following symbols represents in the index:

   J _____

   M _____

   4 _____

2. In which book in the series would you look to locate information on Steven Kellogg?

   _____

3. What pseudonym is listed under Shel Silverstein's name?

   _____ Page _____

4. When was Roald Dahl born? _____ Vol _____ Page _____

5. What is Madeleine L'Engle's real name? _____

   For what book did she receive the 1963 Newbery Award? _____

   _____ Page _____

6. How old was Dick King-Smith when he started writing children's books?

   _____ Page _____

7. Where does Betty Ren Wright like to write? _____

   What is her most awarded book? _____

   _____ Page _____

8. Mavis Jukes had an adventuresome spirit growing up. To what organization did she belong?

   _____ Page _____

REFERENCE #6: *WEBSTER'S NEW GEOGRAPHICAL DICTIONARY*

REF 910.321 Web

In alphabetical order, a geographical dictionary gives the pronunciation, location, and brief facts about places on Earth. *Gazetteer* is another name for a geographical dictionary.

This book will answer questions about size, population, heights of mountains, lengths of rivers, etc. It has special features such as charts, tables, and maps.

Some entries can be difficult to understand because many abbreviations and symbols are used.

1. The table of contents shows where to find the meanings of abbreviations:

    alt _____   co _____

    m _____   nr _____

2. In what state will you find each of these towns?

    Mount Clemens _____

    Logansport _____

3. Give each type of geographical feature below: (river, island, etc.)

    Bois Blanc _____

    Wabash_____

    Kilamanjaro _____

4. How long is the river Nile from its most remote headstream?

    _____

5. What is the maximum depth of the Sea of Japan?

    _____ Page _____

6. In what county is the city of Chicago located?

    _____ Page _____

7. How many square miles does the Sahara Desert cover? _____ Page _____

REFERENCE #7: *ILLUSTRATED FACTS AND RECORDS BOOK OF ANIMALS*

591 Row

This book contains facts about nature from its largest to smallest animal. It contains records of the fastest and slowest creatures. It also describes ordinary animals and strange ones.
Use both the table of contents and the index to answer the questions.

1. The largest fossil remains are of the Brachiosaurus, a fifty-ton dinosaur. In what two countries were the fossils found?

   _____ Page _____

2. The smallest spiders are from Australia. How many inches do their bodies measure?

   _____ Page _____

3. Alligators make nests for laying eggs. How many feet high and wide are the nests?

   _____ feet high, and _____ feet wide Page _____

4. The most dangerous bats are found in tropical America and can transmit rabies and possibly other diseases. What are they named?

   _____ Page _____

5. The fastest domestic dog is the saluki. What is its top speed?

   _____ Page _____

REFERENCE #8: *THE FACTS ON FILE VISUAL DICTIONARY*

REF 423.1 Cor

This dictionary includes over 3,000 illustrations and more than 25,000 terms. It provides pictures for a wide range of subjects.

1. Notice that the dictionary includes three indexes; list them.

    _____

    _____

    _____

2. Label the seven parts of the common table fork.   Page _____

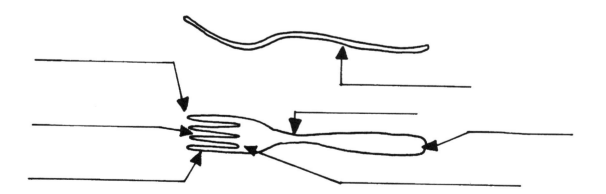

Worksheet continues on page 190.

3. Label the nine parts of an alpine ski boot.

Page _____

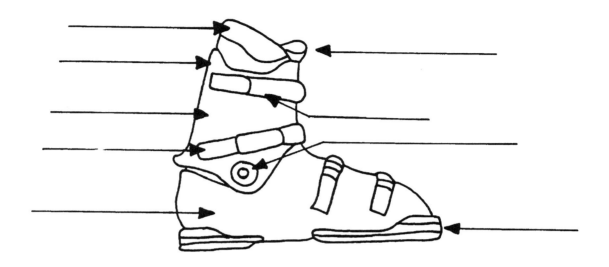

4. Write the Morse Code for the numerals 0–9 below.

Page _____

0 _____	4 _____	8 _____
1 _____	5 _____	9 _____
2 _____	6 _____	
3 _____	7 _____	

REFERENCE #9: *THE STAMP ATLAS*

REF 769.56 Wel

This book tells the history of each stamp-issuing authority, country, or geographic unit and details the changes in the boundaries of countries from earliest times. It contains many maps and over 750 illustrations. *Use the index to locate needed information.*

1. On what date were the first stamps issued in the United States?

   _____ Page _____

2. On what date were the first stamps issued in Canada?

   _____ Page _____

3. When the rulers in Europe created the Royal Posts, how did messengers travel?

   _____ Page _____

4. Who used this service?

   _____ Page _____

5. Look at the map of the Turkish Empire (1683-1923). In what year was the first stamp issued in Turkey? (Hint: See "How to use the maps" on page 9.)

   _____ Page _____

6. How many stars are on the flag shown on the Cuba Correos stamp?

   _____ Page _____

7. What kind of occupation do the two gentlemen who are located on the page about Gibralter have? Can you tell by their clothing?

   Occcupation: _____

   Yes/No _____ Page _____

REFERENCE #10: *LANDS AND PEOPLES*

REF 910 Lan

This book will give you information on the geographic, historical, political, economic, and social development of the North American continent. Looking through the table of contents, you will see that a few places outside the United States are also included.

1. What is the state motto of Indiana? _____ Page _____

2. What is the highest point in Pennsylvania? How many feet or miles? _____ Page _____

3. What was the population of Hawaii in 1990? _____ Page _____

4. What famous explorer discovered Puerto Rico? _____ Page _____

5. The country of Grenada is located in what sea? _____ Page _____

6. What explorer gave Greenland its name? _____ Page _____

7. Which Canadian province is the largest? _____ Page _____

REFERENCE #11: *GREAT LIVES*

REF 920 Gre

In this book you will find short biographies of over 1,000 men and women who play an important part in history and have a story worth telling. It is arranged alphabetically and has portraits of many of those listed. It also notes their birth and death dates and, in small capitals, tells where you can find out more about the same subject. Be sure to use both the *Glossary* and *Index*.

1. Name two people who are listed in the 1880 chronology contents.

   Name   What they were famous for   Page info found

   _____   _____   _____

   _____   _____   _____

2. Why is Chiang Kai-Shek considered important?

   _____

   _____ Page _____

3. Why was the Ides of March important in the life of Julius Caesar?

   _____

   _____ Page _____

4. Impressionism refers to what? _____

   _____ Page _____

5. Name three people listed under Impressionism in the index.

   _____

   _____ Page _____

6. Why was Marco Polo important? _____

   _____ Page _____

7. If you tried to look up Mickey Mouse in the index, where would you be directed to look?

   _____ Page _____

REFERENCE #12: *AMERICAN NICKNAMES*

REF 929.4 Sha

Americans use nicknames more than any other people today. Nicknames are given to family members, enemies, and to almost every object seen or used. This book attempts to list many of the thousands in use. It is arranged alphabetically and uses many cross-references.

1. Other than *the Mile High City*, Denver has *three* more nicknames. List them.

   a. _____

   b. _____

   c. _____ Page _____

2. List the *seven* nicknames Colorado is known by:

   a. _____   e. _____

   b. _____   f. _____

   c. _____   g. _____

   d. _____   Page _____

3. Who has the nickname of *tadpoles*?

   _____ Page _____

4. What is the nickname of Purdue University?

   _____ Page _____

5. Who are *the Rovers*?

   _____ Page _____

REFERENCE #13: *HOLIDAYS AROUND THE WORLD*

REF 394.26 Gae

This book explains the folklore of celebrating in many cultures. Whenever possible, information is given in quotations from people who actually celebrate holidays at home. *Holidays Around the World* includes an abundance of information never before gathered in one source. It especially describes holidays from non-European countries.

1. What are the three kinds of Hindu holidays?

   a. _____ Page _____

   b. _____ Page _____

   c. _____ Page _____

2. When was the League of Nations formally adopted?

   Month _____ Day _____ Year _____ Page _____

3. How many days long is the Jewish holiday Hanukkah?

   _____ Page _____

4. Name three countries that celebrated Thanksgiving before the United States.

   a. _____   c. _____

   b. _____   Page(s) _____

5. Thanksgiving is not a legal holiday, and the President must proclaim it each year. Although the holiday is usually during the last week of November, it actually can be any week during November. However, Thanksgiving must always fall on the same day of the week. What day of the week is that?

   _____ Page _____

6. The Dragon Boat Festival (Tuan Wu) is celebrated in China to honor what beloved Chinese patriot?

   _____ Page _____

REFERENCE #14: *NEW ENCYCLOPEDIA OF SPORTS*

REF 796.097 Hic

This book is an alphabetical list of sports categories, with no table of contents or index. The basic rules and interesting facts of each sport are covered under the sports category. Terms for each sport are briefly defined. Famous athletes are listed under their respective sport.

1. List two gymnasium sports included in this book.

   _____ and _____ Page(s) _____

2. What year was Australian football invented? _____ Page _____

3. From what country did the sport Boccie originate?

   _____ Page _____

4. In what year did cycling have its first recognized race?

   _____ Page _____

5. In golf, what does waggle mean?

   _____

   _____ Page _____

6. In ten-pin bowling, what are the three grips?

   a. _____ Page _____

   b. _____ Page _____

   c. _____ Page _____

7. What Roman sport was the ancestor of golf?

   _____ Page _____

REFERENCE #15: *MACMILLAN DICTIONARY OF QUOTATIONS*

REF 082 Mac

This book contains over 20,000 quotations from many people. The quotations are arranged by more than 1,100 alphabetical headings. Cross-references assist in exploring further quotations related to a heading. (Example: *Ideas—See Also Opinions*)

1. You want to use quotations in a speech. The topic is *character*. Which quotation might you consider using?

    _____

    _____

    Source _____ Page _____

2. In the Keyword Index, find the word *friend*. What does the letter "f" stand for?

    _____

    a. What does the letter "F" stand for?

        _____

    b. On what page would you find "It takes your enemy and your . . ." dictionary?
        Page _____

3. On what page would you locate a quotation by Muhammed Ali about violence? (Hint: Start with the biographical index.) Page _____

    a. Write what Mohammad Ali said about violence.

        _____

        _____

    b. Source of quotation _____

REFERENCE #16: *NEW VIEW ALMANAC*

REF 031.02 New

This almanac is divided into twelve chapters and provides facts and figures on a wide variety of topics including health and nutrition, science and technology, and sports and records. Each topic is accompanied by an easily understood and eye-appealing graphic.

1. What percentage of eighth graders drank alcohol during 1991? _____ Page _____

2. How many deaths per year are caused by alcohol? _____ Page _____

3. List the two states that report the most cases of child abuse. How many cases were reported?

    State _____ Cases _____ Page _____

    State _____ Cases _____ Page _____

4   a.   How many more kids were killed by handguns in 1992 than in 1982? _____

    b.   Name the source of the greatest number of handguns. _____

    c.   Page(s) on which you found these answers _____

5. In the ten-year period between 1982 and 1992, the number of people in prison doubled. How many U.S. inmates where there in 1992? _____

    Page where you found this information _____

6. What are four of the fastest-growing occupations in America? Page _____

    a.   _____   c.   _____

    b.   _____   d.   _____

7. During the 1993–94 school year, what was the percentage of girl athletes? _____

8. What act prohibited gender discrimination against women in sports?

    _____

    This information was found on page _____

REFERENCE #17: *THE COMPLETE BOOK OF U.S. PRESIDENTS*

REF 973.0992 DeG

This book presents information concerning forty of the men who have held the office of the President of the United States. The presidents are listed in this book by their terms of office. Each chapter provides a physical description, the personal and professional life, as well as major contributions of each president. A bibliography of other sources and quotations is available at the end of each chapter.

1. Which president was in office when the atomic bomb was developed?

    President _____ Page _____

2. Which president married Jacqueline L. Bouvier?

    President _____ Page _____

3. What was John Quincy Adams's religion? _____ Page _____

4. Who was Dwight D. Eisenhower's opponent in the 1952 presidential elections?

    _____ Page _____

5. Which president served in office in 1972 when the Consumer Product Safety Act was created?

    President _____ Page _____

    What does this act do for the public?_____

    _____ Page _____

6. How many presidents were Federalists during the first six Congresses?

    Names_____ Page _____

7. The abbreviations DEM and REP stand for which political parties?

    _____ and _____ Page _____

REFERENCE #18: *GOODE'S WORLD ATLAS*

REF 912 Goo

An atlas is a book of maps. Atlases can help you find the locations of cities, the boundaries of countries, roads, and the names of rivers and mountains. Special maps will show you things like the amount of rainfall all over the world, the different religions of the world, or how borders have changed throughout history. Be sure to use the index and table of contents when answering these questions.

1. Find the demographic maps of the United States. What is the average lifetime expectancy in the state of Colorado?

   _____ Page _____

2. Find the U.S. climate maps. How many days are usually frost-free in Florida?

   _____ Page _____

3. Find the U.S. water resources maps. What color denotes very hard water?

   _____ Page _____

4. Find the world nutrition map. As far as calorie supply goes, how does China rate?

   _____ Page _____

5. What is the latitude and longitude of Noblesville, Indiana?

   _____ Page _____

6. Give the latitude and longitude of Denver, Colorado. Which page does the index cite for the Denver map? Index page _____

   Latitude _____   Longitude _____   Page _____

REFERENCE #19: *ENCYCLOPEDIA OF AMERICAN FACTS & DATES*

REF 973.02 Enc

This reference book is a chronological listing of U.S. history from 1492 until 1986. The subject matter is divided into four fields of interest. It is like reading four books at once as you look down each column. Each column continues on the following pair of facing pages. See page IX to view the full entries in each column. The Index Guide is on page 832. The index lists subject, date, and column.

1. On what date was Malcolm X assassinated?

   _____ Page _____ Column _____

2. Where was the first Baseball All-Star Game played?

   _____ Page _____ Column _____

3. The Nobel Prize in Physiology or Medicine was given to Thomas Hunt Morgan on October 20, 1933, for what discovery?

   _____ Page _____ Column _____

4. Who was the first postmaster general for the U.S. Post Office?

   _____ Page _____ Column _____

5. While looking at the back side of the title page of this book, write the copyright date of this book. _____

   The opposite page from the verso page is called the dedication page.

   Who is this book dedicated to? _____

REFERENCE #20: *AUSCHWITZ CHRONICLE 1939–1945*

REF 940.53 Cze

This reference is a complete record of the events and developments over the entire five-year period of Auschwitz and its annexes. Many papers were destroyed, but there was such an extensive paper trail that many documents survived. The records in this book are arranged chronologically from the winter of 1939–40 to January 1945. You will find an index of names, sketches of war perpetrators, a glossary of general and camp terms, maps of both camps at Auschwitz, and a bibliography of other information sources on World War II history.

1. On page 11, what does the sign "Labreit Macht Free" on the main gate of Auschwitz mean?

   _____

2. On September 16, 1941, 900 Russian POWs were killed with gas. Read the footnote (denoted by an asterisk*) at the bottom of the page. What was the name of the commandant who murdered these people?

   _____ Page _____

3. What happened to Jewish men, women, and children who were not "selected" as they got off the train at Auschwitz on October 11, 1942?

   _____ Page _____

4. Adolf Eichmann escaped from an American internment camp during the 1940s and was not located until 1960. To what country did he flee?

   _____ Page _____

5. How was he punished for executing thousands of Jewish people?

   _____ Page _____

6. What do the letters NA represent as used in the bibliography?

   _____ Page _____

7. Look in the Index of Names and select a name. Look on the page that is referenced to see what information is written about that person. What date was this person noted in the Auschwitz Chronology?

   _____ Page _____

REFERENCE #21: *NATIONAL GEOGRAPHIC PICTURE ATLAS OF OUR FIFTY STATES*

REF 912.73 Nat

This U.S. atlas is divided by region first, and then by state. Explicit maps of each state show cities and provide the state bird and flower, the state flag, and topographical information. The atlas also features hundreds of beautiful pictures of people, cultural events, and tourist attractions. "Facts at Your Fingertips" in the back show 1990 census populations, largest metropolitan areas, super facts, and top products by state. At the beginning of the book is a fifty-state map.

1. If it is 10:00 a.m. in Missouri, what time is it in Hawaii? _____ Page _____

2. What mountain range extends through the Mid-Atlantic States?

    _____ Page _____

3. Hawaii is made up of many volcanic islands rising from the ocean's floor. When measured from the ocean's floor, many islands are actually taller than Mount Everest. What is the elevation of the tallest island?

    _____ Page _____

    There are _____ major islands. How many smaller islands surround the major islands? _____ Page _____

4. Which state has a larger population, Wyoming or West Virginia? _____

    Population _____ Page _____

5. What is the name of the highway that connects the Florida Keys?

    _____ Page _____

6. What state is the home of Mount St. Helens? _____ Is it the tallest mountain in the state? _____ Page _____

7. What is the origin of the word Alaska and what does it mean?

    _____

    _____ Page _____

REFERENCE #22: *CHRONICLE OF AMERICA*

REF 973 Chr

American history in pictures and short articles from newspapers and magazines are placed in chronological order from 1492 to 1988. Most often the stories are major happenings of the day, but many articles of lesser importance add to the unique quality of this book.

Beside the detailed index, you will find a map of immigration to the United States from 1820 to 1987, the Amendments to the Constitution, a list of personal facts on U.S. presidents, a diagram of how the U.S. government works, and short summaries about each of the 50 states.

1. During 1908, find the article about the first paper cup. What was the name of the first paper cup?

   _____ Page _____

2. How many people were involved in the assassination of President Lincoln?

   _____

   What year did this happen? _____ Page _____

3. What year was the first Thanksgiving? _____ Page _____

4. What was the name of the program for which the Beatles came to perform in America?

   _____ Page _____

5. What was the name and age of the American who first swam the English Channel?

   Name _____ Age _____ Page _____

6. What year was the Statue of Liberty dedicated? What country gave the statue to the U.S.?

   Year _____ Country _____ Page _____

7. Look up the year you were born and write about something that happened that year.

   _____

REFERENCE #23: *SOMETHING ABOUT THE AUTHOR*

REF 920.03 Som (Vol. 49 & 59)

In *Something About the Author* you find detailed information about authors and illustrators who create children's literature. You find personal information, types of jobs authors have had, and a listing of their works. Each book has a table of contents that tells the names of authors or illustrators included in the book, and an index that guides you to the right volume for a particular author. Each volume lists the authors' biographies in alphabetical order.

1. How is the Table of Contents arranged? _____

2. On what page does the entry about Art Clokey begin? _____

3. For what is Art Clokey most famous? _____

4. Find Pauline Baynes in the Table of Contents. She is not an author; instead she is an illustrator. Name an author for whom she worked and the title of one book she illustrated.

   Author _____

   Book _____

5. Look up Herman Melville. When was he alive? _____

6. For a short time Melville was a captive of cannibals. What was the name of the tribe that held him captive?

   _____ Volume _____ Page _____

7. In which volumes would you find information about S. E. Hinton? _____

   What do the initials S. E. mean? _____

8. Look up the name of the illustrator Mel Fowler. In which volume and on which page could you find one of his illustrations?   Volume _____ Page _____

9. What story is illustrated on page 174 of Volume 59?

   _____

REFERENCE #24: *TIMELINES OF THE ANCIENT WORLD*

REF 930.0202 Smi

This book illustrates pre-history timelines up to A.D. 1500 in chronological order. This format allows you to compare the history of the world by geographic regions.
(For questions 1 and 2 only, review pages 14–15)

1. What are the geographic definitions (areas) used in this book?

   _____ , _____ ,

   _____ , _____ ,

   and _____ .

2. What is the general goal of the Introductory Spread? _____

3. What are the four categories listed under each time period?   Page _____

   _____ , _____ ,

   _____ , and _____ .

4. In what time period did evidence of humans first appear in the Americas?

   _____ Page _____

5. What was happening around the world in Art & Ritual during 800–700 B.C.?

   Americas _____ Page _____

   East Asia and Australia _____

   Middle East and South Asia _____

   Europe _____

   Africa _____

6. What was the first domesticated animal and by whom was it domesticated?

   Animal_____ Domesticated by the _____ Page _____

➤ *Teacher Notes:* This next section includes electronic resources. Instructions for use of each of the programs precede the student worksheets.

ELECTRONIC REFERENCE #25: EBSCO® PERIODICAL SERVICE

This collection of 141 full-text magazines is networked on all school computers.

1. From the Desktop, double click on Mac HD. Double click on EBSCO®. Click on either Load Disk 1 or 2, then click on MAS Full TEXT Elite.

2. The screen will ask if you want to continue. Click continue and a Search Summary Field Box will appear in the upper right corner of the screen.

3. Type a topic (e.g., Olympics) in the box provided and click on the search box. How many articles did the service provide to you? _____

4. A *results list* will tabulate how many articles were found on your topic. The final total will be displayed on the left, with the abstracts of the articles listed below.

If too many articles appear, narrow your topic by adding the words *track* or *diving*. Now, how many articles do you have to choose from? _____

5. Notice the small box to the left of each article. If there is an article that you are interested in, click in that box so you can come back to it. Now preview some other articles. Notice that some say Double Click for Full Text and others do not. Double click articles are Full Text (no pictures), and the other articles offer only an abstract with bibliographic information. You may print a list of these articles for later reference if you leave the check mark in the box. Go to File:

   Which command can you select to obtain this list? _____

   What command will deselect all your checked articles? _____

6. Look at a couple of articles. First select an article that has no "Double Click for Full Text" on it by clicking once on that abstract. Now go to the top and *click on the detailed display box*. What happens?_____

7. Try an article that has the "Double Click for Full Text" at the bottom of its abstract.

   Double click on it and what happens? _____

8. Where is the bibliographic information for each article? _____ and _____

9. The box in the upper left corner is called the _____ and provides a list of all your searches that you have completed so far.

10. Leave the word *Olympics* in your topic box and go below to Search Magazine. Click on the triangle and type the word *time*. Click on search once more. What happens?

    _____

11. When using the Date Range Search how must the date be typed so a specific magazine date can be located? Circle the correct form you should use:

    yymm - yymm   <u>or</u>   mmddyy-mmddyy

ELECTRONIC REFERENCE #26: NEWSFILE®

Over 500 International, national, and local newspapers are provided on this school networked program.

1. From the desktop, double click on Mac HD. Select NewsFile® and double click.

2. Load NewsFile® first (multiple file folders will come up on the screen—ignore them)

3. Select the NewsFile® icon by clicking on it.

4. To do a simple search for a word or phrase appearing anywhere in the text of articles:

    a. type the word or phrase on the first line
    b. click the search button

5. To search for a word or phrase appearing only in a specific portion of articles, such as headlines:

    a. type the word or phrase on the first line
    b. click on the down arrow next to the words "All Text" to pull down the Field Menu
    c. highlight the field you wish to search, then release the mouse button
    d. click the search button

6. Select Display Results. (Wait patiently.) Select an article title on the left by clicking on it. What happens on the right? _____

7. You can print the whole or a highlighted part of an article by selecting what from the File column from the screen menu? _____

8. To use Boolean searching: Use AND, OR, or NOT to connect terms in order to broaden or narrow your searches:

    a. AND—narrows a search when you have too many search choices
    b. OR—broadens a search that found too few articles by adding a word
    c. NOT—narrows a search when you exclude a word from the search

9. Try using a root word followed by an asterisk. Truncate the root word *ecolog** or *del**. What choices do you come up with? _____

    _____

10. When you are searching for articles using words such as *women* or *woman*, use *wom?n* instead. What is the difference in the number of article choices offered?

    woman _____ women _____ wom?n _____

11. Try clicking on Browse Index. Look at the dialogue box. What happens when you move the letter indicator at the top of the Browse box back and forth on the alphabet?

    _____

    _____

12. To Close NewsFile®, go to File and select Quit. Be sure to only use this method to quit or the next person to use NewsFile® will have a hard time getting into it.

ELECTRONIC REFERENCE #27: FACTORY®

Some of the benefits of this computer program are adding, subtracting, learning about degrees, geometry, perception, and reasoning skills. The program is networked on all school computers.

1. From the desktop, double click on Mac HD; double click on Factory® Folder; double click on the Factory® Network icon.

2. The Factory® screen should show up. Before clicking on the start button:

   a. Check out the menu and look to see what is available.
   b. Select easy, medium, or hard.
   c. Select the machines you will work with.

3. Click the start button.

4. If the pattern you select is too hard, where do you go to change the degree of difficulty?

   _____

5. How do you clear all the machines quickly? _____

6. Where do you go to change the shape of the paper? _____

7. What do you select to change how the machines work? _____

   _____

8. How do you turn off the sound? _____

9. How do you change the color of the paper? _____

10. What does the turquoise machine do? _____

11. What does the orange machine do? _____

12. What does the purple machine do? _____

13. Suggest three ways to use this computer program to enhance math curriculum skills or make class lesson plans more enjoyable: _____

   _____

   _____

   _____

ELECTRONIC REFERENCE #28: WRITING CENTER®

This word processing program may be used for keyboarding papers or making a newsletter.

1. From the desktop screen, double click on the Hard Drive icon. Double click on Writing Center®. (If you don't see the Writing Center® icon, scroll up or down to locate it.) Click once again on Writing Center®.

2. What four options do you have? _____, _____, _____, and _____

3. Select Newsletter. What options do you have? _____ and _____

4. Where do you go in the menu to change the font? _____

5. What menu title allows you to double space your work? _____

6. Which menu title helps you check your spelling? _____

7. Where do you go to select a picture? _____

   a. Select picture—click as you drag and select picture.
   b. Select which folder you want and click Open.
   c. Select a picture and go to the place in your document where it will be inserted.
   d. To rotate the picture, go to Picture and select.
   e. To move it, click and drag with the mouse.

8. If you select New, but want to get back to your other page, what do you do?

   _____

9. Where do you go to change the border? _____

10. Where do you go to save your product? _____

    What do you select? _____

11. When saving to your floppy disk, what do you select under File? _____

12. Before you print, always confirm that the printer you want is listed as the target for your command.

13. To select a printer:

    a. Go to the Apple® in the menu bar and click once.
    b. Pull down the menu to select Chooser and let go of mouse.
    c. Select the printer you need from the window offered on the left.
    d. If several printers appear, click to highlight the one you want on the right side of the Chooser screen.
    e. Close Chooser by clicking in the close box in the upper left corner.

14. Select _____ from the File Menu to leave the program when you are finished.

ELECTRONIC REFERENCE #29: WORD MUNCHERS®

This word, letter, and sound recognition program allows students to enjoy a game while receiving practice and support with vowel blends for reading and language arts curricula.

1.   From the Desktop, double click on Mac HD, double click on the Word Munchers® icon. Select the Word Munchers® icon.

2.   If a box comes up and says switch color to 256, go to the Apple® icon on your menu bar and click and drag to the control panel. Select monitors and then select 256. Close the box.

3.   Where do you go on the menu list to turn off the sound? _____
(When you have 25 computers operating, this will be valuable to know!)

4.   Where can you find instructions for this language arts curriculum enhancer?

_____

5.   Try playing a couple of vowel sound boards (practice makes perfect). Which ones did you play?

_____ and _____

6.   If you are interrupted or need to stop play, what options do you have?

_____ or _____

7.   Where can teachers go to modify student playing boards? _____

8.   Where do teachers go to gain Access to Management Options? _____

9.   What are the bad munchers called? _____

10. What are two ways players can be rewarded for good tries? _____
and _____

11. When players do exceptionally well, their names are placed in the Word Munchers®
_____ of _____

12. How do you end Word Munchers®? _____

13. How do you quit? _____

ELECTRONIC REFERENCE #30: CLARISWORKS® WORD PROCESSING

From the desktop, double click on Mac HD. Find and select the ClarisWorks® 4.0 folder and double click on it. Double click again on ClarisWorks®. A screen with six options will appear: word processing, drawing, printing, spreadsheet, database, or communications. Select word processing.

Before you start typing, take a look at the page. Look through the menu bar at the top of the page. Also, at the top you see a text ruler. Notice the vertical bar that is the cursor or insertion point, blinking in the upper left corner. The light lines are page guides showing the boundaries of the text page. The cursor or I-beam moves when you move the mouse or type. The I-beam also helps you insert or highlight text.

Type all or part of the following paragraph. Do not stop to correct errors:

> You can't escape from the Information Age. Ready or not, you are right in the thick of it. For most of us, information overload is now a reality. If you are like most people, piles of unread newspapers, books, and magazines clutter almost every room of your house. You constantly vow to get around to reading them when you have extra time, but invariably you end up throwing them out so they can be replaced by more current material which you also do not read.

If you make an error, you can either backspace and delete, or place the I-beam to the right of the text and highlight by clicking once and dragging across the text to be replaced. Either type over the highlighted area or delete and type new information. Try changing some text on the paragraph you just typed. Try inserting new text into the previous paragraph.

If you want to see the invisible formatting characters (e.g., spaces, paragraph marks) while you type, you can go to the menu and select Preferences. A dialog box will appear and you can click to show invisibles. Use the same procedure to take off the invisible characters. You can also use the shortcuts palette under File.

What happens if you hold the command (Apple®) key down and press the up arrow?

_____

To move text around, click and drag the I-beam through several lines and let go. The text remains highlighted. Choose Copy from the Edit menu and then place the I-beam where you want the copied text. Select Paste from the Edit Menu or click on the Paste button on the shortcuts palette.

➤*Teacher Notes:* We return now to hard copy reference materials.

REFERENCE #31: *CHRONICLE OF THE 20TH CENTURY*

REF 909.82 Chr

Paintings introduce each decade from 1900 to 1995 in the opening pages of this reference book, and then appear as decade dividers in the main body of work. The book is presented in yearly format with monthly calendars sharing the headlines of the day. Black and white and color pictures add to the daily news stories.

1. Which day of the week was June 10, 1958? _____ Page _____

2. Which Alfred Hitchcock thriller is shown on the same page? _____

3. How old was Asa Candler when he died in March 1929? What invention is he famous for?

   _____ Page _____

4. What two sporting ladies were in the August, 1950 news? What were their names? Why were they in the news? Give the date of each article. Page _____

   _____

   _____

5. Give the date and time of the eruption of the 8,366-foot Mount St. Helens. How tall was the volcano after the eruption?

   _____ Page _____

6. Select an article from the month and year you were born. Paraphrase it. _____

   _____

   _____ Page _____

7. What is the significance of the numbers after each index entry? Page _____

   _____

8. Who were the founding partners of United Artist Corporation? Page _____

   _____

REFERENCE #32: *FACTS ON FILE ENCYCLOPEDIA OF THE 20TH CENTURY*

REF 909.8203 Fac

This is a comprehensive, more than 8,000 entry, alphabetical guide to the important people, places, events, and ideas that have shaped the contemporary world.

1. The boldface numbers in the index indicate what? _____ Page _____

2. Why was Ernie Pyle famous? How did he die at 45 years of age? Page _____

_____

_____

_____

3. For what purpose was the Gemini Program designed? _____

_____

_____ Page _____

4. When looking at the map of Djibouti, how many kilometers is Modahtou from Dikhill? _____ In what country is Djibouti? _____ Page _____

5. What famous cartoon character voice was provided by Jim Backus?

_____ Page _____

6. What president was in office in the United States when the Lusitania sank?

_____ Page _____

7. What does the acronym START stand for? What countries were involved in its formation? _____ Page _____

8. In the earlier description of this book, the word *contemporary* is used. Go to the dictionary, select the appropriate definition, and write it here. _____

_____

REFERENCE #33: *U.S.A., A CHRONICLE IN PICTURES*

REF 973 Wen

This book offers a fascinating and informative picture of the growth of the world's greatest nation. Information listed starts with Columbus and ends with Norman Schwarzkopf. A name or the top news stories for each decade are given in the table of contents. Abbreviations for the chronologies are shown after the table of contents. All events are listed in date order.

1. What does the acronym HEW stand for? _____

   _____ Page _____

2. What was the Quartering Act? _____

   _____

   _____ Page _____

3. Locate Calamity Jane's real name, her birth and death dates. Page _____

   _____

4. Who was Charlie Chaplin's young sidekick in the silent film, "The Kid"?   Page _____

   _____

5. Al Jolson was famous for what words? What movie were they spoken in, and what was so special about this movie? _____

   _____ Page _____

6. Jesse Owens was a gold medalist in what Olympics? How many gold medals did he win and in what sport? What Aryan theorized Germany was frustrated while watching Owens capture his gold medals? _____

   _____ Page _____

7. What two news reporters broke the Watergate story in 1972 and kept it in the public eye? What newspaper did they work for? _____

   _____ Page _____

   Who is the author of *Chronicle in Pictures*? Where did he study English? _____

   _____ Page _____

REFERENCE #34: *HISTORIC U.S. COURT CASES 1690–1990*

REF 347.7326 Joh

This book is divided into six parts, and then sub-divided. Therefore, this book can be classified as selective and not comprehensive. Each essay (171 total) is meant to highlight a major legal issue or concern. Some essays have been selected because of fame, others because they represent a large body of important litigation, a few because they are not typical cases, and some because they raised significant legal or historical issues. Finally, a few essays were selected because they examine cases that showcase the role of a particularly famous jurist, lawyer, or litigant.

1. According to *Miranda v. Arizona*, if you can't afford an attorney what happens?

   _____ Page _____

2. What confirmed the conviction of Richard Nixon in *United States v. Nixon*?

   _____ Page _____

3. What was President Roosevelt's concern about the Supreme Court Justices after the *West Coast Hotel Company v. Parrish* trial? _____

   _____

   _____ Page _____

4. What did *California Federal Savings and Loan Association v. Guerra* guarantee?

   _____ Page _____

5. What crime was worse than murder in *United States v. Rosenberg*?

   _____ Page _____

6. How many children from the Tinker family were involved in *United States v. Tinker*? What were their names and grades in school? Why did they want to wear the black arm bands to school? _____

   _____

   _____

   _____ Page _____

7. The pirate Black Beard's real name was given in the court case of *The King v. Bonnet*. What was his real name?

   _____ Page _____

REFERENCE #35: *TIMETABLES OF HISTORY*

REF 902.02 Gru

This famous horizontal linkage reference tells who did what, when, from 4,500 B.C. to A.D. 1990. Facts are separated into seven categories: history and politics; literature and theater; religion, philosophy and learning; visual arts; music; science, technology and growth; and daily life. These categories are listed in chronological order. The index lists each subject with a year and a corresponding category letter.

1. In what year did the Golden Gate Bridge open its toll booths? List the category and the page number where you found this information.

   Year _____ Category _____ Page _____

2. It was reported in 1986 that Rembrandt's portrait of Jacob DeGheyn III had been stolen from the Dulwich Gallery in London _____ times. Page _____

3. What was the previous name of Princeton University, and in what year did that name change? _____ Page _____

4. What item was used in England for the very first time in 1500? Page _____

   Answer _____ Category _____

5. What do the cello and lyre represent in this book? _____

6. Leap year was introduced to the Julian calendar during what year? _____ Page _____

7. What product was first cultivated in Brazil during 1532? _____ Page _____

8. What caused a superstition in 1531, on this same page? A "great _____ "

   What is its true name? _____

9. What do the categories music, science, and daily life have in common during the years 680–691? Why do you suppose they are that way? Page _____

   _____

   _____

10. In 1035, Canute died and his kingdom was divided between his sons. Who were his sons and what did each of them get? _____

    _____

    _____ Page _____

REFERENCE #36: *AMERICAN DESTINY*

REF 973 Ame (Vol. 14 & 20)

American Destiny is a twenty-volume set. Each volume contains one or more aspects of American history, information on its people and involvement with other countries. Each volume not only has a separate title which helps you focus on a particular time period, but also has a separate table of contents and introduction. The index for the whole set is located in the last volume.

1. Name the volume and page that provides information about the Camp Fire Girls?

    _____ Page _____

2. Who was the captain of the Bounty in the movie *Mutiny on the Bounty*?

    _____ Page _____

3. What Indian Chief appears on the old Buffalo Nickel on page 68 of Volume 14?

    _____

4. What caused the Dust Bowl? _____

    _____ Page _____

5. What famous picture, painted by Reginald Marsh, appears on page 10 and 11 of volume 14? This painting is located at the Sheldon Art Gallery in Lincoln, Nebraska. Ask your Media Specialist what a docent does. Write it here. _____

    _____

6. What act created the Tennessee Valley Authority (TVA) in 1933? What did the TVA build?

    _____ Page _____

7. Read the introduction to volume 14. What caused the Great Depression? How long did it last? How many people were unemployed? Who and what brought the depression to a halt?

    _____

    _____

    _____

    _____

    _____ Page _____

REFERENCE #37: *DICTIONARY OF AMERICAN HISTORY*

REF 973.03 Dic (Vol. I, VII, and the Index)

This eight-volume set contains 6,425 American history word entries. The topic words were selected from military, science and technology, political science, the arts, economics, and the general history of the United States. An Abbreviations Used List, an Errata List, and the Index are placed in the last volume. Entries are in alphabetical order.

1. On what pages of which volume will you find the name H. R. Haldeman? With which famous scandal is his name synonymous? _____ Vol._____ Page _____

2. When was the Seiscor Voting Machine invented?_____ Vol._____ Page _____

3. What does the ABC stand for at the ABC Conference? _____

    _____ Page _____

4. Alaska was the last great area on earth to be "_____." When did this happen, and who charted the unknown territory? _____ , and _____
    _____ . What body of water in Alaska is named for him?
    _____ Vol. _____ Page _____

5. How many volunteer lawyers were affiliated with the American Civil Liberties Union in 1976?_____ Why was this union formed? _____

    _____

    _____ Vol. _____ Page _____

6. What is the new name for Aquidneck Island? Who witnessed its purchase?

    _____, _____ Vol. _____ Page _____

7. What were buffalo trails credited for accomplishing? How did the trails get there?

    _____

    _____ Vol. _____ Page _____

8. How often is the U.S. census taken? Why is the census taken? _____ ,

    _____ Vol. _____ Page _____

REFERENCE #38: *BUILDINGS OF COLORADO*

REF 720.9788 Noe

This book contains the architectural history of Colorado from its Native American origins, such as the Anasazi Indians at Mesa Verde, and the villages of Mexican settlers and mining camps hastily constructed during the Pikes Peak gold rush. It features forts, farms, and ranches of pioneers; homes, churches, and schools of early towns; and modern industrial centers and vacation spots. This book is arranged geographically in four regional sections that cover Colorado's major river valleys, by county and in alphabetical site order, and it also includes maps of those regions.

1. In what county is Raynold's Beehive located? _____ Page _____

2. In what region is Raynold's Beehive located? _____ Page _____

3. Greenwood Village is located at what elevation? _____ Page _____

4. How many feet deep is the Mollie Kathleen Mine? _____ Page _____

5. Who were the supervising architects of the First Presbyterian Church of Sterling?

   _____ Page _____

6. In the town of Telluride, what street do you take to reach the power plant?

   _____ Page _____

7. What launches the Central City Opera season each year? _____

   _____ Page _____

8. In what year did the fire occur at the Aurora Fox Arts Center? _____ Page _____

9. Define the word *facade*. _____

   _____

   _____ Page _____

10. What is an oculus? _____

    _____

    _____ Page _____

REFERENCE #39: *NEW YORK PUBLIC LIBRARY DESK REFERENCE*

REF 031 New

This book is organized into 26 subject areas. Sidebars, charts, graphs, tables, and lists make the book attractive and accessible. There is a wealth of information about people, events, movements, and discoveries as well as facts, dates, terms, and symbols.

1. How many holy books of the world are listed? Which religion teaches Taoism?

   _____, _____ Pages _____

2. Who was the philosopher Plato's teacher? _____ Page _____

3. How many U.S. Supreme Court decisions are most significant during the nineteenth and twentieth centuries? _____ Pages _____

4. What pseudonym do you know the famous author Theodore Seuss Geisel by?

   _____ Page _____

5. List #1 and #5 of the 11 possible ways that you can measure without having a ruler.

   _____ and _____

   _____ Page _____

6. When is the White House flag flown? _____

   _____ Page _____

7. Explain what the letters of the international organization "NATO" stand for.

   _____ Page _____

8. One of the Seven Wonders of the Ancient World is the statue of the Supreme God, Zeus. What is this statue made of?_____ and _____ Page _____

REFERENCE #40: *REFERENCE LIBRARY OF HISPANIC AMERICA*

REF 973.0468 REF—Vol. II

This three-volume set has 27 sections, plus an illustrations appendix, a glossary, a chronology, a general bibliography, and an index.

1. Why and where was the League of United Latin American Citizens founded during 1929?

   _____

   _____ , _____ Page _____

2. In the Religion section, what is the Arizona Jesuit Father Kino famous for?

   _____

3. Which professional trade did he learn in order to accomplish this?

   _____ Page _____

4. In the Law and Politics Section, how many Colorado Hispanics have served in the House of Representatives? _____ In the Senate? _____ Page _____

5. What does Caballeros de Labor mean? _____ Page _____

6. Gary Soto is known for his highly _____ works. Page _____

7. What does the word *carpa* mean?_____ Page _____

8. What is the second largest Hispanic *business*, how many people does it employ, where is it located, and how much income does it generate per year?

   _____ ,

   _____ , Colorado, and $ _____ Page _____

9. Who was the first Hispanic female general in the armed services? What rank does she now hold and in which branch of the armed forces does she serve?

   _____ was born _____. She is now a

   _____ in the _____ Page _____

REFERENCE #41: *WORDS THAT MAKE AMERICA GREAT*

REF 973 Wor

This collection of 200 timeless documents and speeches illuminates the American national identity and policy since Columbus, bringing into sharp focus what it means to be an American. The book is divided into fifteen chronological sections with two indexes. One is the normal index listing events, titles, and people, and the other is chronological and presented in the front of the book.

1. What famous Texas Congresswoman argued for President Richard M. Nixon's impeachment after his involvement in Watergate? What year did this take place?

   _____ , _____ Page _____

2. Which three speech events took place in 1946? These are found on page _____

   _____

   _____

   _____

3. Who wrote the "Star-Spangled Banner" and when? Page _____

   _____ , _____

   Which line of this song is your favorite? Why? _____

   _____

   _____

4. In what year, city, and country did Hillary Rodham Clinton present her speech, "Human Rights Are Women's Rights"?

   _____ , _____ , _____ Pages _____

5. Who wrote President Ronald Reagan's speech to the Republican party?

   _____ Page _____

6. Who is the author of *Words That Make America Great?* How many other books has he written?

   _____ , _____ Page _____

REFERENCE #42: *SCIENCE FICTION, FANTASY, AND HORROR WRITERS*

YA REF 808.838 Sci (Vol. 1)

This two-volume set highlights fantasy, science fiction, and horror writers. Eighty biographies include the writers' best books to buy, books turned into film, tidbits of information about their lives, and bibliographic sources. Each volume lists the awards and their recipients for each field and an index for both books.

1. Who received the last Gandalf Award and when?

   _____ Page _____

2. Who does the Hugo Award honor and why was his name selected for this award?
   _____ Page _____

3. How old was L. Frank Baum when he wrote the *Wonderful Wizard of Oz*? How many performances were there of the Broadway version of *Wizard of Oz*?

   _____ , _____ Page _____

4. What was Lewis Carroll's real profession? _____ Page _____

5. How much was Robert A. Heinlein paid for his first story published in *Astounding Magazine*? Why did he have to use pseudonyms? What is a pseudonym?

   _____ , _____

   _____ Page _____

6. How old was Michael Crichton when he learned to type? How old was he when he first published an article? What was his article about? _____ , _____ ,

   _____ Page _____

7. Where would you find the biography on E. B. White? Pages _____

   In which volume would you locate these pages? _____

8. Give the name of the president's wife who liked Roald Dahl's stories so much that she invited him to dinner?

   _____ Page _____

9. How does Roald Dahl practice for his writing trade? _____

   _____ Page _____

REFERENCE #43: *REFERENCE LIBRARY OF BLACK AMERICA*

YA REF 973.049607 Ref (Vol. II)

This set consists of five volumes about Black Americans. Each volume has its own introduction, chronology, index, bibliography, picture, and text credit and covers different aspects of Black American lives. Volume V has an Appendix of African American Recipients of Selected Awards. All pictures are black and white. Only the table of contents matches the volume number with the pages.

1. The introduction shares that this reference book had a different title in 1967. What was the previous title?

   _____ Page _____

2. Tell what the four brief overview statements are at the beginning of Chapter Five, "Africa and the Western Hemisphere," and summarize them. _____

   _____ Page _____

3. How many Black soldiers fought in the Civil War? _____ Page _____

4. By what margin, quoted in the Law Section, was Clarence Thomas nominated as Supreme Court Justice? _____ Page _____

5. In *Gaines v. Canada*, what was the *ultimate* decision? _____

   _____

   _____ Page _____

6. What do the letters NAACP in the index stand for? _____

   _____

7. Look at several bibliographic records. Write in order how that information is placed in the bibliographic record. (Use the terms: city of publisher, publisher, author's name, title of article, and date.)

   _____

   _____

8. Do Seychelles and Sierra Leone share any of the same ethnic divisions? If so, what are they?

   _____ Pages _____

REFERENCE #44: *ENCYCLOPEDIA OF WORLD SPORT*

REF 796.03 Enc (Vol. 1)

This three-volume set describes 300 types of sports from the first Olympics in ancient Greece to the Olympics in Atlanta, Georgia. This book also covers issues such as preserving local customs and traditions, and the legal, medical, and political aspects of sports. One hundred and fifty experts from around the world provide information for this principle reference.

1. What English explorer participated in the most famous game of bowls in 1588?

   _____ Page _____

2. Cooperstown, New York is the famous starting place for baseball. Abner Doubleday invented the game of baseball in what year? _____ Page _____

3. Ballooning originated in what country? What was carried in the basket of the first balloon that flew? _____ , _____ Page _____

4. Young falcons, called _____ , are captured or taken from their nests because falcons do not breed well in captivity.   Page _____

5. How many years after golfer Babe Didrickson Zaharias received $3,400 in 1948 did a woman golfer achieve a salary of $100,000? Who was this woman? _____
   _____ Page _____

6. In Commercialization it was stated that athletes were first paid $1 million in what year?
   _____ Pages _____

7. Determine the increase in the sales price of the Dallas Cowboys football team from 1960 to 1989. _____ Page _____

8. What is another name for *footbag*? _____ Page _____

9. In 1980, what new name was given to the Olympics for the Disabled? _____

   _____ Page _____

REFERENCE #45: MILITARY HISTORY
OF THE UNITED STATES

REF 973 Cha (Vol. 1 & Index)

This sixteen-volume set provides an objective reference work on all wars fought by Americans. The volumes contain over 8,000 entries, presented in chronological order, starting with the Revolutionary War and ending with the Gulf War. Volume sixteen is the main index for the entire set. Each volume has its own table of contents, index, glossary, bibliography, and a table of contents for all other volumes. The whole set includes 1,500 illustrations, maps, for further reference boxes, and color drawings of uniforms and important weapons.

1. How many authors, besides the main author, were involved in writing the volume titled "The Revolutionary War"? Authors: _____

    This information can be located in two places. Identify these:

    Vol. _____ Page _____ and Vol. _____ Pages _____

2. Our first official American flag was the Grand Union Flag. It had another name. What was its second name?

    _____ Page _____

3. Who created the Continental Army?_____ Page _____

4. What was the American victory at Saratoga? _____

5. What did this make France do? _____ .
    What two agreements were signed and became the Franco-American Alliance?

    _____

    _____ and _____ Page _____

6. What was the Turtle? _____ Page _____

7. What was the motivation of Washington's strategic military strike on the Hessian garrisons of Trenton and Brodentwon on December 26, 1776? _____

    _____ Page _____

8. What year did the American Revolution start and when did the last foreign soldier leave the American soil? _____ and _____ Pages _____

9. What does reconnaissance mean? _____

    _____ Page _____

REFERENCE #46: *AMERICAN WOMEN IN SCIENCE: A BIOGRAPHICAL DICTIONARY*

REF 509.2273 Bai

This resource is a concise biography of 400 nineteenth and twentieth century American women scientists who work primarily in the physical or natural sciences. The women selected for this book met specific selection criteria. For example, women who started their careers after 1950 were excluded. Due to lack of documentation, many records are incomplete. In our society a woman generally takes on her husband's last name and this sometimes caused problems with accurate recording. Each chapter represents a letter of the alphabet and the women's names are listed on the chapter divider.

1. The term *scientist* was coined by what person in the introduction? What year did he do this? _____ , _____ Page _____

2. Look up *spectroscopy* in the dictionary and paraphrase what Gladys Amelia Anslow worked on during her career.

   _____

   _____ Pages _____

3. How many years was Marian Koshland employed in the cancer center at M.I.T., and what was her title?

   _____ , _____

   Where does she currently work?_____ Page _____

4. What are Maria Mitchell's two claims to fame? She is the _____

   _____ and she discovered a

   _____ Pages _____

5. What kinds of diseases did Anna Wessels Williams, a bacteriologist, spend most of her life in New York working on?

   _____ , _____ ,

   _____ and _____ Page _____

6. List three symptoms of scarlet fever? _____

   _____

   _____

REFERENCE #47: REFERENCE LIBRARY OF ASIAN AMERICA

REF 973 Ref (Vol. II and one other volume)

The first volume of this three-volume set defines fifteen distinct Asian heritages and lists significant documents having an impact on Asian culture. The second volume covers immigration, refugees, civil rights, diversity, traditions, language, and education. This volume also has extensive statistical data. The third volume focuses on religion, culture, historic landmarks, and speeches. Each volume has black-and-white pictures, graphs, tables and maps, and its own index. Guide words are at the top of each page with information placed under sub-titles.

1. Bruce Yamashita was removed from the Marines because his staff sergeant did not like Asians. How long did it take him to fight this outrage and what did he finally receive as compensation?_____ and he was _____

   _____ Page _____

2. What is an Amerasian? _____

   _____ Page _____

3. Hoang Nhu Tran is recognized for several honors. List them. How many years was he in the United States before he accomplished these feats? _____,

   _____ , _____,

   _____ , _____ Page _____

4. On page 445, what two barriers cause difficulty in adapting curriculum to help Asian students with literature and language arts? _____

   _____

   _____ and _____

5. Using Table 29.37, how many eighth grade Asian and White students study for two hours a day? Which group studies longer? Calculate the difference. _____

   _____ , _____ , _____ , _____ Page _____

6. What Asian astronaut died in the space shuttle explosion on January 28, 1986?

   _____ Page _____

REFERENCE #48: *NEW GROLIER ENCYCLOPEDIA OF WORLD WAR II*

REF 940.53 New (Vol. 1, Home Front)

This encyclopedia about World War II is written from eight points of view. Large print words written at a middle school level, with many old pictures of different countries and peoples, make for an easy and interesting reference set. Copies of newspaper headlines, posters, actual documents, and personal narratives are added to the text and pictures. Students get a good idea about each point of view.

1. What did Winston Churchill become and in what country was his mother born?

   _____,

   _____ Pages _____

2. Mussolini, an Italian dictator, believed that _____ rather than
   _____ would give him power. Page _____ Mussolini, or
   _____ (his nickname), felt physical prowess was important. Page _____

   He proved this by making his men march with him "at the double." He could cover a mile in how many minutes? _____ Page _____

3. A young farm worker in the French resistance, Etienne Achavane, was executed by the Germans for doing what?

   _____

   _____ Page _____

4. In the United States, women replaced men in factories. This changed American lifestyles forever. How did some women in Japan, an Axis country to Germany and Italy, help their home front?

   _____ Pages _____

5. The Netherlands's resistance group was called "the Ondergrondse." Sound this word out and guess what this word means. What was one of their main activities?

   _____,

   _____

   _____ Page _____

REFERENCE #49: *JUNIOR WORLDMARK ENCYCLOPEDIA OF THE CANADIAN PROVINCES*

REF 971.003 Jun (2)

This book provides profiles of the ten Canadian provinces and two territories. The provinces are listed in alphabetical order and each has 40 different headings, which allows students to compare two or more provinces. The reader's guide located in the front of the books lists the forty headings. Each profile has a map of the province, a coat of arms, and a flag. A guide to articles gives the number for each heading. This numbering system is used throughout the book. In the book, a glossary and an abbreviations and acronyms table in the back precedes the index.

1. What are Canada's two territories? Which is larger? _____ and the

   _____ , _____ Pages _____

2. What are the two bodies of water between Greenland and Baffin Island?

   _____ and _____ Page _____

3. What "Star Trek" actor was born in Quebec? _____ Page _____

4. How many liberal premiers have served in British Columbia? Who was the last one?

   _____ , _____ Page _____

5. What is the "Symphony of Fire"? _____

6. If you were touring Ontario, this is something you might want to see:

   _____ Page _____

   Under what heading did you find this information?_____

   _____ Who provides this show? _____

   _____

7. What does the "c.$" before monetary units stand for? _____ Page _____

8. What is the Prime Meridian? _____

   _____ Page _____

9. What animal is located on the coat of arms and on the flag of New Brunswick?

   _____ Page _____

REFERENCE #50: *ELEMENTS: COPPER, SILVER AND GOLD*

REF 546 KNA (Vol. 5)

This fifteen-volume set provides an accessible approach to chemistry. The printing is large, and pictures and diagrams are easily understood. Each volume presents the characteristics, behavior, occurrence, isolation, and uses of the most important elements and their compounds. Laboratory demonstrations are illustrated. A glossary offers useful definitions. Other sections offer key facts about the periodic table and understanding equations.

1. Some element names start with the same letter of the alphabet. When this happens, their element symbols are selected differently. How is this done? (use "Understanding Equations")

   _____

   _____ Page _____

2. How much silver is used industrially for making photographic film? _____

3. What are the two light-sensitive silver salts used in photography?

   _____ and _____ Page _____

4. How much gold does an eighteen-carat necklace have? How many carats does pure gold have?

   _____ and _____ Page _____

5. What does the word *copper* mean? _____ Page _____

   Using the same section used above, answer this next question.

   Which element is the rarest on Earth? _____ Page _____

6. How is copper used by plants and animals? Animals use copper _____

   _____ Page _____

   Plants use copper_____ Page _____

7. Why does gold plating not turn a different color with age? _____

   _____ Page _____

REFERENCE #51: *NEW YORK PUBLIC LIBRARY BOOK OF HOW AND WHERE TO LOOK IT UP*

REF 025.524 New

This book is a one-stop guide to locating the most up-to-date resources. The book uses six major categories: reference books, telephones, government, picture sources, special collections, and electronic databases. Each section lists primary locations of information.

1. Which clothing book would be best to consult on a May Day Festival? _____

    _____ Page _____

2. What does the acronym CD ROM stand for? _____

    _____ Page_____

3. What is the address of the Museum of Television and Radio? Page _____

    _____

4. The New York Botanical Garden Library listed in special collection has how many books in its collection? _____ Page _____

5. Which section of this book would you use to locate EBIS—Employee Benefits Infosource?

    _____

    How often is this information updated? Who provides this source?

    _____ and _____ Pages _____

6. What is the publishing date and who are the publishers and editors of the *Dictionary of Music*?

    _____ , _____ , _____ , and

    _____ Page _____

7. Do we have a copy of Webster's *New Biographical Dictionary* in our reference section? If so, what is its call number?

    _____ , _____ Page _____

8. What makes *Dinosaur Heresies* such a popular book? _____

    _____ Page _____

Worksheet continues on page 234.

➤ *Teacher Notes:* We have included a list of all resources for ease of preparing this unit. We highly suggest that you pull them off the shelves and onto a movable cart.

Reference	Call Number
1. *World Almanac and Book of Facts*	Ref 317.3 Wor
2. *Webster's Biographical Dictionary*	Ref 920.02 Web
3. *Bartlett's Familiar Quotations*	Ref 808.88 Bar
4. *Famous First Facts*	Ref 031.02 Kan
5. *Sixth Book of Junior Authors and Illustrators*	Ref 809.89282 Six
6. *Webster's New Geographical Dictionary*	Ref 910.321 Web
7. *Illustrated Facts and Records Book of Animals*	Ref 591.824 Row
8. *Facts on File Visual Dictionary*	Ref 423.1 Cor
9. *Stamp Atlas*	Ref 769.56 Wel
10. *Lands and Peoples*	Ref 910 Lan
11. *Great Lives*	Ref 920 Gre
12. *American Nicknames*	Ref 929.4 Sha
13. *Holidays Around the World*	Ref 394.26 Gae
14. *New Encyclopedia of Sports*	Ref 796.097 Hic
15. *Macmillan Dictionary of Quotations*	Ref 082 Mac
16. *New View Almanac*	Ref 031.02 New
17. *Complete Book of U.S. Presidents*	Ref 973.0992 DeG
18. *Goode's World Atlas*	Ref 912 Goo
19. *Encyclopedia of American Facts and Dates*	Ref 973.02 Enc
20. *Auschwitz Chronicle 1939–1945*	Ref 940.53 Cze
21. *National Geographic Picture Atlas of Our Fifty States*	Ref 912 Nat
22. *Chronicle of America*	Ref 973 Chr
23. *Something About the Author*	Ref 920.03 Som
24. *Timelines of the Ancient World*	Ref 930.0202 Smi
25. EBSCO® Periodical Service	Computer
26. NewsFile®	Computer

27.	Factory®	Computer
28.	Writing Center®	Computer
29.	Word Munchers®	Computer
30.	ClarisWorks® Word Processing	Computer
31.	*Chronicle of the 20th Century*	Ref 909.82 Chr
32.	*Facts on File Encyclopedia of the 20th Century*	Ref 909.8203 Fac
33.	*U.S.A., A Chronicle in Pictures*	Ref 973 Wen
34.	*Historic U.S. Court Cases 1690–1990: An Encyclopedia*	Ref 347.7326 Joh
35.	*Timetables of History*	Ref 902.02 Gru
36.	*American Destiny*	Ref 973 Ame
37.	*Dictionary of American History*	Ref 973.03 Dic
38.	*Buildings of Colorado*	Ref 720.9788 Noe
39.	*New York Public Library Desk Reference*	Ref 031 New
40.	*Reference Library of Hispanic America*	Ref 973.0468 Ref
41.	*Words that Make America Great*	Ref 973 Wor
42.	*Science Fiction, Fantasy, and Horror Writers*	Ref 808.838 Sci V1
43.	*Reference Library of Black America*	Ref 973.049607 Ref
44.	*Encyclopedia of World Sport: From Ancient Times to Present*	Ref 796.03 Enc
45.	*Military History of the United States*	Ref 973 Cha
46.	*American Women in Science*	Ref 509.2273 Bai
47.	*Reference Library of Asian America*	Ref 973 Ref
48.	*New Grolier Encyclopedia of World War II*	Ref 940.53 New
49.	*Junior Worldmark Encyclopedia of the Canadian Provinces*	Ref 971.003 Jun
50.	*Elements: Copper, Silver and Gold*	Ref 546 Kna
51.	*New York Public Library Book of How and Where to Look*	Ref 025.524 New

➤ *Teacher Notes:* Next we offer a presentation format for students to remember all parts of the resource needed to inform their classmates. We hope you find it useful.

PRESENTATION

Name _____ Date _____ Period _____

    When you present your Research Roundup reference to the class, you will need to have (1) the book, (2) your visual aid, (3) your worksheet, and (4) this form completed. You will need to state the following information on this form in your presentation:

____ Do you have all four items required? (4 points)

____ (A) Author(s) _____

____ (B) Book title _____

____ (C) City where published _____

____ (C) Company or publisher's name _____

____ (D) Date of copyright _____ (5 points)

____ What kinds of information can be found in this book? Give three examples. (3 points)

       1. _____

       2. _____

       3. _____

____ This book is useful for what types of reports? Give two examples. (2 points)

1. _____

2. _____

____ What is the call number of this book? _____ (1 point)

____ Walk to the library shelf and show the class the book's location. (3 points)

Answer this question at the end of *all* presentations:

_____ What did you *learn* about library reference books? This is *metacognition*—a term that means thinking about your thinking. Be specific.

Your answer should be at least five sentences long. (7 points)

_____

_____

_____

_____

_____

____ Visual Aid (10 points)   ____ Research Roundup Questions (15 points)

Total Possible Points: 50 Points   Your points _____

➤ *Teacher Notes:* While this unit is lengthy, we have included it in its entirety so you may use part or all of it. The next chapter presents an overview of the interrelationship of the five STARR components.

Resources and Useful Information

Books

Adams, James Truslow. *Dictionary of American History*. New York: Scribner, 1976–1978.

Agel, Jerome. *Words that Make America Great*. New York: Random House, 1997.

Bailey, Martha J. *American Women in Science: A Biographical Dictionary*. Santa Barbara, CA: ABC-CLIO, 1994.

Bartlett, John. *Bartlett's Familiar Quotations*. Boston: Little Brown, 1855.

Boughton, Simon. *Great Lives*. Garden City, New York: Doubleday & Co., 1988.

Carruth, Gorton. *The Encyclopedia of American Facts and Dates*. New York: Harper & Row, 1987.

Chant, Christopher. *The Military History of the United States*. New York: M. Cavendish, 1992.

Chronicle of America. Liberty, MO: JL International Publications, 1993.

Clifton, Daniel, ed. *Chronicle of the 20th Century*. Liberty, MO: J.L. International Publishing, 1992.

Commager, Henry Steele. *The American Destiny: An Illustrated Bicentennial History of the United States*. New York: Danbury Press, 1975.

Commire, Anne. *Something About the Author*. Detroit, MI: Gale Research, 1971.

Cooke, Tim, and Halliwell, Sarah. *The New Grolier Encyclopedia of World War II*. Danbury, CT: Grolier Educational Corp., 1995.

Corbeil, John Claude. *The Facts on File Visual Dictionary*. New York: Facts on File Publications, 1986.

Czech, Danuta. *Auschwitz Chronicle, 1939–1945*. New York: H. Holt, 1990.

DeGregorio, William A. *The Complete Book of U.S. Presidents*. New York: Dembner Books, 1984.

Drexel, John. *The Facts on File Encyclopedia of the 20th Century*. New York: Facts on File, 1991.

Estell, Kenneth. *Reference Library of Black America*. Detroit, MI: Gale Research, 1994.

Gaer, Joseph. *Holidays Around the World*. Boston, MA: Little, Brown, 1953.

Gall, Susan B. and Natividad, Irene. *Reference Library of Asian America*. Detroit, MI: Gale Research, 1995.

Gall, Timothy L., and Gall, Susan B. *Junior Worldmark Encyclopedia of the Canadian Provinces*. Detroit, MI: UXL, 1997.

Goode, J. Paul, and Espenshade, Edward B. Jr., ed. *Goode's World Atlas*. Chicago: Rand McNally, 1995.

Grun, Bernard, and Stein, Werner. *The Timetables of History: A Horizontal Linkage of People and Events*. New York: Simon & Schuster, 1991.

Harris, Sherwood. *The New York Public Library Book of How and Where to Look It Up*. New York: Prentice Hall, 1991.

Hickok, Ralph. *New Encyclopedia of Sports*. New York: McGraw-Hill, 1977.

Holmes, Sally. *Sixth Book of Junior Authors & Illustrators*. New York: H.W. Wilson, 1989.

Johnson, John W. *Historic U.S. Court Cases, 1690–1990: An Encyclopedia*. New York: Garland Publishers, 1992.

Kane, Joseph Nathan. *Famous First Facts: A Record of First Happenings, Discoveries, and Inventions in American History*. New York: H.W. Wilson, 1981.

Kanellos, Nicholas. *Reference Library of Hispanic America: Hispanic American Almanac.* Detroit, MI: Gale Research, 1998.

Knapp, Brian J. *Copper, Silver and Gold.* Danbury, CT: Grolier Educational Corp., 1996.

Lands and Peoples. Danbury, CT: Grolier, 1993.

Levinson, David, and Christensen, Karen. *Encyclopedia of World Sport: From Ancient Times to the Present.* Santa Barbara, CA: ABC-CLIO, 1996.

MacNee, Marie J. *Science Fiction, Fantasy, and Horror Writers.* Detroit, MI: UXL, 1995.

The McMillan Dictionary of Quotations. New York: Macmillan, 1989.

National Geographic Picture Atlas of Our Fifty States, Second Edition. Washington: National Geographic Society, 1980.

The New York Public Library Desk Reference. New York: Webster's New World, 1989.

Noel, Thomas J. *Buildings of Colorado.* New York: Oxford University Press, 1997.

Rowland-Entwistle, Theodore. *Illustrated Facts and Records Book of Animals.* New York: Arco Publishers, 1981.

Scarre, Chris. *Smithsonian Timelines of the Ancient World.* Washington, D.C.: Smithsonian Institution, 1993.

Shankle, George Earlie. *American Nicknames: Their Origin and Significance.* New York: Wilson, 1955.

Tesar, Jenny E. et al. *The New View Almanac: The First All-Visual Resource of Vital Facts and Statistics.* Woodbridge, CT: Blackbirch Press, 1996.

Webster's Biographical Dictionary. Springfield, MA: G. & C. Merriam Co., 1980.

Webster's New Geographical Dictionary. Springfield, MA: Merriam-Webster, 1984.

Wellsted, R. Raife. *The Stamp Atlas.* New York: Facts on File Publications, 1986.

Wenborn, Neil. *The U.S.A., A Chronicle in Pictures.* New York: Smithmark Publishers, 1991.

What Work Requires of Schools: A SCANS Report for America 2000 by the Secretary's Commission on Achieving Necessary Skills. Washington, D.C.: U.S. Department of Labor, 1991.

World Almanac and Book of Facts 1999. Mahwah, New Jersey: World Almanac Books, 1998.

Electronic Databases

EBSCO®: This is a database of hundreds of thousands of article summaries. http://www.epnet.com, 1-800-653-2726, Ebsco Industries, Inc., 83 Pine Street, Peabody, MA 01960.

NewsFile® (formerly titled NewsBank): Updated bimonthly, this database provides full-text articles from over 500 regional, national, and international newspapers and newswire sources since 1991. http://www.newsbank.com 1-800-762-8182 5020, Tamiami Trail North, Suite 110, Naples, FL 34103.

Software

ClarisWorks®: A multi-faceted program, including word processing, spreadsheet, database, painting and graphics. http://www.claris.com, Apple Computer, Inc., 1-800-325-2747.

Factory Network, Wired for Learning, 1605 Green Hills Road, Scotts Balley, CA 95060, 1-800-321-7511 or 1-408-438-5502.

KidPix Studio Deluxe by Craig Hickman. http://www.Broderbund.com, Broderbund Software, 1-800-973-5111.

Word Munchers Deluxe®: Teaches reading, vocabulary, and grammar skills. http://learningco.com, The Learning Company, 1-800-685-6322.

The Writing Center®. http://www.mattelinteractive.com.

CHAPTER 8

STARR MULTIDISCIPLINARY UNITS

I keep six honest serving-men
They taught me all I knew;
Their names are What and Why and When
And How and Where and Who.

— Rudyard Kipling, "The Elephant's Child," *Just So Stories,* 1902

THE INTERRELATIONSHIP OF THE STARR COMPONENTS

As you read through each STARR component—speaking, technology, analysis, reading, and research—it is our hope that you clearly see the interrelationships. We do not teach these components separately, but on a daily basis they are woven together so that our learners are immersed in a holistic learning experience. One of the major criticisms of public education today is the fragmented nature of the presentation of the curriculum. Hopping from language arts to social studies to math to science and so on in 45- or 50-minute segments with no connections certainly fragments learning. In this curriculum, we try to help students make connections among disciplines and to the real world. We present each component separately in this book to accommodate the limitations of this form of communication. We also want to share multidisciplinary units that truly incorporate all STARR components.

CREATING STARR ENRICHED LEARNING ENVIRONMENTS

Any multidisciplinary curriculum requires collaboration. The teacher, Media Specialist, Technology Coordinator, and other team members together create an abundance of resources. Students find that they have a variety of people who help facilitate their searches. Therefore, the collaboration of staff and students is critical to the learning process.

In addition to human resources, learners in an enriched environment need access to technology, print, and online resources. The minimum requirements include computers equipped with word processing, databases, spreadsheet, and drawing and painting software. Presentation software, CD ROMs, and Internet connectivity have proven to be highly motivating.

And finally, an enriched environment also means a nurturing one where questions can be asked and risks taken. As in the work world, classrooms where learners can think, reflect, and present findings without fear of failure are the ones where students are most successful.

Allow yourself to experiment with the STARR model. Try one of the units or a selection of lessons during a quarter. See what works and does not work. Adapt what we have provided and create a learning environment where you and your students can flourish and where learning is exciting and dynamic.

MULTIDISCIPLINARY UNIT ONE: RENAISSANCE LEARNERS

> *Teacher Notes:* The idea behind this unit came about from a small group of students who had decided to research great artists. These four students, in four separate classes, wanted to know why Michelangelo painted the Sistine Chapel, what cubism is, if there really is a Giverny that inspired Monet, and why European painters seem to be better known than American painters. From these four students the seed for the Renaissance Learners emerged.

Foundation Skills

In this unit all foundation skills and competencies listed in the Secretary's Commission on Achieving Necessary Skills (SCANS) report are integrated. Students locate and interpret information, and communicate thoughts and ideas through writing, listening, speaking, generating new ideas, making decisions, solving problems, working collaboratively, and utilizing technology.

Content Proficiencies

Language Arts

Student read to construct meaning by interacting with the text, by recognizing different requirements of a variety of printed materials, and by using appropriate strategies to increase comprehension. The student:

- Reads a variety of materials including literature, textbooks, and reference materials.

- Comprehends and draws inferences beyond the literal level.

- Recalls and builds background knowledge by exploring information related to the text.

♦ Identifies the author's intent, main idea, and supporting details.

♦ Applies appropriate strategies to increase fluency and adjusts his or her reading rate when reading various materials.

The student produces writing that conveys purpose and meaning, uses effective writing strategies, and incorporates the conventions of written language to communicate clearly. The learner:

♦ Produces creative, expository, technical, or personal writing on an assigned or self-selected topic.

♦ Indicates understanding of a topic through specific, accurate, and sufficient details.

♦ Organizes clearly and sequences ideas logically.

♦ Selects appropriate voice and word choice.

♦ Uses a variety of sentence structures.

♦ Edits and eliminates errors.

Social Studies Proficiencies

♦ The learner demonstrates an understanding of tradition and change by communicating how the past influences the present and the future.

♦ The learner demonstrates an understanding of human diversity by communicating respect for basic human rights and the multicultural nature of societies and the world.

Connecting the Renaissance Unit to Workplace Skills

The introductory Renaissance Scavenger Hunt is designed to connect students with art and the global community. As students participate in this search they begin to immerse themselves in an unfamiliar period. Michelangelo and Florence, Italy, become more real for them. In addition to this connection, we plan a voluntary field trip on a Saturday to the Denver Art Museum. This is usually students' first exposure to this museum. The museum prepares a specific introduction that connects our students to the world of art. Students learn what curators do. They are introduced to the behind-the-scenes workings of the art museum.

Aligning Instructional Practices with Proficiencies and Assessments

As mentioned earlier, this unit aligns with Language Arts and History proficiencies. It also supports art, music, drama, and dance.

Assessments

This unit requires multiple assessment strategies. Students keep journals as they research and meet once a week with the teacher to update progress and challenges. The final product, designed and presented by the student, is the major assessment piece for the portfolio. Please refer to Chapter 9 for additional assistance with assessment ideas.

Instructional Strategies

This is a unit where the role of the teacher is that of facilitator. Each student selects an artist, writer, and a third prominent person who could be a political figure, a scientist, or an activist from the same period of history. Students research their subjects to determine what works they produced, what they were well-known for, and what the impact was of that particular historical period on the people and their works. This connection provides learners with a systemic view of the people and the period.

Remediation Strategies

Adaptations and expectations for this unit can be adjusted to the learners' needs. For example, you may require that students research only one artist for this unit. The grading rubric for the final project would then be based on that adjustment. This unit supports Gardner's Multiple Intelligences theory in that the products our students have produced range from videos to plays to original pieces of art work.

Enrichment Strategies

As with remediation strategies, the adaptations for this unit are limitless. Our gifted and talented students in one class decided they would write an original play based on the movie *Back to the Future* and present each of their historical figures. They not only wrote the play, they did the costuming and scenery and invited parents to a performance complete with a tea. An additional idea would be to have students create a Web site to showcase their knowledge.

Notes to Users of This Unit

Classroom Teachers: Renaissance Learners delve into subjects outside the realm of the standard curriculum. The combination of art, music, literature, and politics becomes highly intriguing once students start to make connections between the artist and the political impact of an era. Our students were amazed that Michelangelo did not always paint or sculpt what he wanted, but what the pope and his paying patrons required. This multidisciplinary unit helps students make connections between art and politics, music and literature, and science and art. The products our students created for their portfolios were creative and polished. We hope you will have as much fun with this unit as we have.

Media Specialists: Your skills and knowledge will contribute to this rich learning experience. Renaissance Learners need direction and guidance on where to locate resources. They need access to art, music, history, sociology, and literature through a variety of media, including print, on-line, video, and recordings. Once students have decided on the period of history and the artists, writers, and political figures they want to research, they will need support in this challenging endeavor. You can provide a variety of resources, as well as sharing information on how to access materials that may not be normally available in a school media center.

Technology Specialists: The Renaissance Learners Unit results in creative, multimedia projects. Your guidance in audio and video editing, as well as help for students to learn more complicated presentational software applications, will enrich the students' experience. You may want to schedule mini-lessons on creating multimedia presentations.

Specific Knowledge

The students will:

* Use decision-making skills to select their research focus.

* Use information management skills of accessing, identifying, locating, sorting, and organizing resources.

* Use collaborative skills in working with others.

* Understand complex interrelationships during a specific period of history.

* Select and apply technology to support and enhance the project.

* Keep a journal of activities for assessment purposes.

* Design, develop, and present a final project to communicate and share learning.

Environmental Considerations

Students will need access to resources in the media center, the computer lab, and the classroom. Students may want to utilize the public library for their project, as well as museums and art galleries. This project supports independent learning.

Assignments and Intelligences Addressed

Assignment	Intelligence
Journals	Linguistic and Intrapersonal
Final Projects	All eight

Why a Renaissance Learners Unit?

When budgets shrink, art and music are among the first areas to get cut. We watched this happen in our own district and felt a need to design a unit that would provide students with an opportunity to explore these areas. But we wanted more. We wanted to help students make connections. In our own educational experiences, no one helped us see what the impact of an historical period was on artists, sculptors, writers, and scientists. We wanted to help our students see the bigger picture and perhaps get them excited about a different way to view history. From the beginning with only four students, we expanded the concept into this unit.

> *Teacher Notes:* We introduce this unit of learning by placing students into teams and sending them on a two-day on-line Renaissance Scavenger Hunt, to create interest and motivation. You may want to have your students do a print scavenger hunt using resources in your media center. This can be adapted to meet your needs.

RENAISSANCE SCAVENGER HUNT

Name _____ Date _____ Period _____

Challenge: You have two days to complete this scavenger hunt. You may use the computers in the classroom, media center, or computer lab. On the third day you will return to class and share what you have learned.

1. Go to Netscape and type in this URL: http://www.ih.k12.oh.us/ms/Woodring/RENAIS/Renaissa.htm

Seventh-grade students like you created this Web site. The following questions are all answered on this Web site.

2. When was the Renaissance? _____

_____

3. What does the word *Renaissance* mean? _____

_____

4. Who were the best-known painters of this era? Select your favorite work and tell about it.

_____

_____

5. Who was Michelangelo? Who forced him to paint the Sistine Chapel? What is the Sistine
Chapel? _____

_____

_____

_____

6. Tell about writers of this era. What did they write? Do you know any of their works?

_____

_____

_____

7. What would it mean if someone said, "Oh, yes, he or she is quite the person, sort of a Renaissance man or woman"? _____

_____

More Instructional Strategies

When students return with the information, have a discussion on what they learned. Remind them that this era is known as the Period of Enlightenment in art, music, literature, and politics. Italy was one of the countries best known for its impact on the world during this era. You may create webs on the board to make connections about what students discuss. Also be sure that students understand the concept of the Renaissance man, a person who has a variety of skills in writing, painting, sculpting, inventing, and thinking. We always expand and update this to include women.

Assignment #1: Selecting an Artist, Writer, and a Third Important Person

Now that you know a little about the Renaissance, it is your turn to become a Renaissance learner. In this assignment, you will research a period and select one artist, one writer, and a third person of prominence. Your challenge is to research them thoroughly and design a creative way of sharing. Where do you begin? Think about different historical periods such as Ancient Greece or Rome, or the American Civil War. Or you may start with an artist or writer you know, such as Picasso, Monet, or Klee. Determine a starting point and begin either an Internet search or use the media center. You have two days to select three people.

Assignment #2: Making Connections

As you research the people and period, keep these questions in mind:

- What major historical events had an impact on this era?

- What were the obstacles to the success of your people?

- How did they overcome these barriers?

- What works of art, major literary pieces, or events were your people famous for?

- Did any of your people know each other? How?

- How were your people connected?

PLANNING QUESTIONS

Name _____ Date_____ Period _____

Directions: Use this checklist as you gather information. This is the kind of information you need to include in your final project.

_____ 1. Where were each of your people born?

_____ 2. In what period of history were they born?

_____ 3. What was their early family life like?

_____ 4. For what were they best known?

_____ 5. What events in history influenced their work?

_____ 6. What person or people influenced their work?

_____ 7. What other famous people were alive during the same time period? (Who were their contemporaries?)

_____ 8. Why did they choose to do their work?

_____ 9. What was their most famous creation?

_____ 10. What did their entire body of work include?

_____ 11. Were they well known when they were living?

_____ 12. What makes their work unique or reflective of the period?

_____ 13. What is your reaction to their work?

_____ 14. What made you select them?

_____ 15. If they were alive today, would their work be considered great? Why or why not?

_____ 16. What did the critics of the period say about their work?

_____ 17. Would you have wanted to live during this time period? Explain.

Assignment #3: Sharing Knowledge

Now that you have found everything there is to know about the three people you selected, how are you going to share what you have learned? As you think about how you want to share, keep in mind that you are required to show the influences and impact of the history and people. Do you need to include charts, graphs, diagrams? Will you design a Web site? Will a HyperStudio® presentation be the best method? Meet with your team and brainstorm how the information will be presented. You may work together or do individual presentations.

Make an appointment with your teacher to discuss options.

> ➤ *Teacher Notes:* Weekly updates with a checklist help students to keep on track with this truly constructivist learning project. We found that students needed assistance in organizing information. We taught them how to create three folders to keep track.

FINAL PROJECT GRADING RUBRIC FOR THE RENAISSANCE LEARNERS PROJECT

Name _____ Date _____ Period _____

Artist _____

Writer _____

Third Person _____

Period of History _____

Describe your final project. _____

_____

Research was in-depth for each person	5	4	3	2	1
Historical period was well described	5	4	3	2	1
Strong connections were made among the three people and historical era	5	4	3	2	1
Analysis, synthesis, and evaluation were evident	5	4	3	2	1
Final project showed creative thought	5	4	3	2	1

Final project grade: _____

Comments:

Unit Two: Hero Research Project

> ➤ *Teacher Notes:* The Columbine Student Body President, Heather Dinkel, in her address at a public memorial on April 25, 1999, reminded us that we are all heroes to one another. It is our sincerest hope that this unit may reflect hope in every human life, that there is a hero in everyone we meet.

The hero unit is part of a larger unit on autobiography and biography and includes elements of the larger unit. Research is a time-consuming and challenging aspect of the STARR curriculum. However, we feel so strongly that our students need to learn the basics of documented research that we try to incorporate two or three research units in our school year. We often integrate research with another area, such as social studies or language arts. For example, when students are studying the Eastern Hemisphere, we may align with the social studies teacher and have each student select an eastern hemisphere country to research. Our language arts tie-in links the study of heroes with Anne Frank, or other everyday heroes who have risen to hero status simply because they rose above seemingly unbearable circumstances. This unit reflects research choices of people whom the students consider past or present heroes.

Learning Objectives

Students will:

- ◆ Be introduced to the basic elements of autobiographies and biographies.

- ◆ Learn or review research basics, such as how to:

  - Use research materials, such as encyclopedias.

  - Use the Reader's Guide to Periodical Literature.

  - Use research databases, such as NewsFile®.

  - Search for quality information on the Internet.

  - Write a business letter for information.

  - Take notes and document sources.

  - Organize information into an outline.

  - Write an introduction, body, and conclusion to a research paper.

  - Write a bibliography.

  - Create a title page.

  - Create a final document in ClarisWorks® slide show.

  - Deliver an informative speech about their subject.

Content Proficiencies

The student will read a wide variety of materials for information, pleasure and to enrich experience. Meaning is constructed by interacting with the materials, recognizing the requirements of different types of readings, and using appropriate strategies to increase comprehension.

Assessments

Qualities of a hero warm-up—short answers

Two column notes: biographies/autobiographies

Web—organization of notes

Outline: organization of research paper

Research progress checklist

ClarisWorks® slide show final research product

Informative speech presentation

Concepts/Skills

The learner will:

♦ Learn about reading for information.

♦ Read for comprehension.

♦ Analyze different types of reading materials for inclusion in a research product.

♦ Organize information in web and formal outline formats.

♦ Produce ClarisWorks® slide show of research product.

♦ Present informative speech.

♦ Collaborate with a partner to prepare the research product.

Instructional Strategies

Literal: (These are lessons directly aimed at instructing students in reading, comprehension, research, and computer application skills and aligns specifically with the curriculum.)

♦ Reading strategies

♦ Comprehension of expository text—techniques

♦ Outlining

♦ Decision-making and problem-solving skills as related to research

- ◆ Computer application—ClarisWorks® slide show

- ◆ Re-teach informative speech

Lateral: (These are adjunct to the literal lessons above.)

- ◆ Multiple Intelligences addressed

- ◆ Collaborative work with a partner

- ◆ Two-column note taking skills

Remediation Strategies

- ◆ Assign strong student with student needing greater assistance to achieve final product

- ◆ Reduce expectations of final product

- ◆ Reduce number and type of sources required

- ◆ Allow additional time to complete project

- ◆ Select research materials written at lower reading level

Enrichment Strategies

- ◆ Web site creation about hero of choice

- ◆ Individual research project comparing/contrasting two heroes from two time periods

- ◆ Videotape interview of local hero

Notes to Users of This Unit

Classroom Teachers: Students who can create a research question and search for answers are well prepared for the workplace. Employers expect employees to recognize and solve problems. We prepare students to resolve problems by seeking information from a variety of sources. We find that this unit works best when we link it with another curricular area such as language arts. Students have a greater buy-in to the work if they know it affects two classrooms and that two teachers are assisting them. Further, because students are allowed to select personal heroes, they truly enjoy the research process. They become more and more excited by the amount of information they gather. A student who receives a personal response from a present-day hero understands that solid primary research leads to a direct link of information.

Media Specialists: Successful research depends on collaboration from the Media Specialist. As you can see from the objectives, most research items listed could be taught collaboratively between the Media Specialist and teacher. Your mission is to provide valuable resources for a wide variety of heroes. It is truly amazing to witness students who struggle all year come alive when they delve into the latest rock star's life through the guidance you offer. Current news and magazine databases, on-line assistance, and whatever hard copy materials you have help them enormously. Working with both the teacher and Technology Specialist elicits the best materials. Although extremely demanding, such collaboration also is incredibly rewarding as students locate information about their personal heroes.

Technology Specialists: Assisting the Media Specialist and teacher in discovering on-line resources and in providing a variety of news and magazine databases will help students achieve their research needs. Further, the culmination of this unit is a production of a ClarisWorks® slide show by each student. The teacher may need you to demonstrate a slide show and explain the steps involved in creating it, including how to import photos and other documents.

> ➤ *Teacher Notes:* The student worksheet below is an introductory lesson to the hero unit. It stimulates student interest and lively discussions about the qualities of heroes.

QUESTIONS FOR HEROES

Name _____ Date _____ Period _____

1. What qualities do we find in a hero? List several adjectives or nouns that describe a hero. (5 minimum)

2. List as many heroes as you can and describe why each is a hero. (Minimum four heroes and descriptions.)

   a. Hero _____ Description _____

   b. Hero _____ Description _____

   c. Hero _____ Description _____

   d. Hero _____ Description _____

3. How does a hero become a hero? _____

4. What special knowledge, skills, vision, communication ability, planning, etc., does it take to be a hero? _____

   _____

5. If you were to interview a hero, what would you ask? (Minimum three questions)

   a. _____

   b. _____

   c. _____

6. If your hero is no longer alive, or if you are unable to interview your hero, where could you look for answers to your questions about his or her life? (Minimum four other resources—THINK!)

   a. _____

   b. _____

   c. _____

   d. _____

7. Is a hero a leader? Why or why not? _____

8. Is a leader a hero? Why or why not? _____

➤ *Teacher Notes:* The last two questions create quite a controversy in the classroom. We have used chart paper to list answers and create a Venn diagram from those responses. We found that students enjoy this type of analytical thinking and discussion.

➤ *Teacher Notes:* The introduction of autobiography and biography expectations was originally created on ClarisWorks® slide show to illustrate what the final technology product might look like. We had students take two-column notes from this presentation, which were graded for completeness.

1. Each student will research and complete a report on a hero of his or her choice.

2. The report will be five paragraphs in length (minimum).

3. Three sources (minimum) must be used and cited in the bibliography.

    Introductory Paragraph (four sentences)

    Sentence 1: Attention Getter: gets the reader's attention.

    Sentence 2: Projected Order Sentence: sets up the topics in order.

    Sentence 3: Topic Sentence: states the reason of the paper.

    Sentence 4: Transition sentence: leads the reader into the body paragraphs.

An example of an Introduction Paragraph follows:

Not very many people know that George Washington did not have wooden teeth. In fact, his false teeth were made out of whale bone. In this research report, topics include George Washington's birth and youth, the years he served as a General in the Continental Army, and his rise to political office. George Washington was a fine man who gave himself to the service of his country. First, George's birth and youth will be reviewed.

Attention Getter Sentence (ask a question, make a startling statement, use a quote)

Did you know that _____ did _____?

Projected Order Sentence (list in order what will be covered in the paper)

This paper will consider these ideas: first, _____, secondly, _____, and finally, _____.

Topic Sentence (purpose of the paper)

_____ was the first person to _____.

Transition Sentence

In the next paragraph, you will read about _____.

Body Paragraphs

The body of your paper will consist of at least three paragraphs. Each paragraph needs to be a minimum of eight sentences in length. These sentences include:

1. Topic sentence

2. Detail sentence

3. Expanding sentence

4. Detail sentence

5. Expanding sentence

6. Detail sentence

7. Expanding sentence

8. Concluding sentence

The order of the body paragraphs is dictated by your projected order sentence in the introductory paragraph, where you state which topic is first, second, and third.

Below are ideas for body paragraphs for your hero. Remember, you will need a minimum of three of these body paragraphs. You may have other ideas.

Body paragraph 1 (eight sentences): Birth and early years

Body paragraph 2 (eight sentences): Family and schooling

Body paragraph 3 (eight sentences): Focus on achievements

Body paragraph 4 (eight sentences): Personal attributes, such as appearance, religious affiliation, belief systems, opinions, etc.

Body paragraph 5 (eight sentences): Marriage and children

Body paragraph 6 (eight sentences): Senior years, death

Conclusion Paragraph

Finally, you need to end the paper. The conclusion paragraph is only three sentences long and restates important information from your introductory paragraph.

Sentence 1: Restate the topic sentence:
In conclusion, George Washington served his country with dignity.

Sentence 2: Restate the projected order:
You have read about George's birth and early years, his service as a military officer, and his rise to political office.

Sentence 3: This is a totally new sentence that leaves the reader with something to think about and wraps up the paper.
Truly, George Washington was a hero who served his new country with great honor.

**Remember that the conclusion paragraph restates the same information in the introductory paragraph, but uses slightly different words.

Bibliography

The last page of your report is a bibliography, which lists sources used for your research. Bibliographies are alphabetized by the first word of each entry. Below are correct formats for different sources. Please pay attention to punctuation and indenting. Follow this same pattern for your report's bibliography. You have this same information in your bibliography packet.

Book
>Author's last name, author's first name. *Title of Book.* City of Publication: Book Publisher, Copyright date.

Magazine
>Author's last name, author's first name. "Title of magazine article." *Title of Magazine.* Date of magazine, pages of article.

Newspaper
>Author's last name, author's first name. "Title of article." *Name of Newspaper.* Date of newspaper, section of newspaper, page number.

Electronic Periodical
>Author's last name, author's first name. "Title of Article." *Name of Electronic Periodical.* Date of periodical. *Name of Electronic Source.*

Internet Source
>Use your handout for Internet citations.

Documenting your information

In class, we discuss ways to avoid plagiarism. These include quoting the source and summarizing, paraphrasing, and writing an opinion about material read. If you recall, opinions do not belong in research.

The best bet for research notes is to paraphrase. Use abbreviations and short phrases. Every note you write should include a reference to the source from which you took the notes.

Your note cards or research notepaper should include this information:

1. Your name and period

2. The source information—see the bibliographic requirements above

3. The topic this piece of information fits—see the ideas for body paragraphs

4. Include the page number where the information is found

5. You must have a minimum of ten different facts or pieces of information

GRADE SHEET

This is your grade sheet and must be handed in when you do your class presentation.

Name _____ Date _____ Period _____

Miscellaneous Report Expectations

1. Your report will be written in rough draft format first and include a title page.

2. Three peer edits and a rewrite will be attached to your first draft. Peer editing will be conducted on the rewrite for further refinement. Your title page should include the name of your hero, your name, your period, and the date.

3. Follow the pattern for the report outlined in this packet.

4. The paper must be double spaced and completed in ClarisWorks® Slide Show.

5. The font size must be at least 14 and preferably 18 point. Acceptable fonts are Palatino, Helvetica, New York, or Monaco.

6. USE SPELL CHECK. Read your slide show out loud to find typing errors. You will need at least one peer editor to read your report on the monitor.

7. Turn this page in when you do your presentation.

Write your presentation date here _____

Grading Matrix

_____ Title page	5 points
_____ Intro	5 points
_____ Body #1	10 points
_____ Body #2	10 points
_____ Body #3	10 points
_____ Conclusion	5 points
_____ Bibliography	15 points
_____ Research notes	50 points
_____ Mechanics (Spelling, punctuation, capitalization, word choice, indenting, and organization)	20 points

_____ Editing   15 points

_____ Parent edit bonus   10+

_____ ClarisWorks® Slide Show   30 points
      (includes at least one graphic,
      preferably a photo of your
      hero or an object directly
      related to your hero)

Presentation Points

_____ Posture   5 points

_____ Voice Projection   5 points

_____ Word Enunciation   5 points

_____ Gestures   5 points

_____ Eye contact   5 points

_____ TOTAL POINTS (Total possible=210 including parent edit bonus)

Comments

RESEARCH QUESTIONS

➤ *Teacher Notes:* The following worksheet is for your use to track student progress as the research continues. It offers students the opportunity to identify problem areas and ask for help.

Name _____ Period _____ Date _____

1. Who are you researching? _____

2. How is your research progressing? _____

   _____

3. Are you having any problems? _____

   _____

4. What resources have you found? _____

   _____

5. Please show me your notes.

   Paraphrase?_____ Quotes? _____ Document properly? _____

EXTRA CREDIT ASSIGNMENTS

➤ *Teacher Notes:* There are always students who want to do more, or who need enrichment activities. We offer the following extra credit opportunities for our students.

Biography/Autobiography

You may choose *one* extra credit assignment below to complete. The extra credit assignment you choose will be worth up to 25 points, depending on the quality of your work and the effort you have put into it. Do your best to earn the highest grade possible.

1. Collage: Prepare a collage on a large poster board representing the person you read about in your biography or autobiography. Remember that *neatness* is a critical factor in this type of project. Include the following elements in your collage:

   a. +4 Something about the subject's family.

   b. +4 A picture or map that represents the setting of the story. For example, if your subject was John Glenn, an astronaut and U.S. senator, you could have two different settings—either a space capsule (he was in a Mercury spacecraft), or a picture of the U.S. Capitol (or Senate) in Washington, D.C.

   c. +4 An example that represents a hardship or trial that this person had to overcome to achieve greatness. An example would be that Abraham Lincoln failed numerous times before he was elected. How could you show that your person achieved greatness through strength of character, positive attitude, family encouragement, or whatever is the case for your subject? You may have to use words cut from newspapers or magazines for this. However, your example should truly describe how your subject became a person worthy of having a book written about him or her.

   d. +4 A photo or carefully created drawing that shows what your subject did that made him or her great, such as:

   > Thomas Edison and a light bulb.

   > Agatha Christie and a mystery book.

   e. +4 A quote from your subject about his or her life experiences can be carefully written in large letters, or cut out of magazines or newspapers. It should be something that you can identify with and truly represents the quality of this person. (For example, John F. Kennedy said, "Ask not what your country can do for you. Rather, ask what you can do for your country.")

   f. +5 On a separate sheet of paper, explain each of the five elements above and explain how you have shown them on your poster. Glue the explanation to the back of your poster. Include your name and class period.

Worksheet continues on page 264.

2. Biographical sketch: Write a biographical sketch about an *adult* who greatly affected your life, either in what they taught you, helped you with, or how they generally improved the quality of your life. For example, I might write about my sixth grade teacher, Miss Endicott, who greatly influenced me in my desire to excel in schoolwork. She was an outstanding educator who encouraged students to achieve to the best of their abilities. I greatly admired and respected her. She was a wonderful person. (At this point, I could continue by telling how she helped me and encouraged me, what teaching methods she used, and how all of this helped design my future life.) Take your idea of your "most unforgettable person" and write at least a 300-word essay on:

   a. +4 Why was this person unforgettable? Describe what made him or her special.

   b. +4 How did he or she influence your life? Explain exactly what he or she did.

   c. +4 What affect did he or she have on your life? What did you learn from him or her?

   d. +4 How will you model your life on what you have learned from this person? Can you see yourself doing something similar? Why or why not?

   e. +5 Out of all the people who have had an affect on your life, why did you choose this person? Have you ever told him or her how you feel? Why or why not? Will you be willing to share this report with this person? Why or why not? If you do share it, and the person is willing, have him or her sign your essay for bonus points (+5).

   f. +4 Use proper introduction, body, and conclusion parts of an essay. Use quality sentence structure. Carefully watch spelling, punctuation, and capitalization. Edit carefully for maximum points.

HOW TO OUTLINE

Name _____ Period _____ Date _____

➤*Teacher Notes:* The following example is adapted from *Write Source 2000*, an outstanding student resource, and follows an initial student attempt to organize research information by creating a web.

Example:

Subject	Trees
Topic Sentence	Many trees can be used for landscaping
Subtopic	Some trees are best suited for cold climates
Supporting detail	Evergreens are hardy and provide year-round color
Specific example	Norway pine
Specific example	Scotch pine
Supporting detail	Maples hold up well and provide brilliant seasonal color
Specific example	Red maple
Specific example	Silver maple
Subtopic	Some trees are better suited for warm climates

This example would be converted to one paragraph!

OUTLINE FRAMEWORK

Use the example and your web to create your outline below. After you look over your web, select the topic to begin your first body paragraph. This topic will become your first topic sentence.

Subject (Name of your hero)

Topic Sentence for first body paragraph

Subtopic

    Supporting Detail

        Specific Examples

    Supporting Detail

        Specific Examples

Subtopic

    Supporting Detail

        Specific Examples

    Supporting Detail

        Specific Examples

Topic Sentence for second body paragraph

Subtopic

    Supporting Detail

        Specific Examples

    Supporting Detail

        Specific Examples

Subtopic

    Supporting Detail

        Specific Examples

    Supporting Detail

        Specific Examples

Now continue your outline neatly on the back of this paper. Remember that a minimum of three body paragraphs is required, so you need three topic sentences and support in your outline to get a C or D grade. When finished, turn in this paper with your notes. To receive a passing grade, your notes must have correct source information. Good luck!

Some FINAL THOUGHTS

These units with an interdisciplinary focus are intended to provide you with insights into how we weave the five elements of speech, technology, analysis, reading, and research together. The final chapter discusses management, assessment, and evaluation.

Resources AND USEFUL INFORMATION

Books

Ehrich, Eugene and DeBruhl, Marshall. (eds.) *The International Thesaurus of Quotations.* New York: Harper Perennial, 1996.

Sebranek, Patrick, Meyer, Verne, Kemper, Dave, and Krenzke, Chris. *Write Source 2000.* Burlington, WI: Write Source Educational Publishing House, 1992.

What Work Requires of Schools: A SCANS Report for America 2000 by the Secretary's Commission on Achieving Necessary Skills. Washington, D.C.: U.S. Department of Labor, 1991.

Electronic Databases

NewsFile®. http://www.newsfile.com. This site provides information about NewsFile®, which is a resource that allows access to the full-text articles from more than 500 regional and international newspapers and newswire sources from 1991 to the present. You may reach the organization at 1-800-762-8182.

Software

HyperStudio® is a multimedia presentational software package developed by Roger Wagner. Ordering and product information is available at http://www.hyperstudio.com.

Web Sites

http://www.ih.k12.oh.us/ms/Woodring/RENAIS/Renaissa.htm

CHAPTER 9

MANAGEMENT, ASSESSMENT, AND EVALUATION

"Man is always more than he can know of himself; consequently, his accomplishments, time and again, will come as a surprise to him"
—Golo Mann, *The Liberation of an Unloved One,* 1987.

Management, assessment, and evaluation are daily issues for teachers. Real, practical concerns must always be considered. Questions plague us. For example, "How can I teach rich, engaging lessons and still prepare students for standardized tests in the spring?" "How should I convince parents and the community that what I teach meets these standards?" "How do I know that I am meeting these standards?" "When do I get to teach and quit doing the other myriad intrusive things society and the school district say I have to?" "Why can't I do what I love to do, teach?"

These complex questions have no easy answers. However, in STARR, we revitalized the joy of learning for many frustrated students. By allowing students to pursue topics of interest to them, the learning becomes engaging. At the same time, teaching moves from a monotonous repetitive preparation of lessons to the creation of an exciting learning environment. Assessment and evaluation include self, peer, and parent evaluations, as well as teacher evaluations. Students begin to be more responsible for their own learning.

STARR's implementation and management takes time. STARR's educational philosophy is about depth and breadth in learning. STARR provides learners with opportunities to question, think, reflect, and grow cognitively, socially, and emotionally. It is a process that takes careful consideration of learning styles and learners' needs.

From a practical sense, then, how do you get there? The first step is to rid yourself of preconceived notions about your role as a teacher. The STARR classroom is a student-centered learning environment. Here, students are provided with experiences to reach multiple intelligences. The learning is active, exploratory, and inquiry-based. Students ask questions, reflect, and make informed decisions. Students learn technology as they need it and as they see a reason for using it. The teacher provides facilitation to move students through each process.

What does this look like on a daily basis? We attempt to complete each research project within nine weeks. Sometimes it works; sometimes we extend it into the next quarter. Research-based inquiry does not always fit into artificial borders. And we honor that process while understanding that students also need to learn about expectations and deadlines. Please keep in mind that the ongoing skills and processes are intertwined. So, a typical nine-week plan looks like this:

Week 1: The research question is identified. As you can see from Chapter 4, this is a complex process in our classroom. We highly value well-developed research questions and take the time to allow students to think, revise, and share. During this first week while research questions are formulated, a mini-lesson on Writing Center®, a creative word processing program, might take place. Students work independently and in groups to conceive questions and learn new software. The teacher meets with individuals and teams to answer questions and check on progress. On Monday of this first week, a mini-lesson on formulating research questions is presented to the whole class. The Media Specialist may elect to teach this lesson. Students work in small groups to start the questioning process. (See Chapter 4 for details.) On Tuesday, a mini-lesson on Writing Center® software is presented by a student who is proficient on the program. Students continue to meet in small groups to refine research questions. Computers are assigned on a rotation basis for students to practice new software. On Wednesday, the teacher meets with small groups to answer questions and discuss research questions. On Thursday, the Media Specialist presents a mini-lesson on available print resources in the library. On Friday, students present their questions in a round-robin format to the entire class. Research questions are turned in for final teacher approval.

Week 2: Students begin accessing, sorting, and organizing information. On Monday, after research questions have been returned, students are given the rubric used to assess the research project. Students read over this rubric and ask questions for clarification. Multiple resources are required for the project, so there are always questions about how many. "How many books, magazines, on-line resources, and people do I have to use?" "What if I can't find . . .?" After anxiety subsides or increases, as the case may be, students list possible resources. Students spend Tuesday in the library or on the Internet beginning their searches. The teacher acts as a guide for the whole quarter. On Wednesday, students have a lesson on how to refine searches on the Internet and the differences among various search engines. In our classes, students do not print on-line resources until they learn how to select pertinent ones. On Thursday and Friday, accessing, sorting, and selecting materials continues.

Week 3: Students learn how to organize accumulated materials. You might ask, "Why don't we present the organizing lesson first?" We want students to experience information overload. Then we go back and help them sort and organize, within a system that works for them. On Monday, students learn a variety of ways to organize. We introduce them to file folders, binders with dividers, and large envelopes. We teach them how to use folders for storage on the computer too. Tuesday is spent applying their organizational skills. On Wednesday and Thursday, while students are continuing their search, the teacher meets with individual students for a resources check. On Friday there is an introduction to giving a three-minute informative speech, a requirement for this quarter.

Week 4: Students read and take notes on the materials they have collected thus far. A short review of two-column note-taking refreshes their memories, as well as a mini-lesson of how to use 3" x 5" index cards. The teacher uses this week for individual progress reports. Students reflect on what they have accomplished so far and where their challenges are. These reports go home for an update and are returned with a parent signature.

Week 5: Students wrap up the information collection week. At the end of this week, students complete a resources check, because the writing begins next week. Students normally collect last-minute pictures and diagrams.

Week 6: On Monday, the teacher and students review writing requirements for the research paper. The first draft is due on Wednesday. In-class writing time is provided Monday, Tuesday, and Wednesday. Students work in small groups during this process. The teacher reads the drafts and provides ongoing feedback. On Thursday, the three-minute informative speech is reviewed and students write and practice speeches on Thursday and Friday.

Week 7: The rough drafts are returned. Students work in collaborative groups to revise and edit papers and work on speeches. Second drafts are due Friday and speeches begin Monday.

Week 8: Speeches are given on Monday and Tuesday and the second drafts are returned. The rest of week eight is spent working on technology requirements. Students select how they will share through technology. Small group lessons focus on how to use a camcorder, import a graphic, or bar code a laser disc. The teacher and students act as coaches and mentors.

Week 9: Final technology presentations are given and final papers are turned in. Students complete self-evaluations and peer evaluations, and the teacher provides feedback. The final Friday is reserved for class reflection and feedback to the teacher. What has happened during this nine-week period can be used to inform and revise the process for the coming quarter.

As you can see, multiple activities take place to provide opportunities for learning. Students work individually and collaboratively and act as coaches and mentors to one another. The teacher in the STARR classroom teaches, facilitates, provides feedback, and manages the learning environment to maximize time and resources.

ASSESSMENT AND EVALUATION

How do we grade this process? Students access information, sort through numerous resources, organize information, take notes, mentor, read, write, give speeches, learn software, and present the final products. Sounds a bit overwhelming? To provide ongoing feedback to students in this type of learning environment, we use multidimensional assessment and evaluation. What does that look like?

First, what is assessment? Assessment is defined as any method used to better understand the current knowledge that a student possesses (Dietel, Herman, and Knuth, NCREL, 1991). Second, what is evaluation? Evaluation is the careful appraisal and study of something to determine its feasibility and effectiveness.

The ongoing assessment in STARR is formal and informal. It is both performance-based and standardized. Formative and cumulative, it involves self, peer, parent, and teacher evaluations. Developed by students and teachers together, it is linked to instruction and learning. STARR is indeed multidimensional.

How would you assess and evaluate the nine-week research process? Here are some options we use. In week one, when the research question is identified, we provide students with the scoring rubric. This rubric is completed with student feedback and goes home to parents. For the Writing Center® lesson, students are given the option to take a pretest. If they test well, they are designated mentors on that software and can assist other students. For those just learning the software, they have until the seventh week of the quarter to take a test. This test is a hands-on application of their skills.

During the second week of the quarter, the students are given the rubric that evaluates their final research project presentations. These rubrics are given prior to a project so students know exactly how they will be evaluated. Our rubrics have been revised over several years with student input. We use the same process with the rubric for the written paper. In the third week, when students are learning organizational skills, we use an informal show-and-tell assessment. Students work in small groups to organize information and share strategies with other students. To conclude this week, we create the rubric students will use during their three-minute speeches. After the mini-lesson on how to give an informative speech, students help design the grading rubric. Students are very clear about expectations and enjoy helping to create the rubrics.

Throughout the research process, informal feedback occurs. Students solicit feedback from classmates and learn how to provide constructive information.

During the fourth week, when students are taking notes, the teacher again provides feedback. Sometimes, as an example, we may pull aside a small group and restate note-taking techniques or outlining skills when students need extra help. Then, at the end of the fifth week, students categorize and list resources, comparing this list against the grading rubric. They find additional information for any missing data. Their checklist is turned in for a grade.

During the writing process, students receive a variety of feedback. They work in small groups, writing, reading, editing, and revising papers. Peer editing helps them revise for clarity. Students turn in two drafts and receive teacher feedback. Neither draft receives a formal grade, but students complete a rubric for each draft they hand in.

The final speeches are evaluated using student rubrics. The teacher and three peers evaluate each speech. Only the teacher evaluates the final research papers, and a student/teacher writing conference provides feedback on the final draft. Final technology-based presentations are self, peer, and teacher evaluated. On the final Friday of the quarter, we take time to record what we learned during the quarter. Students answer questions in their journals such as "What new information did you learn?" "What new software did you learn?" "What was the most challenging part of the quarter for you?" "What do you need to work on?" "How will you change what you do next quarter?" We use their responses to inform and revise our teaching processes.

As you can see, the assessment and evaluation options are broad. We feel the power of assessment and evaluation is that it is ongoing. Students receive continual feedback and are provided with opportunities to revise. Eventually, they understand that learning is an ongoing process. The end of a quarter does not signal the end of learning, but the application of new knowledge to the next project.

OPTIONS FOR ASSESSMENT AND EVALUATION

- Present speeches
- Use performance-based evaluations, using rubrics
- Videotape for portfolio assessments
- Enter local speech contests
- Assess technology skills
- Administer checklists
- Assess through pre- and post-tests

- Demonstrate competencies through hands-on experiences
- Apply skills through the development and design of projects
- Participate in presentations and performances
- Apply analysis strategies
- Use problem-solving techniques
- Write reflection journals
- Peer evaluate
- Self evaluate
- Design student- and teacher-constructed grading rubrics
- Apply thinking maps
- Incorporate and improve reading skills
- Participate in a young author's fair
- Publish a quarterly literary newsletter
- Create an on-line database of recommended readings
- Design interactive book reports
- Seventh graders write and illustrate a book for third graders on the water cycle or planets
- Research
- Create rubrics
- Write formal research papers
- Participate in small group discussions
- Participate in teacher/student conferences

STUDENT PORTFOLIOS

A portfolio is a collection of student work that shows the quality and range of student work over a period of time. A variety of methods can be used to compile and evaluate portfolios. In student portfolios, we include representative work from the five STARR components each quarter. Our portfolios include videotapes of speeches and performances, computer floppy disks with technology projects, and print copies of materials. Both students and teachers select materials.

Performance-Based Assessment

In this form of assessment, students demonstrate what they learn and what they can do with their new knowledge. The Office of Technology Assessment defines performance assessment as testing methods that require students to create an answer or product that demonstrates knowledge or skills. Performance-based assessment ranges from writing the diary of a Civil War soldier to presenting multiple viewpoints of the American Civil War using a PowerPoint® slide presentation. Students apply their learning in a variety of ways. We utilize performance-based assessment as one of our methods for assessing and evaluating students.

COMMUNITY SHOWCASE

Exhibits are a positive way to communicate with parents and the community what students have learned over the year. We produce the STARR Showcase in May. Students apply to present the best of their work from the year on that evening. Every student is encouraged to participate. This extravaganza takes organization, but it is well worth the effort. Our showcase begins at 6:00 p.m. The schedule of presentations is posted at the school's entrance and students act as guides. The halls are filled with exhibits and the rooms are filled with students presenting.

DISTRICT TECHNOLOGY FAIR

The district technology fair is produced in the spring by our school district and spans several days. Our students actively participate by presenting technology-based projects. Students clamor to show off their work to teachers and interested community leaders. Not only do students proudly display their learning of technology, they are also given one more opportunity to demonstrate speech skills in a real-life setting.

EVALUATION OF THE STARR PROGRAM

Just as we evaluate our students, we in turn are evaluated. In addition to ongoing conversations and communications with parents, we elicit feedback at the end of each school year through a survey. We have students complete an evaluation and send a separate survey home to parents. Past responses from parents include: "The benefit is that these are areas of learning that are true to the workplace and the more practice they receive the better employees they will make." "All the skills she learned in this program are expected of her in high school, college, and life. The more she does this, the better she will become at it." Here is an example of the survey we sent to parents:

Dear Parent/Guardian:

STARR (Speaking, Technology, Analysis, and Reading Through Research) classes would like your assistance in evaluating this year's program. As you are aware from previous information, STARR is based on the needs of students as defined by the documents *Colorado 2000* and *Workforce 2000*. Businesses are telling educators that students need more skills in the areas of speaking, technology, reading, analysis, research, and collaboration. They must be flexible and work in teams. Given this information, please help by letting us know how we are doing. The information you provide will be used to revise the curriculum for the next school year. Thanks, in advance, for your help.

Which of the following lessons, assignments, or activities do you feel increased your child's skills?

Lesson/Assignment/Activity

My child learned:	0=nothing, 3=somewhat, 5=really learned from this					
Speaking	0	1	2	3	4	5
Speech Outline	0	1	2	3	4	5
Oral Presentations	0	1	2	3	4	5
Using Visual Aids	0	1	2	3	4	5
Technology	0	1	2	3	4	5
Word Processing	0	1	2	3	4	5
Keyboarding Skills	0	1	2	3	4	5
Presentation Software (HyperStudio®)	0	1	2	3	4	5
Videotaping	0	1	2	3	4	5
Analysis	0	1	2	3	4	5
Problem Solving	0	1	2	3	4	5
Decision-Making	0	1	2	3	4	5
Reading	0	1	2	3	4	5
Comprehension	0	1	2	3	4	5
Fluency	0	1	2	3	4	5
Reading for information	0	1	2	3	4	5
Research	0	1	2	3	4	5
Accessing Resources	0	1	2	3	4	5
Taking Notes	0	1	2	3	4	5
Writing a Formal Paper	0	1	2	3	4	5

Do you feel STARR was: _____ too easy? _____ too hard? _____ just right?

What recommendations or suggestions do you have to help us create a better STARR program for next year?

Please return this to your child's STARR teacher.

EXAMPLES OF EVALUATION AND ASSESSMENT TOOLS

Rubrics for Speeches

5—The student gathers information from teachers, resources, and experiences to build a speech that informs, explains, demonstrates, or persuades.

4—Student self-selects written material and can assimilate pertinent information to support the topic. Student utilizes outside resources and life experiences to access information that will benefit his or her speech. All materials are independently accessed.

3—Student pools information from written material, outside resources, and life experiences to compliment his/her speech. Student can access materials with little or no teacher involvement.

2—Student needs assistance in finding resources for the topic. Has difficulty extracting information that supports the speech.

1—Student needs constant assistance from the teacher. Has difficulty collecting information that will help support the speech.

0—No effort was made.

HyperStudio® Proficiency Checklist

The student is able to:

_____ Locate and open the HyperStudio® program.

_____ Create new cards.

_____ Link cards in a stack.

_____ Create buttons.

_____ Appropriately use transitions and sounds.

_____ Import graphics.

_____ Resolve basic computer problems.

_____ Apply basic principles of design to the creation of a stack.

RESEARCH GRADING RUBRIC

Name _____ Date _____ Period _____

Directions: Three evaluations are due for this project. You complete the self-evaluation and have a parent complete their evaluation, and I will complete the teacher evaluation.

Research

1.	Outline	5	4	3	2	1
2.	Title Page	5	4	3	2	1
3.	Introduction	5	4	3	2	1
4.	Body of Paper	5	4	3	2	1
5.	Conclusion	5	4	3	2	1
6.	Five sources	5	4	3	2	1
7.	Mechanics, spelling, grammar, and punctuation	5	4	3	2	1
8.	Typed, word processed, or written in black ink	5	4	3	2	1
9.	Research question was answered	5	4	3	2	1
10.	Analysis, synthesis, and evaluation evident	5	4	3	2	1

Comments _____

_____

_____

Self-evaluation grade _____

Parent evaluation grade _____

Teacher evaluation grade _____

Multidimensional assessment and evaluation provides the learner, parent, and teacher with a variety of tools to help students gain skills. We find that when students are given the opportunity to self-assess and to have input about their own rubrics, the investment in learning has greater meaning. We encourage you to create meaningful assessments that provide information about where the student is in the learning experience and how they can achieve the quality of learning to move to where they want to be.

RESOURCES

Books

Andrews, Robert (ed.). *The Columbia Dictionary of Quotations.* New York: Columbia University Press, 1993.

What Work Requires of Schools: A SCANS Report for America 2000 by the Secretary's Commission on Achieving Necessary Skills. Washington, D.C.: U.S. Department of Labor, 1991.

Software

HyperStudio® is a multimedia presentation software package developed by Roger Wagner. Ordering and product information is available at http://www.hyperstudio.com.

PowerPoint® is presentational software developed and available through Microsoft at http://www.microsoft.com.

The Writing Center® is a multipurpose program that includes word processing, spreadsheets, and more. It is available through Mattel at http://www.mattelinteractive.com.

Web Sites

This policy statement on redesigning the National Assessment of Educational Progress provides insight into assessment design. http://www.nagb.org.policy1.html.

The North Central Regional Educational Laboratory is one of ten regional labs that supports educational research and innovation. http://www.ncrel.org.

INDEX